Wrexham Football Club

Official Yearbook 2006-2007

Wrexham Supporters Trust

By:
Gavin Jones, Lindsay Jones
and Peter Jones

We would like to thank the following people for their contributions to this project:

Kevin Baugh, Bruce Clapton, Gareth Collins, Steve Cooper, Dave Davies, Gareth Davies, Les Evans, Alan Fox, Arfon Griffiths MBE, Shaun Holden, Mike Hughes, John Humphries, Barry Jones, Marc Jones, Bryn Law, Colm O'Callaghan, Richard Owen, Geraint Parry, Wayne Price, Gary Pritchard, Paul Sleeman, Alun Thomas, Len Willett, Mark Williams, Martin Wright, and Rob Wynne.

Without the following pre-subscribers, this book would never have been possible. A warm thank you goes out to:

1. Gordon Williams Rhostyllen
2. Aggo Taraborelli Wrexham
3. Peter Beatty Wrexham
4. Paul Lindsay Wrexham
5. Simon Williams Stourbridge
6. Dyfan Owen Trefynwy
7. Sioned Roberts Ruthin
8. David Lemmon Burton on Trent
9. Ken Peters Kidderminster
10. Phil Egan Warrington
11. Phil Egan Warrington
12. Lorcan Adrian Whitchurch
13. Ivor Hewitt
14. Neil Sanderson Oswestry
15. Alan Roberts
16. Paul Matthias Gwersyllt
17. Neil Thomas Wrexham
18. Mark Drury Dudleston Heath
19. Owen Preece Rhosddu
20. Rae Benjamin Bradford (Ontario)
21. Alan Hinton Ellesmere
22. Dave Taylor Rhyl
23. Jamie Kelly Manchester
24. Neil Haslum Telford
25. Roger Jones Worthing
26. Nathan Davies Inverness
27. Richard Dixon Oxfordshire
28. Lou & Alan Morgan Wrexham
29. Glyn Davies Wrexham
30. Eifion Pugh Higher Kinnerton
31. John Connah
32. Tony Williams Deeside
33. A Valentine Wrexham
34. Mark Waters Ruabon
35. Tony Graham Wrexham
36. Tracey Tanner Holywell
37. Alison & Sylvia Holywell
38. David Lemmon Burton on Trent
39. Harri & Megan Lucas-Jones Wrexham
40. David Peters Flintshire
41. Anthony Bourne Buckinghamshire
42. Anthony Bourne Buckinghamshire
43. Anthony Bourne Buckinghamshire
44. Ken "Dapper" Davies Newtown, Powys
45. Patrick J Davies Oswestry
46. Dave Inskip Clacton on Sea
47. Hywel, Lucy & Glyn Roberts Swanley, Kent
48. James Nicholson Southampton
49. Kevin Salisbury Chatham, Kent
50. Bryn Jones Buckley
51. Peter George Wrexham
52. David Preece Bolton
53. Mark Williams Johnstown
54. Rob Griffiths Northwich
55. Louise Roberts Acton
56. Richie Garrett Wrexham
57. Alan Constantine Hightown
58. The Twigg Family Chirk
59. Naomi Davies Brynteg
60. Andrew Maggs
61. Aaron Jones Warrington
62. Ian Parry Leicester
63. Stuart Roberts Windsor
64. David McMinn Leeds
65. Mark Slawson Aylesbury
66. Alun Thomas Stamford, Lincs
67. Gary Pritchard Ynys Mon
68. Simon Summers Whitchurch
69. Rob Wynne Rhos
70. Jacko Acrefair
71. Steve Robinson Acrefair
72. Brian Davies Shrewsbury
73. Richard Purton Wrexham
74. Andrew Davies Gwersyllt
75. Dave Davies Brynteg
76. Bryan Davies Brynteg
77. Mark Harber Moss
78. Tony Morgan Prestatyn
79. David Butler Bridgenorrth
80. Nigel Evans Malpas
81. David Griffiths
82. Mary Pritchard Ellesmere Port
83. Ian Cheetham Watford
84. Neville Cheetham Watford
85. Nigel Wynn Wrexham
86. Paul "Kizza" Davies Wrexham
87. Nathan McCarthy Wrexham
88. Jenny Jones Wrexham
89. Gwenda Millar Wrexham
90. Haydn Taylor Wrexham
91. Paul Jones Bradley
92. Ray Clarke Wrexham
93. Morgan Owain Denby Hope
94. Peter Roberts Sheffield
95. Amy Simpson Sheffield
96. John Humphreys Shrewsbury
97. Steve Rogers
98. Dyfan Jones Bwlchgwyn
99. Laura Watson
100. Paul Lloyd Williams Buckley
101. Robert Geraint Lloyd Wrexham
102. Robert Gareth Lloyd Wrexham
103. Elizabeth Lloyd Wrexham
104. Aled Huw Lloyd Wrexham
105. Clare Chiddicks Winsford
106. Mark Roberts Ynys Mon
107. Linda Williams Rhyl
108. Denise & Martin Jones Llay
109. Lesley Griffiths Coedpoeth
110. David Hughes Rhyl
111. Gareth Griffiths Rhudllan
112. Ken Pemberton Haverford West
113. Jack Jones Plas Madoc
114. Stu Roberts Llangollen
115. John Valentine Wrexham
116. Gareth Collins Newark, New Jersey
117. Anne & Tony Crane Sydney, Australia
118. Peter Morris Shotton
119. Bryn Williams Rhos

Wrexham Supporters Trust

First published in Great Britain in 2006 by :

Wrexham Football Supporters' Society Limited, PO Box 2200, Wrexham, LL12 9WG

Introduction

Review of 2005/2006

Preview of 2006/2007

Heritage

I am delighted to have been asked to write the foreword to the new Wrexham Yearbook. It has been many years since the club had such a publication and I am positive that this Annual will become a much-anticipated feature of every new season at Wrexham. I know that a lot of people have worked very hard on this project and I wish them every success with it.

The past two years have been amongst the most difficult in the clubs long and proud history. I know from speaking to many supporters, both at the match and around the town, how stressful it has been for all of you. At times the outlook was very bleak indeed as we went into administration, were relegated and then faced expulsion from the League.

Such an outcome would have been a disaster for the town of Wrexham and Welsh football.

Those anxious days are now behind us and I am confident that our victory in the legal battle coupled with the long awaited takeover by Neville Dickens and Geoff Moss will lead to better days for our club.

Wrexham is a footballing town and the potential for a well-run club is enormous. We now need to build on the momentum generated through the struggle to save the club and work together to build a brighter future for Wrexham.

During my career at Wrexham as a player and as manager, I was fortunate to have worked with many of the greatest names in the clubs history. I do not have space here to list them all but I am sure you know who they are.

We had some fantastic days during the 70s and even today people will say to me that a certain player, or a performance, or a team was without a doubt the "best ever" in Wrexham's long history.

That is very kind but I would have to take issue with those sentiments because, as every football fan knows, the "best" is yet to come.

In that spirit I am looking forward to the new season with a great deal of optimism and I would urge every Wrexham fan to get behind Denis Smith and his team.

A lot of work still needs to be done on and off the pitch but these are exciting times for Wrexham fans and the rebuilding of Wrexham FC starts from here.

Arfon Griffiths MBE

Mae'n bleser gennyf gael y cynnig i ysgrifennu rhagair i Blwyddlyfr newydd Wrecsam. Mae'n flynyddoedd lawer ers i'r clwb gael y fath gyhoeddiad a dwi'n hyderus y bydd y Blwyddlyfr yn dod yn rhan hanfodol o bob tymor newydd yn Wrecsam. Mae'n amlwg fod llawer o bobl wedi gweithio'n galed iawn ar y prosiect yma a dymunaf yn dda iawn iddynt.

Mae'r ddwy flynedd diwethaf wedi bod gyda'r mwyaf anodd yn hanes hir a balch y clwb. O siarad efo llawer o gefnogwyr, yn y gemau ac o gwmpas y dre, gwn mor galed mae hi wedi bod i chi gyd.

At adegau, roedd y dyfodol yn dywyll iawn wrth i ni ddod dan law y gweinyddwyr, disgyn cynghrair a wynebu cael ein taflu allan o'r Gynghrair.

Byddai'r fath sefyllfa wedi bod yn drychineb i'r dref ac i bêldroed Cymru.

Mae'r dyddiau blin yna y tu cefn i ni bellach a dwi'n hyderus y bydd ein llwyddiant yn y llysoedd ynghyd â Neville Dickens a Geoff Moss yn cymryd yr awennau yn arwain at ddyddiau disglair unwaith eto i'r clwb.

Tre pêldroed ydi Wrecsam ac mae'r potensial i glwb dan reolaeth dda yn anferth. Bellach mae angen adeiladu ar y momentwm a godwyd i achub y clwb a gweithio gyda'n gilydd i greu dyfodol gwell i Wrecsam.

Yn ystod fy nghyrfa yn Wrecsam fel chwaraewr a rheolwr, bues i'n ffodus i weithio efo llawer o'r enwau mwyaf disglair yn hanes y clwb. Does dim lle yma i'w rhestru nhw i gyd ond rydach chi'n gwybod pwy ydyn nhw.

Cawsom ddyddiau anhygoel yn y 70au a hyd heddiw mae pobl yn dweud wrthyf fod ambell i chwaraewr neu berfformiad neu tîm gyda'r gorau erioed yn hanes Wrecsam.
Mae hynny'n garedig iawn and dwi am herio'r sentiment yna gan fod pob cefnogwr pêldroed yn gwybod fod y "gorau" dal i ddod.

Yn yr ysbryd yna, edrychaf ymlaen at y tymor newydd yn llawn optimistiaeth a gofynnaf i bob cefnogwr Wrecsam uno y tu cefn i Denis Smith a'i dîm.

Mae angen llawer o waith o hyd ar - ac oddiar - y cae ond mae'n gyfnod newydd i gefnogwyr Wrecsam ac mae adfywiad Wrecsam yn cychwyn yma.

Arfon Griffiths MBE

At last! It is a relief to be able to discuss football rather than property deals and consortiums and League restrictions and deadlines.

We have just come out of administration after what seemed a lifetime and I am confident that our club now has a bright future. Everyone connected with Wrexham is on a high and we now need to translate that into results on the pitch.

This is my 25th season as a football manager and I can assure fans that everybody at the Racecourse is focussed on moving the club forward. I do not see any point in being happy just stabilising our position; we must aim higher than that. The top of the table is the only place to be and that is our aim.

Last season was a disappointment in playing terms. We expected to make the play-offs and would have done bar a disappointing end to the campaign.

For this season we have been able to strengthen the playing squad and I have to say that I am delighted at the quality of players we have been able to recruit. Wrexham is a marvellous place to play football. We have a great stadium, fantastic training facilities and a passionate and knowledgeable support. Above all else, Wrexham is what I would call a proper football town.

Of course the majority of our new recruits already know this because they already have strong links to the area. Much has been made of this over the summer months, but the facts are very straightforward.

I don't just sign players because they are local or Welsh but if I had a choice between two similar players and one was Welsh and one English, I'd choose the Welsh lad.

Local players do feel it more. They get feedback from the fans, good and bad, all the time. I am from Stoke and was lucky enough to play for my local club. When I pulled on the shirt I knew that my family and friends would be watching me. I did not want to let them down and would have run through a brick wall for the cause.

Fifteen of our current squad are products of the academy or local men. You can also add to that Welshmen Matty Crowell and Chris Llewellyn.

However, the main reason these lads are here is that they all have ability. The make up and versatility of the current squad means that we are not tied to the 3-5-2 formation we have used for the last few years. During the pre season I experimented with 4-4-2 and also 4-2-3-1. It's great that we have these options and we may see all of them employed during the coming season.

There is more pressure on us to win promotion this season, as we've no excuses. But I've been living with this kind of pressure for 40 years since I started playing football and it won't make any difference to me now. I relish the challenge.

Local owners, Local players, Local pride

Let's get this club moving!

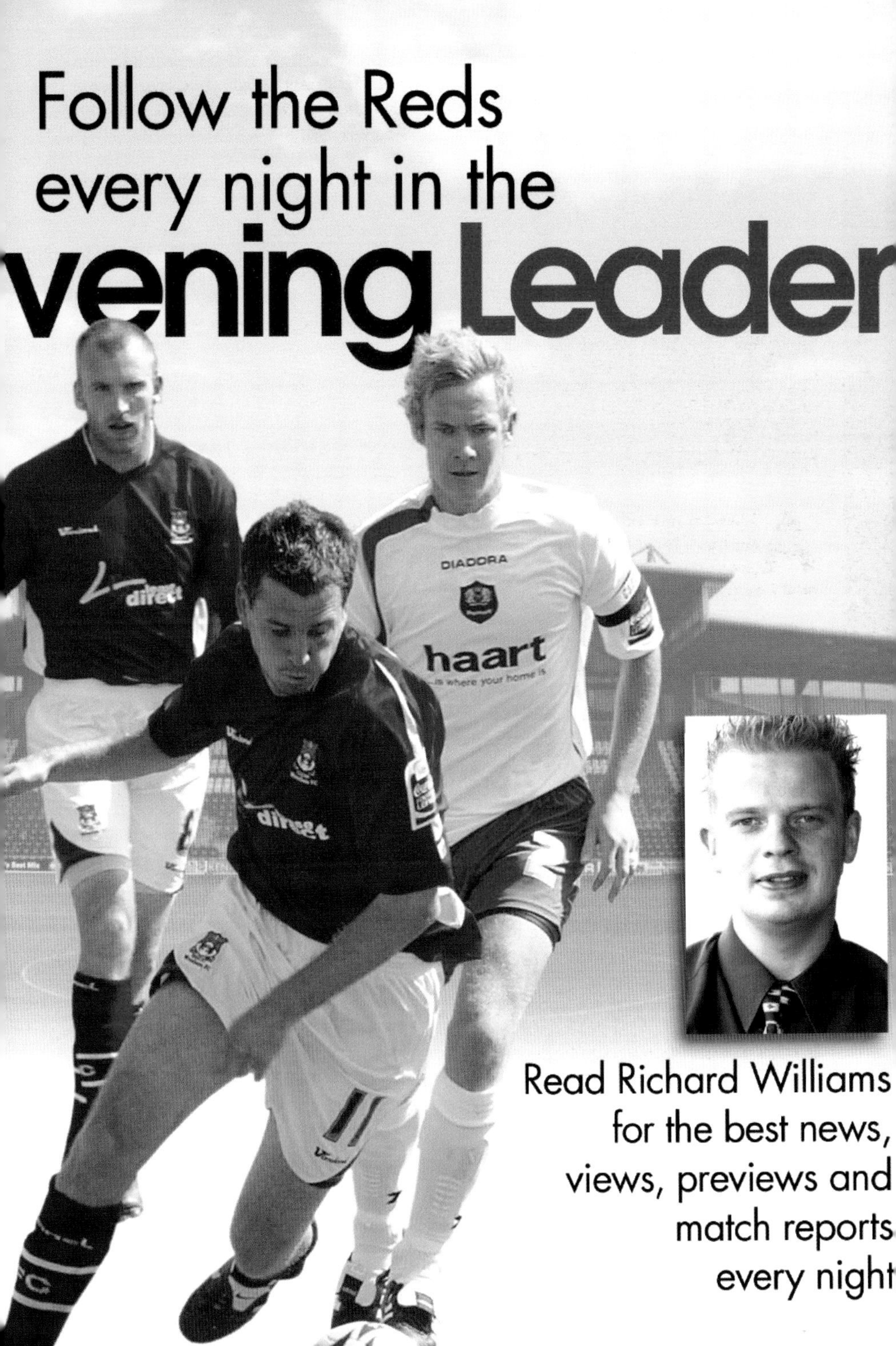
Follow the Reds
every night in the
vening Leader
DIADORA
haart
Read Richard Williams
for the best news,
views, previews and
match reports
every night

Two words dominate all analysis of our most recent on-field season in league football. They are the words 'defensive' and 'lapse'. And they pockmark virtually every review and match report from last season so badly you'd think we'd over-dosed as a squad on cheap smack. How many times did we ruck-up last year with Matt Smith on 'The Championship' on Sunday mornings to re-live some of the costliest give-aways since Nigel Lawson's post-election budget in 1988? How often did we contribute handsomely to our own defeats? And just how many half-hit clearances, deflections and badly judged offside appeals can any one club endure in an eight-month period?

But while we were in an especially generous mood at the back all year, still yearning for a leader, shouter and organiser in the traditional Carey/Davis/Hardy mode, we were flaccid at the other end too, and regularly went more than one game without scoring. And while its easy and obvious to recall the non-stop havoc caused by Trundle and Morrell during the last promotion season, the fact is that since they left, we've lacked natural poachers and real-deal finishers up front. And no more so than last season, when we were often crying out, literally, for someone, anyone, to get a late touch in the six-yard box.

If any one moment defined the past season in microcosm, it was surely the very last play of our very last away game at Darlington? Having enjoyed plenty of possession from the off and having taken a deserved first-half lead, our patched-up team of loanees, youths and assorted journeymen eventually succumbed to yet another set-play.

Despite the handful of clear-cut chances we'd created on the break but were unable to put away, three points became one-point, another draw grasped from the arms of a rare away victory. And so we finished the season in mid-table, anything but comfortable. Displaying relegation form throughout the final two months of the season, had the league programme gone on for four or five weeks more, our eventual landing may not have been so

Mark Jones starts off another attack

soft. Indeed to the uninitiated, the first-half of that game at Darlington's over-ambitious and under-populated all-seater, could well have been two Conference sides lashing away in an FA Vase semi-final.

All of that said, back in August 2005, given the general mayhem around the club and the restraints under which we were operating, most of us would have taken survival ahead of promotion or relegation as a realistic target for the season. But two months in, once we'd scanned the opposition and the standard of the league became apparent, automatic promotion or a play-off place looked eminently attainable, in or out of administration.

At least until the re-scheduled home game with Chester when, after a promising first-half-hour, we drifted out of the game to such an extent that not only were we fortunate to escape with the spoils, but whatever passion we'd worked so hard to muster all season seemed to drain from us visibly. The alarm bells had gone off and the veiled doom-warnings echoed infrequently all season by the managers had now manifested themselves. Simply put, we'd hit the wall.

Of course, the truly frustrating thing is that last year's league was generally quite poor, and certainly far more so than when we last went up. Carlisle for example, the best side in the division pound-for-pound, made hard work of beating us both at home and up at Brunton Park. And it was this inability to generate anything of substance from teams in the Top six and, towards the season's close, teams in the Bottom six too, that eventually saw our chances evaporate. All the more galling seeing as how we threw points away all season like confetti at weddings, both the away games at Carlisle and Torquay being the extremes and the cases in point. And while Denis Smith will look back now from the comfort of being out of administration knowing he's at least helming a club that's officially alive again, he's been around long enough to know that, with more penetration down the flanks, less flakiness at the back and a more poachy threat up-front, we could have been genuine contenders.

Last season, then, was a disappointment and the manager and his staff will privately concede as much. Far too often we weren't simply strong or physical enough. Some of our big, imposing players were repeatedly horsed off balls and out of 50-50 challenges when they should have been able to assert themselves more readily. And none more so than when we relinquished our LDV crown during a pantomime up at Blackpool in October, setting a tone of sorts for the rest of the season.

Having come behind from a 0-2 deficit to take a deserved lead late on, two defensive calamities saw any hopes of a second successive extended campaign dashed in extra-time. On the night we hardly deserved to be beaten and, in many respects, bossed an away game against supposedly better opponents only to come away with nothing.

The defeat had been squarely of our own doing, of course, and this was a game we could, and should, have won. This in itself became a mantra over the course of a season where, regardless of how well we were playing at any given time, a sense of inevitability hung in the air everytime our opponents slung balls into our box.

We went out of both the FA and League Cups by odd goals to Championship 1 opponents, beaten 0-1 by Doncaster in The Carling Cup in August and 1-2 away at Port Vale in the FA Cup, again playing tidy patterns and sparring comfortably against allegedly stronger sides but without ever really threatening. Someday we may actually win a tie in one of these competitions again, and my wish is that we're all around to witness this.

Candidates for our best player, then, during what was without question the

most fraught and disconcerting season in our club's proud history? Well, Danny Williams for consistency at a club gone mad and the fact that he looked like he actually wanted to pull on the shirt week after week. Mark Jones for his spectacular goals, the fact that he's one of our own and the fact that he's got so much untapped potential that he can only get better. And Matt Derbyshire, for his pace his goals and for reminding us what out-and-out strikers look like. Honourable mentions to Matt Crowell and Jonathan Walters, both of whom kept on fighting, when often those around them appeared to not especially care one way or the other.

The home performance of the season, without question, was against Wycombe, when we took on a gamey, strutting team on the up and made them look like a most ordinary side. And by doing so, showed just what we were capable of ourselves when we had the basics in place. Sam Williams' diving headed goal was a result of one of the few times last season we actually got quality crosses beyond the first man. The fact that the cross was swung in by Crowell - who had a most efficient season for us in the engine room - raises the wing back question in a roundabout way. Because for most of last season, our favoured wing backs looked uncomfortable whenever they crossed half-way, and far too often we were over-hesitant in the second third, before imploding with stage-fright in front of goal.

One would expect that next season we'll revert to a more traditional formation with two out-and-out wide-players - simply put, 3-5-2 depends on the ability of the wide-players to show up well defensively and at the same time threaten when in offensive positions and that, sadly, was where we came unstuck most last season.

It's a bit familiar now, I guess, to harp on about the impact of administration on our performances last season, regardless of how the two are inter-linked. But in a roundabout way, our season under Bebgies Traynor generated some positive yields on the field as well, and it's important to accentuate these. Because of administration, we've been forced into blooding the best of our youth crop - possibly too early in some cases - where previously we may have been more reluctant to do so. Very often last year, our bench looked like it had been staffed with an over-flow from one of the local crèches, but its here that the real positives are, and enough of them too to get us worked up over the summer and excitedly through to the start of a new season.

The confidence of teenage goalkeeper Michael Jones - when playing behind an often ponderous and erratic back five - was a massive bonus, and in a season where we often desperately required both physical and verbal leadership at the back, it was the youngster who often provided it most whenever he played. In fact at Torquay - a dark, dark day if ever - he was the only one who sounded like he wanted to be heard.

The long-awaited emergence of Matt Done as a carefree, out-and-out winger will have pleased Denis Smith no end, and his elevation as a genuine first-team candidate gives us a decent option next season, especially if we go 4-4-2. Mark Jones too gave us several reasons to be cheerful, even if he faded badly into the final third of the season. Perhaps too much was expected of him during his first full season as a first-teamer, both by the staff and the supporters, and while his goals will long remain in the memory [especially his volley away at Oxford], it's clear that he's still very much a work in progress, a point he has acknowledged himself. In which case another season in the basement will only serve him well, with one eye on the longer game.

Mike Williams too showed up very nicely during his infrequent appearances at the back and seems to have played himself

Danny Williams scoring against Mansfield

into contention for a regular starting spot next season. A confident, well-built youngster who knows exactly what he's about and is happy with the ball at his feet, he'll not be unduly fazed by what he comes up against every week from August onwards.

That all of the above-mentioned are graduates of our Centre of Excellence and have come through our schoolboy system is both a tribute to the under-stated expertise and dedication of the staff there - full-time and voluntary - and also a nod to exactly how this football club can extract itself from the mire of League 2. All four are resourceful home-grown youngsters and in a squad that now also boasts the likes of Danny Williams, Steve Evans, Ryan Valentine, Simon Spender, Levi Mackin and Shaun Pejic, there's a distinct pattern emerging to the core of our squad.

This coming season, we'll be looking for far more consistency of performance and, on the back of that, maybe a run of some consequence. Last season, for instance, we never once won three games on the bounce. We'll also be looking for an improvement in our away form; - last season we bucked the trend set the previous year, when we played far better and more excitingly on the road.

As I write, the management and staff are re-convening after holidays, although they've already earmarked potential signings and loanees from far out. Much transfer business is yet to be concluded, both through the 'in' and the 'out' doors. What is certain even now though is that, free from the restraints of administration, and buoyed by the formal arrival into the mix of two local owners and an increasingly homespun squad, much will be expected from our beloved Reds this coming season.

Last year the club realised its most important twin targets - survival in its league and survival as a football club. To that end, 2005/06 was an unqualified success even if, as supporters, we'll remember last season most for what might, and maybe should have been, on the field of play, at least.

Wrexham started well without ever threatening the Boston goal, although McEvilly did well to go past two defenders before his early shot was charged down. Both teams exchanged corners, but the defences remained on top, with the Wrexham back three looking composed against the experience of the Boston front two – Julian Joachim and Noel Whelan.

With the game going through a lull, it sprang back into life in the 23rd minute when Welsh under-21 international Mark Jones took Shaun Pejic's pass in his stride and unleashed an unstoppable 25-yard right-foot shot into the side-netting of the far post with Boston keeper Abbey flapping at the ball.

The referee then took centre stage, with Gary Lewis cautioning Danny Williams and Lee Cannoville for a scuffle on the edge of the Boston area, when a ticking off would have been more appropriate. Mark Jones then stole the ball from Holland with a clever challenge, but as he advanced away from the midfielder he was clipped on the ankle but it was Jones who went in the book for diving!

Wrexham continued their dominance in the second-half and created more chances on goal as Boston had to play a more open game as they went in search for the equaliser.

McEvilly had the ball in the net but was denied by the offside flag when he was played clean through.

Moments later the striker had another opportunity following good work from Mark Jones. Jonah picked the ball up in midfield before advancing to the edge of the area, where he picked out McEvilly with a neat pass, but the striker did not connect with his shot and scuffed it across the face of goal, where Jon Walters was agonisingly close to converting it at the far post.

Walters then went close after Andy Holt dispossessed the Boston full back and lifted the ball into the path of Walters, but the striker slipped at the wrong moment, but still managed to lift his shot over the stranded Abbey only to see it strike the far post. The ball rebounded away from goal and despite McEvilly being close-by, the Boston defence regrouped to clear the danger.

Ferguson curled a 20-yard free-kick around the wall that Abbey turned away for a corner, but as the game entered the last 10 minutes, Wrexham got the second that killed off Boston's slim hopes. Substitute Dean Bennett ran half the length of the pitch, turning four Boston players inside out, before squaring the ball to Lee Roche after the winger had cut into the penalty spot and he made no mistake by blasting the ball past an exposed Abbey.

There was still time left for Boston to have their first shot on goal, but Ingham went down at his near post to collect the long- range shot from Danny Thomas.

Referee: Gary Lewis (Cambridgeshire)

Wrexham 2	**Boston United 0**
Mark Jones 23'	
Lee Roche 83'	

Attendance: 4,503

Lee Roche re-opens his Wrexham account.

Starting XI:

01 Michael Ingham
18 Shaun Pejic
04 Dave Bayliss
06 Dennis Lawrence
15 Lee Roche
08 Danny Williams
17 Mark Jones
10 Darren Ferguson
07 Andy Holt
09 Jon Walters
11 Lee McEvilly 72'

Subs:

03 Alex Smith
12 Dean Bennett 72'
13 Michael Jones (GK)
19 Levi Macken
20 Simon Spender

Stats:

Shots on Goal: 5
Shots on Target: 5
Possession: 49%
Fouls Conceded: 8
Corners: 11
Yellow Cards: 2
Red Cards: 0

Starting XI:

01 Nathan Abbey
02 Lee Canoville
15 Mark Greaves
05 Ben Futcher
03 Austin McCann 57'
07 Bradley Maylett
17 Stewart Talbot
11 Chris Holland
14 Gavin Johnson 45'
19 Julian Joachim
18 Noel Whelan 78'

Subs:

06 Alan White
12 Simon Rusk 45'
16 Danny Thomas 57'
21 Rob Norris 78'
26 Chris Wright (GK)

Stats:

Shots on Goal: 3
Shots on Target: 2
Possession: 51%
Fouls Conceded: 21
Corners: 12
Yellow Cards: 2
Red Cards: 0

The Boston midfield halt Fergie - this time.

Dennis Lawrence heads clear.

A tentative start to the game from both teams in front of a subdued crowd. The first attack coming from the home side. The County right winger got a yard on Andy Holt and delivered a low cross that Pejic failed to cut out, but Wrexham were lucky as the ball travelled across the face of goal without a County player getting a touch.

Wrexham's first chance of note fell to Mark Jones after his quick turn allowed him to break free from his midfield marker, but his dipping shot from outside of the area went narrowly over the bar. Ferguson then gave the ball away in midfield, and Wrexham were on the back foot, but as McMahon approached the penalty area he sent his shot high over the bar.

Mark Jones was Wrexham's most lively player, and he again sent a cross over the bar, but with over 30 minutes gone both keepers had not been tested with a shot on target. This was to change soon after when Ingham pulled off a superb save to deny County the opening goal.

Notts County won free-kicks around the edge of the box, but when County won the initial header, a red shirt was always well placed to hack the ball clear. Wrexham were getting closer, with Danny Williams firing a header narrowly wide from the edge of the area, but moments later County should have been down to ten men.

A well-worked move from the Red Dragons resulted in Mark Jones being clean through on the edge of the area after McEvilly dummied Roche's infield pass but, as Jones was about to burst into the box, he was cynically brought down by Pipe. Unbelievably the referee did not show him a yellow card, let alone a red for a professional foul! From the resulting free-kick, Andy Holt blasted the ball straight at the wall and the opportunity was lost.

Wrexham continued to dominate as Jones had a long-range shot that went wide, and substitute Dean Bennett, on for Lee McEvilly, failed to test Pilkington after his shot from the edge of the area lacked any power after further good approach play.

With Wrexham failing to convert their chances, they were hit by a 90th minute sucker punch, although it did look as if Dennis Lawrence was fouled in the build up to County's late winner. Lawrence laid flat out and the Wrexham defence were one man down, with Shaun Pejic outnumbered two-to-one, the ball was played outside him for substitute Stacy Long to round Ingham and slot the ball into the empty net.

Lawrence did not play the seven minutes of injury time left, but there was still time for Bayliss to be booked for a high challenge from behind, although he could have easily been shown red for a challenge that indicated his frustration at the late winner.

Referee: Mike Thorpe (Suffolk)

Notts County 1 **Wrexham 0**
Stacy Long 90'

Attendance: 4,382

Mark lets fly.

Starting XI:

01 Kevin Pilkington
06 Brian O'Callaghan
08 Julien Baudet
20 Kelvin Wilson
17 Robert Ullathorne
02 David Pipe
04 Michael Edwards
24 Lewis McMahon
12 Chris Palmer 74'
25 Andy White 88'
16 Steve Scoffham 81'

Subs:

07 Matthew Gill 88'
10 Glynn Hurst 81'
14 Saul Deeney (GK)
22 Stacy Long 74'
26 Daniel Martin

Stats:

Shots on Goal: 12
Shots on Target: 8
Possession: 51%
Fouls Conceded: 12
Corners: 3
Yellow Cards: 1
Red Cards: 0

Starting XI:

01 Michael Ingham
18 Shaun Pejic
04 Dave Bayliss
06 Dennis Lawrence 90'
15 Lee Roche
08 Danny Williams
17 Mark Jones
10 Darren Ferguson
07 Andy Holt
09 Jon Walters
11 Lee McEvilly 75'

Subs:

03 Alex Smith
12 Dean Bennett 75'
13 Michael Jones (GK)
19 Levi Mackin 90'
20 Simon Spender

Stats:

Shots on Goal: 14
Shots on Target: 6
Possession: 49%
Fouls Conceded: 11
Corners: 5
Yellow Cards: 2
Red Cards: 0

Rooster not happy about the County goal.

Bennett makes his feelings known.

It was difficult to separate the two sides during the game, to be honest. Both tried to play football, but neither was really up to it, which is of course why they are in the equivalent of Division Four. Ferguson was clattered early, and not for the first time (what happened to the "Man On" shout, by the way?), and none of our midfielders seemed to want to take men on, or to put their foot on the ball for a second.

Ingham's sharp save, from a narrow-angled Sabin volley, was one of the few highlights, whilst we were grateful more than once for the linesman's flag. A long-range effort from Jones and a sudden intake of breath as their keeper Harper dropped an innocuous cross, were about the only highlights of the first period.

The second-half continued in much the same vein, that is to say disappointing for the very vocal visiting contingent, which, incidentally, included some of our friends from Cardiff. Both Roche and Holt out wide, though readily available, crossed poorly and our passing generally was sub-standard. A plus was that the back three of Pej, Bayliss and Lawrence were generally on top of things and Ingy, some of his kicking apart, looked confident and competent.

For the second game running, Evil was replaced by Dean Bennett, who at least added some pace to the attack, and his involvement led to our only real chance, Walters's intelligent cutback finding Jonesey, whose finish, from fifteen yards, wasn't one for the scrapbook.

At the death we broke and found ourselves with what looked like a three-on-one situation. A linesman's flag brought us up short, and from the resulting counter Ingy was lobbed, the ball bouncing off the bar and over. To lose one game in a week to a last-minute goal could be seen as unfortunate – to lose two would have been unforgivable.

Denis Smith: "While I was looking for nine points this week, overall I thought a draw was a fair result today and Northampton certainly deserved something from this game. The changing conditions in the second-half certainly took its toll and I was satisfied with point. We know we have to do more up front, but we have a good base on which to work and improvements will follow. To come to Northampton and keep a cleansheet is no mean feat and from what I have seen today, both teams should be there or thereabouts come next May. The obviously wanted to impress after what has been a poor start for them, and that certainly showed. From what I have seen so far, these are the kind of players I would be happy to be in the trenches with!"

Referee: Carl Boyeson (East Yorkshire)

Northampton Town 0 **Wrexham 0**

Attendance: 5,075

Holty takes control.

Starting XI:

01 Lee Harper
20 Pedj Bojec 53'
16 Sean Dyche
05 Luke Chambers
02 Jason Crewe
10 Joshua Low 85'
12 David Hunt
07 Ian Taylor
27 Lawrie Dudfield
11 Eoin Jess
18 Eric Sabin 62'

Subs:

08 Andy Kirk 62'
13 Mark Burn (GK)
15 Brett Johnson 53'
17 Bradley Johnson
28 Ryan Gilligan 85'

Stats:

Shots on Goal: 9
Shots on Target: 6
Possession: 58%
Fouls Conceded: 13
Corners: 5
Yellow Cards: 0
Red Cards: 0

Starting XI:

01 Michael Ingham
18 Shaun Pejic
04 Dave Bayliss
06 Dennis Lawrence
15 Lee Roche
08 Danny Williams
17 Mark Jones
10 Darren Ferguson
07 Andy Holt
09 Jon Walters
11 Lee McEvilly 69'

Subs:

03 Alex Smith
12 Dean Bennett 69'
13 Michael Jones (GK)
19 Levi Mackin
20 Simon Spender

Stats:

Shots on Goal: 10
Shots on Target: 7
Possession: 42%
Fouls Conceded: 7
Corners: 4
Yellow Cards: 0
Red Cards: 0

Jon Walters powers a goal bound effort.

"They shall not pass".

In a frantic first-half there were sufficient chances for the game to be 3-3 by half-time, but both teams had left their shooting boots at home. Wrexham should have been two behind before they had their first attempt on goal, as Carlisle spurned two great chances.

Hawley spun away from Pejic and with only Bayliss to beat, he under hit his pass to the unmarked Holmes with Ingham reading the situation well by coming out and smothering the pass at the feet of Holmes.

Carlisle continued to look dangerous on the break, with Karl Hawley again the thorn in Wrexham's side but, despite all his neat approach play, his shooting and crossing failed to hit their intended targets. In one move he turned Bayliss on the edge of the area, but fired his cross across the face of goal when the Carlisle players were waiting for a cut back on the penalty spot.

In an end-to-end game, Wrexham were denied when Carlisle failed to clear a corner, but Mark Jones' 25-yard shot was again blocked but this time by Andy Holt who was just getting up after challenging for the corner!

The second-half was a timid affair compared to the first, but that all changed in the 62nd minute when the game exploded into life. Dennis Lawrence took a poor throw in to Danny Williams, and this resulted in a 50/50 challenge with two players on the ground.

The ball got trapped under the Carlisle player and substitute Simon Spender, who had replaced Lee Roche towards the end of the first-half, lost his head and lunged in two footed on the Carlisle player. This sparked a ruck involving the majority of the players and, when this eventually calmed down, referee Darren Drysdale showed Spender a justified red card.
Wrexham were not organised for the resulting free-kick and despite Michael Ingham saving well, he could only palm it out to Brendon McGill who made no mistake from close range to fire Carlisle into the lead. Carlisle should have added a second to put the game beyond Wrexham in the last 15 minutes after Bayliss was dispossessed on the Carlisle right. The centre was perfect for Hawley, but Pejic made up a lot of ground to block the shot away for a corner. Ingham was beaten again by Hawley, but Holt got back in time to clear the ball off the goal line to keep Wrexham's chances alive.

To cap it all, Jon Walters missed a late penalty, fluffing his shot after a long delay.

It was just one of those days.

Referee: Darren Drysdale (Lincolnshire)

Wrexham 0	**Carlisle United 1**
	Brendon McGill 63'

Attendance: 4,239

Dennis goes close.

Starting XI:

01 Michael Ingham
18 Shaun Pejic
04 Dave Bayliss
06 Dennis Lawrence
15 Lee Roche 34'
08 Danny Williams 78'
17 Mark Jones
10 Darren Ferguson
07 Andy Holt
09 Jon Walters
11 Lee McEvilly 69'

Subs:

03 Alex Smith
12 Dean Bennett 69'
13 Michael Jones (GK)
19 Levi Mackin 78'
20 Simon Spender 34'

Stats:

Shots on Goal: 10
Shots on Target: 4
Possession: 53%
Fouls Conceded: 12
Corners: 11
Yellow Cards: 3
Red Cards: 1

Starting XI:

CARLISLE UNITED FOOTBALL CLUB

01 Anthony Williams
15 Paul Arnison 67'
05 Danny Livesey
06 Kevin Gray
21 Zigor Aranlde
07 Brendon McGill
11 Adam Murray
04 Chris Billy
19 Paul Simpson
10 Karl Hawley
09 Derek Holmes 74'

Subs:

03 Peter Murphy 67'
16 Glenn Murray
18 Simon Hackney
20 Kieren Westwood (GK)
22 Raphael Nade 74'

Stats:

Shots on Goal: 12
Shots on Target: 5
Possession: 47%
Fouls Conceded: 6
Corners: 4
Yellow Cards: 0
Red Cards: 0

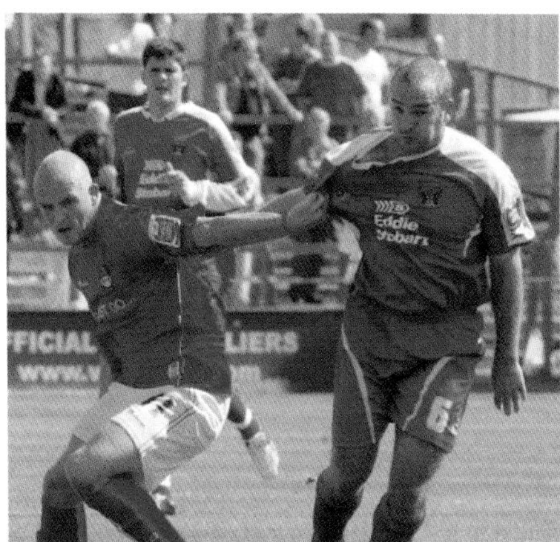

Can we swap shirts at the end Lee?

Denis can't believe we lost this one.

In a game where you could count the number of shots on target from both teams on one hand, it was hardly surprising that it took just a single goal to separate the teams at a sparsely populated Racecourse.

When Doncaster scored with four minutes left, it was arguably against the run of play as Wrexham controlled the second-half, but despite all their possession they could only muster shots from outside of the area.

Mark Jones was the most likely player to score for Wrexham having a better game from the weekend and had Andy Warrington at full stretch when he curled a shot wide of the near post.

Jonah was brought down as he quickly changed direction on the edge of the area, but although his free-kick had power, it was going well off target until a Doncaster defender deflected it back into the area, but Rovers managed to scramble the ball clear.

Wrexham started the second-half positively, and at least started to have shots on goal. Darren Ferguson went close as he collected a knock-down from Walters, but he failed to get a clean contact on the ball and in the end Warrington had a simple save to make diving low to his right to turn the ball around his near post, although the shot was actually going wide.

Wrexham continued to press with Walters forcing Warrington into a save and despite the shot from the edge of the area being scuffed, the Rovers keeper made a meal of it by turning the ball away for a corner. Despite Wrexham forcing eight corners, the absence of Dennis Lawrence limited the options for Ferguson and Doncaster had no problems clearing the danger.

Wrexham continued to play the ball well around midfield but lacked the decisive pass as they advanced to the Doncaster area. On too many occasions they reverted to passes back, as the wing backs did not offer many options and when they did collect the ball, the crosses in from either flank were of a poor standard.

Wrexham's injury problems increased with 10 minutes left as Dean Bennett limped off to be replaced by Levi Mackin. This forced Paul Warhurst into the wing back position, with Danny Williams dropping back into defence and Mackin slotting into midfield.

Michael Ingham had to rush off his line and make a challenge at the feet of Guy but, as the game entered the last five minutes of normal time, Wrexham conceded the vital goal - although they had at least three chances to clear the danger before substitute Adam Hughes scored from close range.

Referee: Jonathon Moss (West Yorkshire)

Wrexham 0	**Doncaster Rovers 1**
	Adam Hughes 86'

Attendance: 2,177

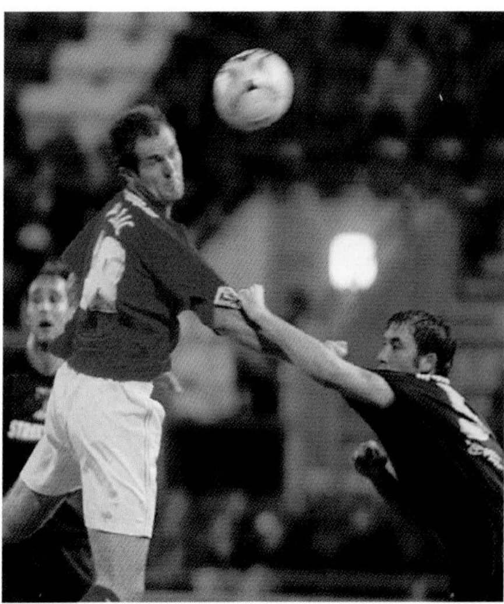

Pejic's goal bound effort.

Starting XI:

01 Michael Ingham
18 Shaun Pejic 62'
04 Dave Bayliss
07 Andy Holt
12 Dean Bennett 81'
08 Danny Williams
17 Mark Jones
10 Darren Ferguson
03 Alex Smith
09 Jon Walters
14 Robbie Foy 89'

Subs:

05 Paul Warhurst 62'
06 Dennis Lawrence
13 Michael Jones (GK)
19 Levi Mackin 81'
22 Matt Done 89'

Stats:

Shots on Goal: 10
Shots on Target: 2
Possession: 52%
Fouls Conceded: 10
Corners: 8
Yellow Cards: 2
Red Cards: 0

Starting XI:

01 Andy Warrington
05 Philip McGuire
15 Nick Fenton
23 Stephen Foster
03 Tim Ryan
26 James Coppinger 71'
30 Dave Mulligan
19 Ricky Ravenhill 59'
21 Michael McIndoe
07 Lewis Guy
13 Leo Fortune-West

Subs:

14 Paul Heffernan
17 Richard Offiong 71'
18 Sean McDaid
24 Adam Hughes 59'
31 Barry Richardson (GK)

Stats:

Shots on Goal: 6
Shots on Target: 2
Possession: 48%
Fouls Conceded: 15
Corners: 4
Yellow Cards: 3
Red Cards: 0

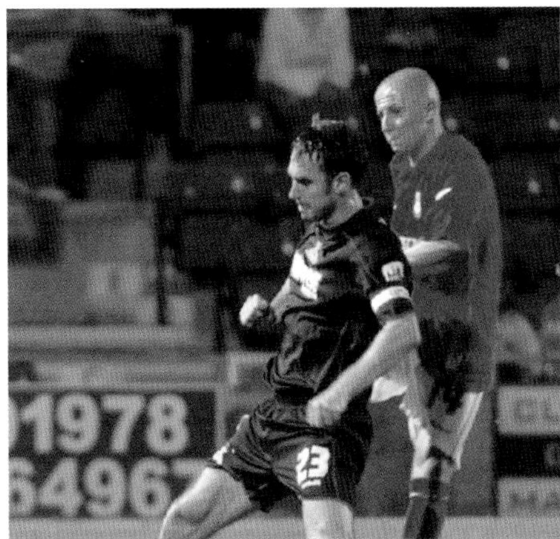

Foy shoots for goal.

Fergie makes another surge forward.

Wrexham's dismal goalless run ended in bizarre fashion, but it wasn't enough to earn them their first win since the opening day of the season.

Denis Smith's men had fired blanks for four games and the boss had been working hard all week to bring new faces and better luck to The Racecourse. And luck certainly played a part as they re-found their scoring touch.

But they were undone by some shaky defending as Bury's new Welsh signing Matthew Tipton earned a point for the home side. It could have been worse, though, were it not for a superb save in the closing stages by Michael Ingham as Tipton burst into the box and fired in a hard, low shot.

After strong early pressure by the home side, Lee McEvilly gave the visitors the lead - their first goal in more than 400 minutes of football - the ball bobbling into the net off his shin after Jon Walters delicate through-ball left the home defence flat-footed.

The lead lasted just two minutes though. A clearance by Reds keeper Michael Ingham hit Jon Newby who centred for Tipton.

His shot was blocked on the line but the ball fell to Brian Barry-Murphy who slotted home from 15 yards.

Then Robbie Foy, who replaced McEvilly, forced another mistake in the Bury defence and raced towards the edge of the box where home captain Dave Flitcroft made a lunging challenge the ball looping into the top corner of the net.

Wrexham's defensive frailties showed up again early in the second-half when Tipton was given far too much time and space to curl home Bury's second equaliser from 25 yards.

McEvilly had received treatment on his injured ankle before kick-off and joins the queue for the Racecourse treatment room.

Centre-half Shaun Pejic will be out for two months with knee ligament damage and hernia victim Lee Roche is another long-term casualty, with six more in the queue for the treatment room. And centre-half Dave Bayliss added to Smith's woes with a straight red card in the last few minutes for smashing Tipton in the face as he threatened to break.

Wrexham's Paul Linwood could have had a debut goal, but the former Tranmere defender, who signed on Friday, directed a free header over the bar from six yards out. Mark Jones put in another impressive performance and was denied a goal by the fingertips of Bury's Welsh keeper Neil Edwards.

Referee: Paul Robinson (Yorkshire)

Bury 2	**Wrexham 2**
B. B.Murphy 13'	Lee McEvilly 11'
Matthew Tipton 52'	Dave Flitcroft (og) 24'

Attendance: 2,468

You silly boy Bayliss!

Starting XI:

01 Neil Edwards
12 Paul Scott
05 David Challinor
19 John Hardiker
16 Simon Whaley
08 Dwayne Mattis
07 David Flitcroft 81'
11 Brian Barry-Murphy 72'
03 Thomas Kennedy
29 Jon Newby 87'
22 Matthew Tipton

Subs:

02 Lee Unsworth 72'
04 John Fitzgerald
14 Stuart Barlow 87'
18 Jake Sedgemore 81'
21 Craig Dootson (GK)

Stats:

Shots on Goal: 17
Shots on Target: 10
Shots off Target: 7
Possession: 48%
Fouls Conceded: 14
Corners: 6
Yellow Cards: 0
Red Cards: 0

Starting XI:

01 Michael Ingham
21 Paul Linwood
04 Dave Bayliss
06 Dennis Lawrence
05 Paul Warhurst
08 Danny Williams
17 Mark Jones
10 Darren Ferguson 86'
07 Andy Holt
09 Jon Walters
11 Lee McEvilly 20'

Subs:

03 Alex Smith
13 Michael Jones (GK)
14 Robbie Foy 20'
19 Levi Mackin 86'
23 Gareth Evans

Stats:

Shots on Goal: 10
Shots on Target: 4
Shots off Target: 6
Possession: 52%
Fouls Conceded: 17
Corners: 4
Yellow Cards: 2
Red Cards: 1

The lads celebrate with Lee McEvilly.

Flitcroft's own-goal.

It was a frantic start to the game with Wrexham opening the scoring after only 36 seconds. Virtually from the kick off Paul Warhurst played a defence-splitting pass to send Mark Jones free and his inside ball picked out Jon Walters. His shot was blocked by Tynan, but Mark Jones had followed up well and swept the ball home as the Bees watched in despair.

The early goal did not knock Barnet out of their stride though and they had an opportunity of equalising when Ingham failed to collect a low cross. However, there were no strikers present to attack the loose ball and Ingham claimed it at the second attempt. Alex Smith then miscued his clearance, but Grazioli did not take advantage of the mistake shooting straight into the arms on Ingham.

Grazioli let Wrexham off the hook when he placed his shot wide of Ingham's far post, after being clean through courtesy of Holt missing a simple ball on the edge of the area. The miss proved costly as Wrexham went up the other end of the pitch and scored after winning a corner. Ferguson played it to Foy on the edge of the box and, after lining up a shot, he hit it straight at Warhurst. He controlled the ball well in the area before placing it under Tynan from 12 yards.

Wrexham, or rather Dennis Lawrence, handed Barnet a life-line in injury time after he was nutmegged on the right touch line by Sinclair and after the striker advanced into the box, Lawrence clattered into him from behind for a clear penalty. Ian Hendon stepped up and although Ingham had gone the right way, the power on the short meant the ball went under his body and bounced up into the roof of the net.

Wrexham had a couple of scares at the start of the second-half but, with Ingham in such dominant form, he was able to collect all that was thrown at him with ease, as Wrexham put the victory beyond doubt just before the hour.

It was another flowing move that left the Barnet defence in pieces, as Wrexham simply cut through them with their slick passing. Wrexham worked the ball around the back three, before Lawrence found Holt on the touch-line. He fired in a pass to Jon Walters, who controlled the ball well, before laying the ball off for Mark Jones. A neat drag back from the midfielder created the space required to play the ball inside to Foy and the Liverpool striker showed great composure on the ball, finding the top corner with a floated shot from the edge of the area.

Referee: Trevor Parkes (West Midlands)

Wrexham 3	**Barnet 1**
Mark Jones 1'	Ian Hendon 45' (pen)
Paul Warhurst 32'	
Robbie Foy 59'	

Attendance: 3,768

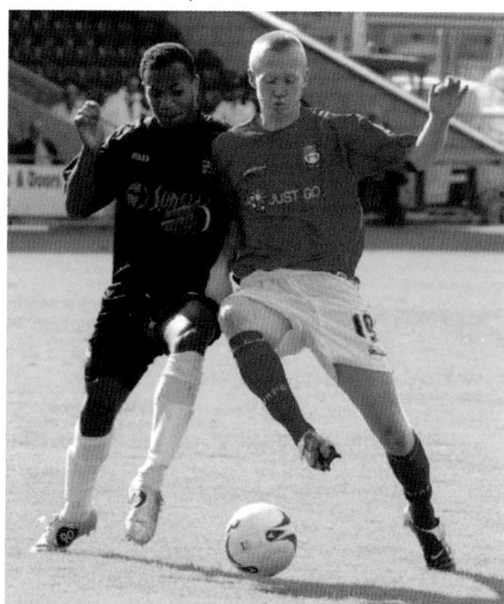

Levi Mackin wins this midfield battle.

Starting XI:

01 Michael Ingham
21 Paul Linwood
06 Dennis Lawrence
07 Andy Holt
05 Paul Warhurst
08 Danny Williams
17 Mark Jones 73'
10 Darren Ferguson
03 Alex Smith
09 Jon Walters
14 Robbie Foy

Subs:

13 Michael Jones
19 Levi Mackin 73'
22 Matt Done
24 Mark Harris
27 Jamie Reed

Stats:

Shots on Goal: 13
Shots on Target: 7
Shots off Target: 6
Possession: 47%
Fouls Conceded: 13
Corners: 5
Yellow Cards: 2
Red Cards: 0

Starting XI:

18 Scott Tynan
04 Ian Hendon
03 Simon King
06 Anthony Charles
05 Adam Gross
10 Den Strevens 68'
02 Nick Bailey
17 Dwane Lee
08 Dean Sinclair
11 Richard Graham 71'
09 Giuliano Grazioli

Subs:

01 Ross Flitney (GK)
12 Lee Roache 71'
15 Damien Batt
19 Ben Bowditch
21 Louis Soares 68'

Stats:

Shots on Goal: 7
Shots on Target: 1
Shots off Target: 6
Possession: 53%
Fouls Conceded: 11
Corners: 4
Yellow Cards: 2
Red Cards: 0

Paul Warhust scoring from close range.

Foy and Walters celebrate the third.

Wrexham dominated the first-half from the start and could have been a goal up before Andy Holt opened the scoring in the eighth minute. The visitors failed to clear a Ferguson corner and Jon Walters was denied his first goal in a Wrexham shirt, when a Cheltenham player cleared his shot off the line.

Wrexham were not to be denied and from another Ferguson corner Andy Holt found himself unmarked and he planted a header into the roof of the net, that cleared the jumping Cheltenham player on the goal line.

With Cheltenham reverting to one up front, they never put Wrexham under any pressure, but in Kayode Odejayi, they had a striker who had the physical presence to play the lone striker role. Odejayi created a couple of opportunities for himself, after Warhurst initially struggled to cope with his power, but when he reached the Wrexham area, the final ball lacked any quality and Ingham was largely a spectator in the Wrexham goal for the first-half hour.

Walters was full of running up front and went close again, but this time Shane Higgs managed to turn his shot around the near post following further good approach play by Ferguson but, despite their dominance, Wrexham could have gone in at half time all square as they gifted the visitors an opportunity to equalise in first-half stoppage time.

Cheltenham reorganised at half-time, matching Wrexham's 3-5-2 formation with Bird replacing Finnigan and this almost paid dividends as Odejayi out paced the Wrexham defence early in the second-half.

But again he rushed his shot on reaching the area and dragged the ball wide into the side netting of Ingham's near post. Soon after Simon Spender replaced Paul Linwood, with the on-loan Tranmere defender limping off the pitch.

Wrexham got the second goal their performance fully deserved with 20 minutes left and this put the game beyond Cheltenham. It was another flowing move from Wrexham, with Williams picking out Mark Jones and his short pass found Walters in enough space to curl the ball around the dive of Higgs and into the net off the near post. It was a good strike from Walters for his first goal in a Wrexham shirt, but the pass from Jones was weighted perfectly.

Walters then beat Higgs to the ball on the edge of the area, but he got it tangled up in his legs and this allowed Cheltenham to clear the danger. At the other end of the pitch, Ingham did well rushing out to palm the ball away in his area and then completing the clearance with a kick into touch. Cheltenham threw balls into the box but Ingham's handling was superb all afternoon and the last attempt came when Vincent blazed the ball high over the bar.

Referee: Russell Booth (Nottinghamshire)

Wrexham 2 **Cheltenham Town 0**
Andy Holt 8'
Jon Walters 69'

Attendance: 3,671

Walters wraps it up.

Starting XI:

01 Michael Ingham
21 Paul Linwood 50'
05 Paul Warhurst
07 Andy Holt
12 Dean Bennett
08 Danny Williams
17 Mark Jones 83'
10 Darren Ferguson
03 Alex Smith
09 Jon Walters
14 Robbie Foy 86'

Subs:

11 Lee McEvilly
13 Michael Jones (GK)
19 Levi Mackin 83'
20 Simon Spender 86'
25 Mike Williams

Stats:

Shots on Goal: 13
Shots on Target: 7
Shots off Target: 6
Possession: 55%
Fouls Conceded: 7
Corners: 10
Yellow Cards: 1
Red Cards: 0

Starting XI:

01 Shane Higgs
02 Jeremy Gill
15 Michael Townsend 79'
06 Michael Taylor
03 Jamie Victory
07 Brian Wilson
08 John Finnigan 45'
11 Grant McCann
22 John Melligan
10 Damien Spencer 67'
17 Kayode Odejayi

Subs:

05 Gavin Caines 79'
12 Scott Brown (GK)
14 David Bird 45'
18 Ashley Vincent 67'
21 Michael Rose

Stats:

Shots on Goal: 10
Shots on Target: 4
Shots off Target: 6
Possession: 45%
Fouls Conceded: 5
Corners: 4
Yellow Cards: 1
Red Cards: 0

Danny clears the danger.

Fergie takes control.

Wrexham's three match unbeaten run ended with a 2-0 defeat at Lincoln, as Nat Brown and Dean Keates struck for the Imps.

Lincoln looked second best early on as the Dragons created a number of chances, with Mark Jones picking out Robbie Foy with a clever pass for the best of them, only for the striker to lose control as the ball ran away from him.

Wrexham's Jon Walters then got in front of his marker, but saw his header saved by Lincoln goalkeeper Alan Marriott but it was the hosts who broke the deadlock in the 63rd minute.

A corner from Scott Kerr was fumbled by Wrexham keeper Michael Ingham and in the scramble that followed Nat Brown forced the ball home.

Four minutes later, Ingham produced a backward diving save to keep out a long-range shot from Kerr, before Dean Keates smashed in a shot from 20 yards, which flew inches over with Ingham rooted to his line.

Wrexham's frustration began to show with Alex Smith and Paul Warhurst yellow-carded for fouls and Lincoln clinched the game in stoppage time when a mistake by Warhurst let in Francis Green, who set up a tap-in for Keates.

Denis Smith:

"I can't say that this didn't hurt, because it did, but we were beaten by the better side tonight. We were never in the game and as good as we were Saturday, we were poor tonight. Fair play to them, they worked hard and once their got their goal, their tails were up."

Referee: Andy Penn (West Midlands)

Lincoln City 2 Wrexham 0
Nat Brown 64'
Dean Keates 90'

Attendance: 2,905

League 2 Table to date

Pos	Team	Pld	W	D	L	GD	Pts
1	Notts County	8	4	4	0	5	16
2	Grimsby Town	8	5	1	2	3	16
3	Carlisle United	8	4	2	2	2	14
4	Rochdale	8	4	1	3	6	13
5	Chester City	8	3	4	1	3	13
6	Darlington	8	3	4	1	3	13
7	Leyton Orient	8	4	1	3	-1	13
8	Wycombe Wanderers	8	2	6	0	5	12
9	Cheltenham Town	8	2	5	1	2	11
10	Lincoln City	8	2	5	1	2	11
11	**Wrexham**	**8**	**3**	**2**	**3**	**2**	**11**
12	Peterborough United	8	3	2	3	2	11
13	Northampton Town	8	2	5	1	1	11
14	Barnet	8	3	2	3	0	11
15	Stockport County	8	1	6	1	0	9
16	Shrewsbury Town	8	2	3	3	-1	9
17	Bristol Rovers	8	2	3	3	-2	9
18	Oxford United	8	1	5	2	-2	8
19	Macclesfield Town	8	2	2	4	-3	8
20	Boston United	8	1	4	3	-5	7
21	Rushden & Diamonds	8	1	4	3	-5	7
22	Mansfield Town	8	1	3	4	-3	6
23	Bury	8	1	2	5	-6	5
24	Torquay United	8	1	2	5	-8	5

Holty off injured again.

Starting XI:

01 Alan Marriott
17 Colin Cryan
05 Paul Morgan
06 Jamie McCombe
02 Lee Beevers
11 Scott Kerr
22 Dean Keates
23 Nat Brown
07 Derek Asamoah 76'
08 Gary Birch 87'
03 Paul Mayo

Subs:

04 Gareth McAuley 87'
09 Francis Green 76'
18 Oliver Ryan
25 Maheta Molango
26 Marvin Robinson

Stats:

Shots on Goal: 15
Shots on Target: 5
Shots off Target: 10
Possession: 60%
Fouls Conceded: 7
Corners: 11
Yellow Cards: 0
Red Cards: 0

Starting XI:

01 Michael Ingham
06 Dennis Lawrence
05 Paul Warhurst
19 Andy Holt 41'
12 Dean Bennett
08 Danny Williams
17 Mark Jones
10 Darren Ferguson
03 Alex Smith
09 Jon Walters
14 Robbie Foy 64'

Subs:

11 Lee McEvilly 64'
13 Michael Jones (GK)
19 Levi Mackin
20 Simon Spender
21 Paul Linwood 41'

Stats:

Shots on Goal: 2
Shots on Target: 1
Shots off Target: 1
Possession: 40%
Fouls Conceded: 8
Corners: 5
Yellow Cards: 2
Red Cards: 0

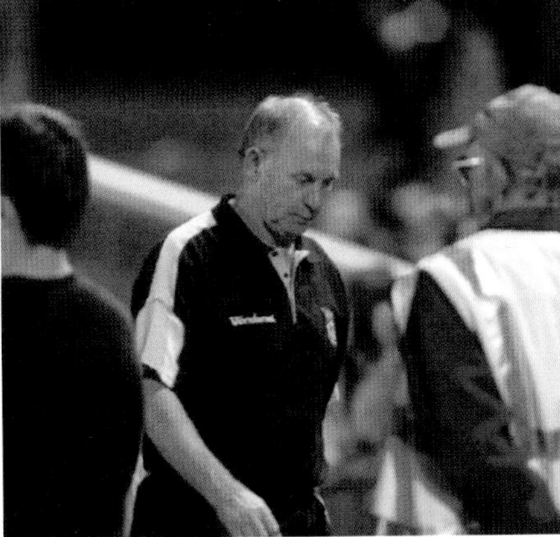

Smith: "We were never in the game."

Walters battles with the Lincoln defence.

After the usual early flurries from the home side, in which Bennett and Linwood distinguished themselves and Carrots held onto a long-range drive to give him a confidence boost, we settled into our familiar role as the better footballing side. There was some decent stuff on offer, with Ferguson always involved (just as well, with Jonah out of sorts) and Foy looking lively early on.

Orient saw a couple of efforts whistle high and wide, while Wrexham's final ball, or cross, was always a bridge too far. Lawrence's barnstorming run, before setting up Jonah, who scuffed his shot, was probably the highlight of the half.

As the second period began, the force seemed to remain with us, as Bennett and Smith got forward with pleasing regularity, although the former does tend to over-elaborate. Walters, not the most mobile, but a willing grafter, also impressed, but the goal took everyone by surprise. The ball broke to Ferguson thirty yards out, and he had a clear run in on the keeper, but our skipper, presumably painfully aware of his lack of pace, instantly unleashed a low drive past home gloveman Glyn Garner. A tremendous, beautiful goal.

In fact the strike seemed to go to Fergie's head – he had two efforts from similar distance saved within 10 minutes of the goal, but our play became scrappier as the half wore on, and old doubts resurfaced. The referee didn't help matters with some over-officious stuff, one of which brought a free-kick to the O's which would have caused more trouble to the driver of a nearby crane (if he'd been there) than Carrots. Our young keeper also held on to a swerving long-range free-kick, but he's a bit hesitant on crosses and 10 minutes from time this proved partly our undoing as the hosts' Alexander, unmarked incidentally, headed in from close range.

That was about it, really, although Denis's late triple substitution came too late to have any effect. Warhurst for Williams a bit sooner would have made more sense.

Denis Smith: "That was a fair result over the course of the 90 minutes, but having taken the lead we should not have conceded it so late in the game. It was not the best of spectacles for the neutral, as both sides seemed cancel each other out for long periods. We have been encouraging Darren to get forward more and it was good to see him score, although I don't think that the Orient manager will have the same view of it! I was pleased by Michael Jones' display and you would have been hard pressed to know that he was a young lad making his first full start. I take some of the blame for the result, as we started to look a little ragged towards the end and I should have made the substitutions then, but my timing was off on this occasion!"

Referee: Bob Desmond (Wiltshire)

Leyton Orient 1	**Wrexham 1**
Gary Alexander 80'	Darren Ferguson 53'

Attendance: 3,733

Carrots makes his full debut.

Starting XI:

01 Glyn Garner
15 Justin Miller
14 Gabriel Zakuani
06 John Mackie
03 Matthew Lockwood
08 Craig Easton
04 Michael Simpson
17 Daryl McMahon
07 Wayne Carlisle 61'
09 Gary Alexander
19 Jabo Ibehre 74'

Subs:

02 Donny Barnard
11 Joe Keith
12 Glen Morris (GK)
16 Shane Tudor 61
22 Efe Echanomi 74'

Stats:

Shots on Goal: 11
Shots on Target: 2
Shots off Target: 9
Possession: 50%
Fouls Conceded: 10
Corners: 3
Yellow Cards: 0
Red Cards: 0

Starting XI:

13 Michael Jones
21 Paul Linwood
04 Dave Bayliss
06 Darren Ferguson
12 Dean Bennett
08 Danny Williams 84'
17 Mark Jones 84'
10 Darren Ferguson
03 Alex Smith
09 Jon Walters
14 Robbie Foy 84'

Subs:

05 Paul Warhurst 84'
11 Lee McEvilly 84'
19 Levi Mackin 84'
20 Simon Spender
25 Mike Williams

Stats:

Shots on Goal: 5
Shots on Target: 4
Shots off Target: 1
Possession: 50%
Fouls Conceded: 16
Corners: 0
Yellow Cards: 3
Red Cards: 0

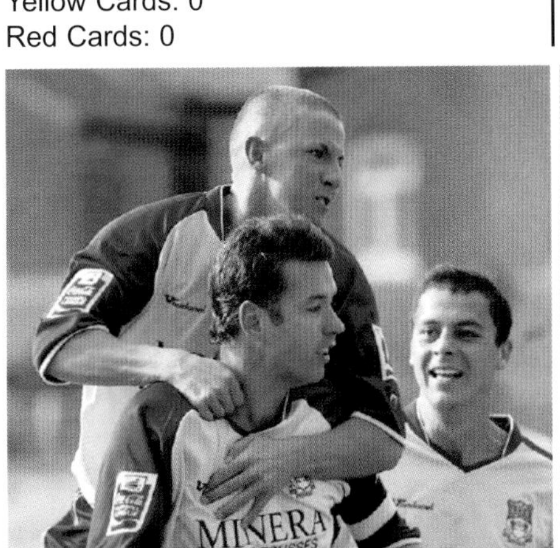

Fergie celebrates with the lads.

Jon Walters is denied by Glyn Garner.

With Macclesfield opting for one up front it was clear they had come for a draw, with the Silkmen conceding a lot of possession to Wrexham. This was a feature of the game as a whole but, despite Wrexham seeing a lot of the ball, they failed to muster any early chances. Mark Jones went closest with a low drive, but it was a comfortable save for Fettis. Further long-range efforts followed, but the only one to test Fettis was a drive from Danny Williams with 20 minutes on the clock.

Wrexham's defence was disrupted with Michael Ingham limping off with a groin injury and he was replaced by teenager Michael Jones in the Wrexham goal. This was compounded with Wrexham reduced to 10 men for almost 10 minutes, after what looked to be an accidental elbow on Paul Warhurst, required the defender to leave the pitch for stitches.

Wrexham did up the tempo for the second-half and Ferguson in particular was the catalyst for the improved play, but the best chances fell to the visitors, as Macclesfield hit Wrexham on the counterattack. In one move, a simple ball over the top, sent Townsend clean through on goal, but Linwood tracked back well and made a last ditch challenge on the striker to dispossess him on the edge of the box.

Wrexham went closest to breaking the deadlock, when they were awarded a free-kick on the edge of the area following a foul on Mark Jones. Ferguson laid the ball back to Bennett and with Fettis' view blocked by Lawrence, the keeper watched helplessly as the ball agonisingly cleared the cross bar.

Wrexham were not to be denied when they finally penetrated the stubborn Macclesfield backline, with the opening goal in the 65th minute. Wrexham won a corner that Ferguson swung out from the left and, with Lawrence and Linwood taking all the markers to the near post, Danny Williams was free to power a header past Fettis to round off a well-worked corner routine.

After 72 minutes, striker Allan Russell replaced Barras and this move paid off for Macclesfield, with the substitute equalising within two minutes of coming on.

Paul Warhurst had appeared to be in control of the situation on the edge of the Wrexham area, but Russell somehow managed to dispossess Warhurst. He turned Warhurst and Linwood, before firing a well struck shot into the bottom corner, that gave Jones no chance of saving.

Danny Williams then went close to regaining the lead when he connected well with a Ferguson lay-off, but his goal bound shot was deflected behind for a corner. Simon Spender was played into acres of space on the right, but he was denied by a good save from Fettis. Spender was again free on the right and this time he picked out Mark Jones inside the six-yard box, but he could only stop the ball rather than turn it in, although the flag had already been raised for offside.

Referee: Dermot Gallagher (Oxfordshire)

Wrexham 1	**Macclesfield Town 1**
Danny Williams 65'	Alan Russell 72

Attendance: 3,830

Dennis wins this aeriel duel.

Starting XI:

01 Michael Ingham 25'
21 Paul Linwood
05 Paul Warhurst
06 Dennis Lawrence
12 Dean Bennett
08 Danny Williams
17 Mark Jones
10 Darren Ferguson
03 Alex Smith
09 Jon Walters
14 Robbie Foy 70'

Subs:

04 Dave Bayliss
13 Michael Jones (GK) 25'
19 Levi Mackin
20 Simon Spender 70'
22 Matt Done

Stats:

Shots on Goal: 13
Shots on Target: 6
Shots off Target: 7
Possession: 56%
Fouls Conceded: 9
Corners: 6
Yellow Cards: 1
Red Cards: 0

Starting XI:

01 Alan Fettis
16 Tony Barras 70'
04 David Morley
05 Danny Swailes
19 Michael Briscoe
12 Danny Whitaker
07 Paul Harsley
14 Kevin McIntyre
03 Kevin Sandworth 45'
06 Martin Bullock
09 Kevin Townson

Subs:

10 John Miles
11 David Beresford
22 Tim Deasy (GK)
23 Andrew Smart 45'
25 Allan Russell 70'

Stats:

Shots on Goal: 4
Shots on Target: 2
Shots off Target: 2
Possession: 44%
Fouls Conceded: 12
Corners: 8
Yellow Cards: 1
Red Cards: 0

Danny heads home for the Reds.

Jon Walters is beaten this time.

You knew Wrexham were going to be in for a difficult evening, when Wycombe had two goals disallowed for offside in the opening quarter of an hour. To even come away from Adams Park with a draw would require the team to dig in, but this effort was missing as the game proved to be a match too far for the injury-ravaged side.

With Wycombe looking dangerous with every attack by making full use of the flanks, the manner of their opening two goals was disappointing. A simple ball from the right flank caught out the Wrexham defence with Bayliss, who had been limping from an earlier tackle, hopelessly appealing for offside as Tyson chased the ball down. Michael Jones rushed off his line and reached the ball before Tyson, but misjudged the bounce as the ball went over him and Tyson was presented with his easiest goal of the season, finishing with a diving header on the line!

Wrexham players were struggling to keep their footing on a sodden pitch, but it was obvious that Wycombe were using the correct studs and a further slip from Bayliss resulted in the second goal midway through the first-half. Bayliss looked to be cutting out the low ball through but his slip sent Betsy clear of the offside trap and he advanced into the box before slotting the ball under Jones and inside of the near post.

Wrexham some how managed to hang on until half time as the first-half followed a predictable pattern with Wycombe appearing to attack at will and Wrexham were grateful to a challenge from Lawrence that deflected a shot from Bloomfield wide of the far post.

Wycombe started the second-half where they left off and a good tip over from Michael Jones kept the deficit to two, when he reacted quickly to Torres's snap shot from the edge of the area.

This could have been the turning point, as within ten minutes of the restart Wrexham had halved the deficit with a well-taken goal from Mark Jones. Jones picked up a through ball from Williams and a quick turn allowed him to break clear of his marker. Robbie Foy did well to take the defender away from Jones and this allowed the midfielder to measure a shot that bounced just in front of Talia and the wet surface zipped the ball into the net.

Tommy Mooney effectively put the game beyond Wrexham when he restored the two-goal advantage.

If anything, the third goal sparked Wrexham's best period of the game, with Bennett seeing his deflected shot narrowly missing the far post. Quick passing between Smith and Walters resulted in Ferguson bursting onto the lose ball in the box, but he was denied by a last ditch diving challenge.

The combination of Betsy, Tyson and Moody proved too much for the Wrexham defence and all three players combined for Wycombe's fourth and last goal.

Referee: Gary Lewis (Cambridgeshire)

Wycome 4	**Wrexham 1**
Nathan Tyson 16' 81'	Mark Jones 54'
Kevin Betsy 22'	
Tommy Mooney 58'	

Attendance: 4,166

Mike Williams made his debut at Wycombe.

Starting XI:

01 Frank Talia
02 Danny Senda
05 Roger Johnson
06 Mike Williamson
03 Clint Easton
22 Sergio Torres 73'
10 Matt Bloomfield
04 Stefan Oakes
07 Kevin Betsy
16 Tommy Mooney 87'
09 Nathan Tyson 90'

Subs:

08 Joe Burnell 73'
11 Ian Stonebridge 90'
12 Russell Martin
18 Jonny Dixon 87'
21 Steve Williams (GK)

Stats:

Shots on Goal: 13
Shots on Target: 10
Shots off Target: 3
Possession: 51%
Fouls Conceded: 17
Corners: 5
Yellow Cards: 0
Red Cards: 0

Starting XI:

13 Michael Jones
21 Paul Linwood 45'
04 Dave Bayliss
06 Dennis Lawrence
12 Dean Bennett
08 Danny Williams
17 Mark Jones
10 Darren Ferguson
03 Alex Smith
09 Jon Walters 79'
14 Robbie Foy

Subs:

19 Levi Mackin
20 Simon Spender
22 Matt Done
25 Mike Williams 45'
27 Jamie Reed 79'

Stats:

Shots on Goal: 5
Shots on Target: 5
Shots off Target: 0
Possession: 49%
Fouls Conceded: 13
Corners: 8
Yellow Cards: 0
Red Cards: 0

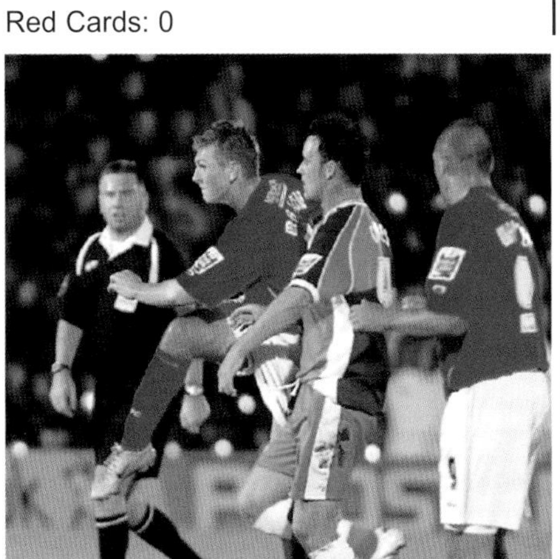

Mark Jones fires in another goal.

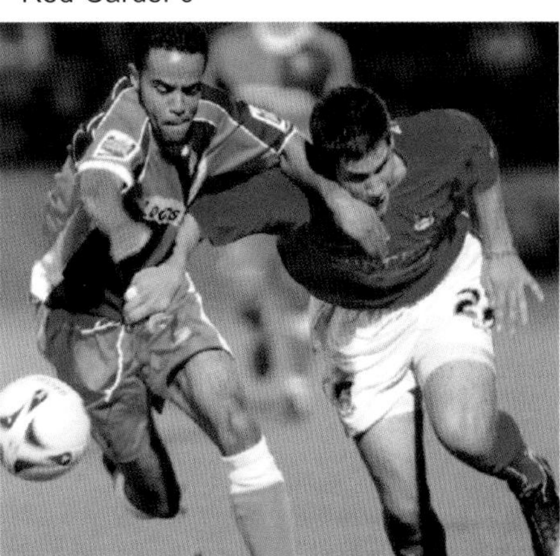

Jamie Reed was another debutant.

With Wrexham replacing Robbie Foy up front with wing back Dean Bennett, Simon Spender made his first start or the season on the right. The move initially paid off with hard running from Bennett and Walters up front combining well, as Wrexham forced two early chances without ever threatening the Stockport goal.

The game turned as early as the seventh minute when Stockport were reduced to ten men, when striker Ludovic Dje was shown a red card for violent conduct after he appeared to elbow Paul Linwood. Referee Nigel Miller had not seen the incident, but after discussing it with his assistant, he was left with no alternative to dismiss the Stockport striker.

Wrexham broke the deadlock after a fine effort from Jon Walters midway through the first-half. The striker received the ball with his back to goal from the lively Mark Jones and after turning his marker he struck an unstoppable left footed shot from twenty yards that went into the stanchion off the far post.

The County keeper then collected the ball just outside of the area but, after no yellow card was shown, Darren Ferguson curled the resulting free-kick over the bar. Wrexham were then grateful to the positioning of Danny Williams, as he cleared a certain equaliser off the line in first-half injury time. Michael Jones came for a corner, but failed to collect it, and the rebound fell kindly to Ashley Williams but his shot was cleared off the line by Williams and Wrexham eventually cleared the resulting corner.

Wrexham started the second-half in control and a brace from Mark Jones within six minutes ended the game as a contest. Six minutes after the restart a simple ball into the box was not cleared and instead the defensive header found Mark Jones unmarked on the edge of the area. His first touch got the ball under control, before he picked out the corner to the keeper's right with a low shot. Jones's second goal was almost identical to his first, when another shot from the edge of the area, was driven through the County players. This unsighted the keeper, who was wrong footed and could not adjust in time, as the ball found the same corner of the net.

County made a triple substitution to liven their game up, but it was Mark Jones who had the next opportunity as he went in search of his hat trick, but his effort curled wide of the post. County will have a long hard season based on this display.

Referee: Nigel Miller (County Durham)

Wrexham 3	**Stockport County 0**
Jon Walters 21'	
Mark Jones 51' 57'	

Attendance: 4,153

Linwood was elbowed in the red-card affair.

Starting XI:

13 Michael Jones
21 Paul Linwood
04 Dave Bayliss
06 Dennis Lawrence
20 Simon Spender
08 Danny Williams
17 Mark Jones
10 Darren Ferguson 84'
03 Alex Smith
09 Jon Walters 86'
12 Dean Bennett 75'

Subs:

01 Michael Ingham (GK)
11 Lee McEvilly 86'
14 Robbie Foy 75'
19 Levi Mackin 84'
25 Mike Williams

Stats:

Shots on Goal: 14
Shots on Target: 3
Shots off Target: 11
Possession: 59%
Fouls Conceded: 9
Corners: 4
Yellow Cards: 0
Red Cards: 0

Starting XI:

21 Carl Ikeme
02 Robert Clare 63'
05 Michael Raynes
28 Tony Vaughan
18 Ross Greenwood
07 Matthew Hamshaw
08 Keith Briggs 63'
06 Ashley Williams
03 Mark Robinson
14 Ludovic Dje
23 Michael Malcolm 63'

Subs:

01 James Spencer (GK)
09 Tesfaye Bramble 63'
16 Chris Williams 63'
20 Danny Griffin
27 Dean Crowe 63'

Stats:

Shots on Goal: 7
Shots on Target: 1
Shots off Target: 6
Possession: 41%
Fouls Conceded: 6
Corners: 3
Yellow Cards: 2
Red Cards: 1

C'mon the Town!!

Mark Jones celebrates another 20-yarder.

Wrexham's first chance came from a poor decision by the officials, when a ball played forward deflected off a Torquay defender, who was retreating from an offside position. With no flag from the linesman, Walters controlled the ball and headed towards goal, but his shot lacked any power and it was a comfortable save for Andy Marriott in front of the Kop.

Wrexham did not have to wait long for the opening goal, as the deadlock was broken in the 17th minute following a flowing move down the left. Holt was playing in defence as a replacement for the rested Dennis Lawrence, but strangely found himself ahead of Alex Smith in the left wing-back position. A ball was played inside the full back that Holt took in his stride and after side-stepping Woods in the area, he squared the ball across the six-yard box for Walters to convert from close range.

The game then went into a quiet spell as both sides picked up bookings and the only shot of note came from Walters, although his long range drive was blocked by strike partner Dean Bennett. As the game headed towards half-time, Wrexham struck for the second time in the afternoon, breaking quick from a Torquay corner that Wrexham were lucky not to concede an equaliser from.

A scramble following a corner in the Wrexham area resulted in Ingham making a good save from Kuffour and as Wrexham cleared the danger Mark Jones made a quick break from midfield. Jones advanced to the half-way line, before delaying his pass to split the Torquay defence to find Bennett free down the left channel. Bennett had checked his run to remain onside and accelerated away from the defenders. After steadying himself in the area, he tucked a low left footed shot past Marriott for a crucial second a minute before half time.

Wrexham scored again within four minutes of the restart and it really was game over for Torquay. Alex Smith was afforded too much space down the Wrexham left and this allowed him to measure across into the box. The ball broke kindly to Walters and his drive was only parried out by Marriott and Spender timed his run from the right flank well to slam the ball in from twelve yards.

Despite Wrexham controlling the game, they allowed Torquay a glimmer of hope following a howler from Mike Ingham. Ingham did well to save at the feet of Bedeau.

The defence advanced to the half way-line, Ingham rolled the ball out for a kick up-field - unfortunately, he forgot to look behind him and a lurking Bedeau nipped in front of him to square the ball for Alan Connell to side foot into the empty net.

Walters then planted a header straight at Marriott before Wrexham steadied themselves courtesy of Walters' second goal of the afternoon from close range with fourteen minutes left. Substitute Lee McEvilly did well to head back Smith's deep cross back across goal, where Walters was unmarked inside the six-yard box to convert first time from close range.

As the game entered injury time, Wrexham conceded another sloppy goal, when a free-kick from the right touch line was swung in for Kuffour to glance in unmarked at the near post.

Referee: Neil Swarbrick (Lancashire)

Wrexham 4	**Torquay United 2**
Jon Walters 17' 76'	Allan Connell 66'
Dean Bennett 44'	Tony Bedeau 90'
Simon Spender 49'	

Attendance: 4,301

"I can play in this division with my eyes shut."

Starting XI:

01 Michael Ingham
21 Paul Linwood
04 Dave Bayliss
07 Andy Holt 26'
20 Simon Spender
08 Danny Williams
17 Mark Jones
10 Darren Ferguson
03 Alex Smith
09 Jon Walters
12 Dean Bennett 73'

Subs:

05 Paul Warhurst 26' 68'
11 Lee McEvilly 73'
13 Michael Jones (GK)
14 Robbie Foy
19 Levi Mackin 68'

Stats:

Shots on Goal: 9
Shots on Target: 5
Shots off Target: 4
Possession: 62%
Fouls Conceded: 10
Corners: 5
Yellow Cards: 2
Red Cards: 0

Starting X1:

01 Andy Marriott
18 Steve Woods
05 Craig Taylor
03 James Sharp
11 Kevin Hill
19 Mamadou Sow 52'
06 Darren Garner
04 Matthew Hewlett
10 Jo Kuffour
07 Tony Bedeau
08 Alan Connell 83'

Subs:

09 Leo Constantine 52'
12 James Bittner (GK)
22 Richard Hancox
23 Liam Coleman 83'
26 Morike Sako

Stats:

Shots on Goal: 8
Shots on Target: 4
Shots off Target: 4
Possession: 38%
Fouls Conceded: 8
Corners: 10
Yellow Cards: 3
Red Cards: 0

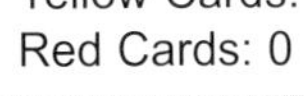

Walters gets a brace today.

Simon Spender gets on the scoresheet.

Holders, Wrexham bowed out of this year's LDV Vans Trophy with an awful defensive display at Blackpool. With Andy Holt passing a late fitness test to play, there was only one change for the visitors - Trinidad international Dennis Lawrence returning in place of Paul Linwood, who had been recalled on Monday by Tranmere Rovers.

Although there few other defensive options open to Dragons boss Denis Smith, the switch was looking decidedly dodgy after only 90 seconds when, with keeper Mike Ingham odds-on favourite to collect a long ball, the big central defender inexplicably headed it over his team-mate and Matt Blinkhorn had the simplest of tasks to score.

Lawrence was immediately moved to the right of the back three, with Dave Bayliss given the task of directing defensive operations as Wrexham set about repairing the damage.

The introduction of substitute Lee McEvilly for Simon Spender after 62 minutes gave an added presence up front, but it signalled a revival by the home side and former Racecourse favourite McGregor saw his goalbound effort through a crowded box blocked.

Foy replaced Bayliss with 17 minutes left and Wrexham went 4-3-3 in a bid to salvage something. Almost immediately we got a reward. Walters found space on the right to pick out Jones' run and his shot from 20 yards slid under Pogliacomi's body. Two minutes later, Walters was on the other flank and, though his cross missed Ferguson, Jones obliged once more with stunning accuracy to the delight of the 200 travelling fans.

With six minutes to go McGregor turned on a poor defensive clearance to lash the ball past Ingham and force extra time.

Dragons captain Darren Ferguson restored Wrexham's lead with a fine shot in the 96th minute, but two horrendous defensive mix-ups in the space of six crazy minutes allowed Keith Southern and Scott Vernon to snatch victory with 15 minutes to spare. The holders dumped out of the competition at the first time of asking.

Referee: C Oliver (Northumberland)

Blackpool 4	**Wrexham 3**
Blinkhorn 2'	Jones 77' 78'
McGregor 84	Ferguson 96'
Southern 99'	
Vernon 104'	

Attendance: 3,239

Mark misses his hat-trick by inches.

Starting XI:

25 Les Pogliacomi
12 Danny Coid 29'
02 Mark McGregor
06 Peter Clarke
30 Chris Armstrong
17 Simon Wiles
04 Keith Southern
08 John Doolan
16 Jamie Burns 41'
14 Matthew Blinkhorn
26 Timmy Wright 65'

Subs:

01 Lee Jones (GK)
05 Tony Butler
10 Scott Vernon 65'
11 Rory Prendergast 41'
20 Simon Grayson 29'

Stats:

Shots on Goal: 18
Shots on Target: 10
Shots off Target: 8
Possession: %
Fouls Conceded: 18
Corners: 6
Yellow Cards: 3
Red Cards: 0

Starting XI:

01 Michael Ingham
06 Dennis Lawrence 90'
04 Dave Bayliss 73'
07 Andy Holt
20 Simon Spender 62'
08 Danny Williams
17 Mark Jones
10 Darren Ferguson
03 Alex Smith
09 Jon Walters
12 Dean Bennett

Subs:

11 Lee McEvilly 62'
13 Michael Jones (GK)
14 Robbie Foy 73'
19 Levi Mackin 90'
25 Mike Williams

Stats:

Shots on Goal: 19
Shots on Target: 8
Shots off Target: 11
Possession: %
Fouls Conceded: 10
Corners: 8
Yellow Cards: 1
Red Cards: 0

Smith: "We were easily the best side."

Jon Walters goes close.

Overall this was a poor game of football and you have to say that the points were thrown away after we took a lead on the hour.

In the first-half Jonah hit the post from 30 yards, but that was about it really and the teams went in level, neither side deserving a lead.

The second period followed the same pattern of the first and when Wrexham took the lead after 57 minutes it came out of the blue. Mark Jones was fouled by Craig Disney 35 yards out from the goal and this earned the Rovers midfielder a yellow card. Ferguson swung the ball into the box where Andy Holt climbed well to head the ball towards goal and Dennis Lawrence stole in unmarked to force the ball past Shearer from inside the six yard box.

Simon Spender did not make enough of the freedom he had down the right, and after he over-hit another cross, you could overhear Danny Williams shouting 'f**king hell Spends!'

Wrexham did not take notice of the obvious danger from set plays and appeared to concede foul after foul, which just invited further pressure.

Eventually the pressure was too much and the cracks finally appeared in the Wrexham back-line.

From another free-kick the ball was swung in and with the free-kick only partially cleared, Forrester crossed to the other side of the area where striker Richard Walker was in acres of space and he planted a free header into the bottom corner that just evaded Dennis Lawrence on the line.

Wrexham were shocked at this and Mark Jones could not keep control of his emotions and blasted the ball away after a free-kick was awarded against Wrexham. A costly mistake as this was his fifth booking and meant he will be suspended for the Darlington game next Saturday.

There was still time for Wrexham to hit the self-destruct button once again, this time conceding a corner deep into injury time. Wrexham failed to clear the danger and Campbell swung in a cross from the left for Richard Walker to have another free header. He made no mistake turning the ball in from twelve yards.

Referee: Pat Miller (Bedfordshire)

Bristol Rovers 2	**Wrexham 1**
Richard Walker 88' 90'	D.Lawrence 57'

Attendance: 5,730

The lads are off to a great start.

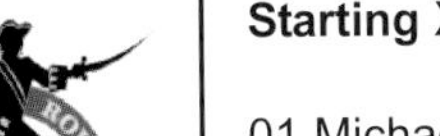

Starting XI:

23 Scott Shearer
32 Aaron Lescott
02 Craig Hinton
06 Steve Elliott
03 Robbie Ryan
19 Alistair Gibb 86'
08 James Hunt
20 Craig Disley
11 Chris Carruthers 71'
10 Richard Walker
09 Junior Agogo 81'

Subs:

07 Stuart Campbell 86'
14 John Anderson
18 Jamie Forrester 71'
26 Lewis Haldane 81'
33 Martin Horsell (GK)

Stats:

Shots on Goal: 10
Shots on Target: 8
Shots off Target: 2
Possession: 55%
Fouls Conceded: 9
Corners: 5
Yellow Cards: 1
Red Cards: 0

Starting XI:

01 Michael Ingham
06 Dennis Lawrence
04 Dave Bayliss
07 Andy Holt
20 Simon Spender
08 Danny Williams
17 Mark Jones
10 Darren Ferguson
03 Alex Smith
09 Jon Walters 79'
30 Juan Ugarte 45'

Subs:

05 Paul Warhurst
11 Lee McEvilly 79'
13 Michael Jones (GK)
14 Robbie Foy 45'
19 Levi Mackin

Stats:

Shots on Goal: 7
Shots on Target: 5
Shots off Target: 2
Possession: 45%
Fouls Conceded: 7
Corners: 2
Yellow Cards: 1
Red Cards: 0

The inquest begins into Rovers' 93' winner.

The fans can't believe what just happend.

For once we weren't the better side to start off with and we were grateful for some profligate Posh shooting and wasteful crosses in the first 15 minutes. Our attacks were sporadic to say the least – a couple of Lawrence leaps and a brace of Walters wallops, one onto the roof of the stand, much to the amusement of the assembled pizza-munchers. It was to get worse for Walters. Midway through the half, though, there was cause for optimism. A Wrexhamesque move involving seven or eight passes, culminated in Ferguson's long ball being intelligently laid back by Smith to Holt, whose cross found McEvilly looping a header over the goalie and onto the roof of the net. Generally, though, our passing wasn't great.

Posh's was better and it took a quite breathtaking tipover from Ingham to deny them as the half hour approached. On exactly 30 minutes, their loanee Lee Thorpe got away on the right in acres of space, had time to weigh up his options and picked out the long-serving David Farrell, who will never score an easier goal, being unmarked, dead centre, six-yard line.

Two minutes later it could have been worse. Thorpe was again the provider, as ex-Norwich man Danny Crow thundered a shot against the underside of the bar. The ball rebounded to Dennis Lawrence, who appeared transfixed as Crow mishit his second attempt for Ingy to gather safely.

After the break, Posh continued to pressurise us and a swerving centre from Farrell deceived everyone, before bouncing off the bar. Play switched to the other end and around the hour mark, we had two glorious chances to equalise. A terrible backpass saw Evil beat the 'keeper to the ball, only to fire criminally into the side netting, and a minute later a spell of pinball in the home area saw the ball break to an unmarked Walters, six yards out, left of centre. His ghastly finish (high, wide and far from handsome) contrived to be both unbelievable and unforgivable.

The introduction of the energetic Foy, for Smith, was a step in the right direction, but really the home side should have sewn things up with ten minutes left. Crow was sent clear and his shot beat Ingham only to hit the top of the bar, our 'keeper claiming the rebound at the second attempt. And so to the final, desperate assault. A free-kick, headed behind for a corner, which met the same fate. This time, Ferguson's kick from the right, was aimed at the near post where Andy Holt arrived at speed to head in. It was a just reward for Holty, a whole-hearted player if ever there was one. He kept plugging away even though, unusually for him, he was subdued by the mediocrity around him. Levi Mackin came on for the ineffective Danny Williams, as we comfortably saw out the final seconds.

Referee: Mick Russell (Hertfordshire)

Peterborough United 1	**Wrexham 1**
David Farrell 30'	Andy Holt 88'

Attendance: 4,014

Holty rescues a point.

Starting XI:

01 Mark Tyler
11 Adam Newton
05 Sagi Burton
06 Mark Arber
12 Sean St. Ledger
02 Dean Holden
25 Jamie Hand
04 Paul Carden
07 David Farrell 86'
22 Danny Crow 90'
26 Lee Thorpe

Subs:

03 Peter Kennedy 86'
09 Trevor Benjamin
10 Calum Willock 90'
19 Richard Logan
20 Ryan Semple

Stats:

Shots on Goal: 13
Shots on Target: 8
Shots off Target: 5
Possession: 53%
Fouls Conceded: 15
Corners: 9
Yellow Cards: 1
Red Cards: 0

Starting XI:

01 Michael Ingham
05 Paul Warhurst
04 Dave Bayliss
06 Dennis Lawrence
07 Andy Holt
08 Danny Williams 84'
10 Darren Ferguson
03 Alex Smith 66'
17 Mark Jones
09 Jon Walters
11 Lee McEvilly

Subs:

13 Michael Jones (GK)
14 Robbie Foy 66'
19 Levi Mackin 84'
20 Simon Spender
25 MikeWilliams

Stats:

Shots on Goal: 12
Shots on Target: 4
Shots off Target: 8
Possession: 47%
Fouls Conceded: 8
Corners: 5
Yellow Cards: 0
Red Cards: 0

Mark Tyler foils Lee McEvilly.

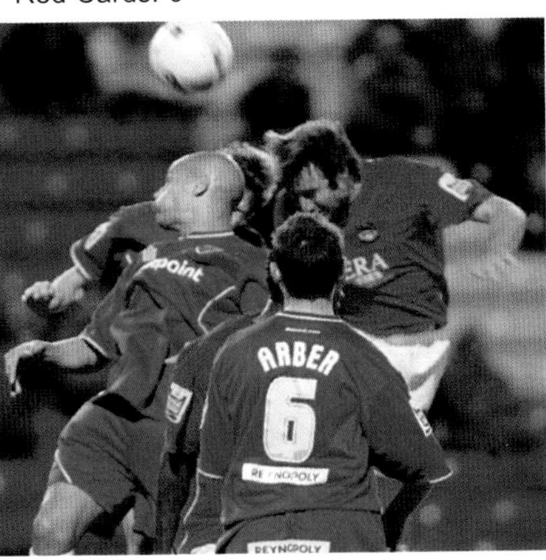

Warhurst wins this aerial battle.

In a game that offered nothing in the first 89 minutes, except for countless fouls committed by Darlington, it suddenly sprung into life when many fans had written the game off as a drab goalless draw. When the arguments had ended following the award of a penalty, Lee McEvilly kept his composure and waited for the keeper to dive before he thumped the ball down the middle for the only goal of the game.

Anybody watching the opening fifteen minutes would have found it difficult to predict that the remaining 75 would be so boring. McEvilly came closest to opening the scoring when he collected the ball 25 yards out and sent in a rasping right-footed shot that just cleared the cross-bar.

You could sense the nerves in the Wrexham defence and these were not helped by a mis-judgement from Michael Ingham. He tried to shield the ball back in the area, but allowed Neil Wainwright to nip in, but his touch took the ball too wide and the resulting shot from the ex-Wrexham player was cleared from the six-yard box by Dave Bayliss.

The second-half was almost an event-free period, with little in the way of chances for either side. However, the game was about to explode at the death.

With five minutes left, Foy took the ball forward and was clattered by Matthew Clarke. It was definite foul, but you could have imagined the ground's surprise when the referee was pointing to the spot, especially as Foy was at least a yard outside the box!

The foul happened in the 85th minute, but the penalty was not taken until the 89th, as it took the three officials four minutes to calm down the resulting melee. Darlington's Russell and Clarke ended up in the book, with Crowell also collecting a caution for Wrexham.

During the four-minute delay, McEvilly kept away from the melee and when it was time to take the penalty, he waited for the keeper to dive to his left and then sent the ball down the middle for the crucial winner.

There was still time for Walters to be booked for time wasting and even when the final whistle was blown, there was still more disciplinary problems for Darlington, as their defender Joey Hutchinson was sent off for foul and abusive language, although you have to sympathise with the lad.

Referee: Garry Sutton (Lincolnshire)

Wrexham 1 **Darlington 0**
Lee McEvilly 89' (pen)

Attendance: 4,881

Jon Walters closes down.

Starting XI:

01 Michael Ingham
06 Dennis Lawrence
04 Dave Bayliss
07 Andy Holt
15 Lee Roche
08 Danny Williams
19 Levi Mackin 31'
10 Darren Ferguson
03 Alex Smith 78'
09 Jon Walters
11 Lee McEvilly

Subs:

13 Michael Jones (GK)
14 Robbie Foy 31'
16 Matt Crowell 78'
20 Simon Spender
27 Jamie Read

Stats:

Shots on Goal: 8
Shots on Target: 1
Shots off Target: 7
Fouls Conceded: 11
Corners: 4
Yellow Cards: 4
Red Cards: 0

Starting XI:

23 Sam Russell
12 Shelton Martis
06 Joey Hutchinson
05 Matthew Clarke
17 David Duke 24'
07 Neil Wainwright
21 Anthony Peacock 71'
10 Jonjo Dickman
02 Ryan Valentine
11 Simon Johnson
20 Akpo Sodje

Subs:

04 Matthew Appleby
14 Stephen Thomas 24'
22 Neil Maddison
24 Guylain Ndumbu-Nsungu 71'
27 Gavin Parkin

Stats:

Shots on Goal: 1
Shots on Target: 1
Shots off Target: 0
Fouls Conceded: 25
Corners: 2
Yellow Cards: 4
Red Cards: 1

Lee safely dispatches penalty.

Job done!

Wrexham crashed out of the cup at Vale Park on a cold Friday night. Although a division below the Burslem club, we did not look out of place and the 1,000 travelling fans saw their team put up a creditable display in front of a disappointing crowd of 5,000.

Port Vale almost took the lead early on when the Wrexham defence stood off Birchall and his shot from outside of the area was parried by Ingham. None of the Wrexham defenders reacted to the loose ball and Ingham did well again to block the rebound shot from Nathan Lowndes.

Vale opened the scoring on 20 minutes. Wrexham were slow to react to a set piece only sending Spender out for a short corner, but he was outnumbered. This allowed Birchall to get a better angle to cross in from Wrexham's right. Although the ball lacked any quality, it somehow got to the near post, where Ingham did well to parry the initial shot from Husbands. The ball rebounded back to Husbands, who this time made no mistake from close range.

Wrexham then had a decent penalty shout turned down when Walters went down under a heavy challenge by Dinning, but the referee waved play on and Walters eventually required treatment off the pitch.

Wrexham started a lot brighter in the second-half with McEvilly having a chance from a Ferguson free-kick. The goal came just after the hour.
Bayliss had the ball in his own half and he delivered it forward for Walters to flick on. The Port Vale defenders just stood there appealing for offside as McEvilly made his way into the box before tucking the ball past Goodlad for a well taken equaliser.

Wrexham fans' joy was only short lived, as Port Vale forced a corner within a minute of the restart. Wrexham had sufficient opportunities to clear the ball as it rebounded around the back post before it broke to Constatine. He made no mistake, burying the ball under Ingham for a debut goal from only six yards.

It was no surprise that Simon Spender was replaced by Robbie Foy with 20 minutes left, as Wrexham reverted to 4–3–3 to go in search for the equaliser. Foy was lively when he came on and went close within a minute of being on the pitch, when he drove narrowly wide of the near post from the edge of the area. At the end Vale were hanging on and their time-wasting tactics were testimony to the scare that Wrexham had given them.

Referee: Darren Deadman (Cambridgeshire)

Port Vale 2	**Wrexham 1**
M. Husbands 20'	Lee McEvilly 63'
Leon Constatine 65'	

Attendance: 5,046

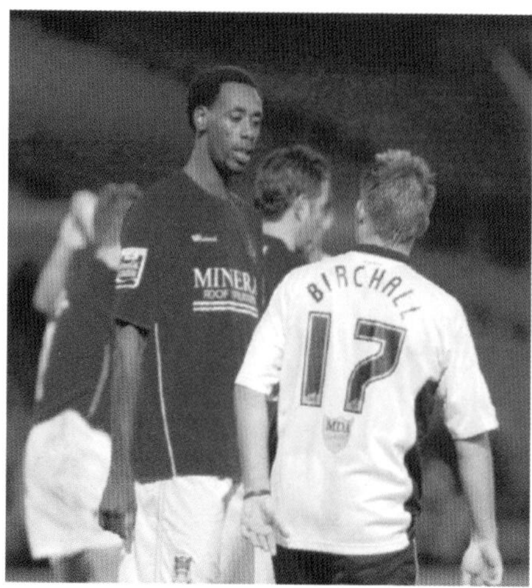

"Do you fancy playing for Trinidad?"

Starting XI:

01 Mark Goodlad
16 Steve Rowland
02 George Pilkington
12 Tony Dinning
20 Mickey Bell
17 Christopher Birchall
18 Mark Innes 80'
03 Craig James
30 Michael Husbands 67'
09 Nathan Lowndes
33 Leon Constatine

Subs:

11 Jeff Smith 67'
21 Joe Cardle
24 Jonny Brain (GK)
26 Andy Porter 80'
34 Louis Briscoe

Stats:

Shots on Goal: 16
Shots on Target: 9
Shots off Target: 7
Possession: 49%
Fouls Conceded: 15
Corners: 6
Yellow Cards: 3
Red Cards: 0

Starting XI:

01 Michael Ingham
20 Simon Spender 71'
04 Dave Bayliss
06 Dennis Lawrence
15 Lee Roche
08 Danny Williams
17 Mark Jones
10 Darren Ferguson
03 Alex Smith
09 Jon Walters 84'
11 Lee McEvilly

Subs:

12 Dean Bennett 84'
13 Michael Jones (GK)
14 Robbie Foy 71'
16 Matt Crowell
25 Mike Williams

Stats:

Shots on Goal: 10
Shots on Target: 5
Shots off Target: 5
Possession: 51%
Fouls Conceded: 10
Corners: 4
Yellow Cards: 2
Red Cards: 0

McEvilly levels it for the Town.

"These cup competitions!"

Patched-up Wrexham got their first away win of the season at the Kassam Stadium as Denis Smith maintained his unbeaten run against his former club. Danny Williams looked assured at the back and won almost every challenge that came his way. A couple of these challenges were crucial midway through the first-half, when Oxford broke quickly from a Wrexham attack and Williams found himself defending one on one against striker Eric Sabin.

With Wrexham having to soak up some pressure they took the lead six minutes before half time following a mistake by defender Willmott, who slipped while chasing the ball with Jon Walters. This allowed Walters to break free down the right wing and his cross to the centre was perfect for the unmarked McEvilly. The Wrexham striker took one touch to control the ball and smashed his shot under Turley from about 12-yards out.

Oxford made three changes at the break and this had a visible impact as they attacked Wrexham from the start of the second-half, although two of the players, Davies and Griffin, were booked within five minutes of coming on. Dean Bennett rescued Wrexham eight minutes after the re-start when a simple ball forward caught the Wrexham defence out. Steve Basham ran onto the loose ball and lobbed the advancing Ingham, but Bennett appeared from nowhere to hack the ball behind for a corner.

When it looked as if the home side were getting on top of Wrexham, it was the Dragons who scored a crucial second. Good play down the left by Mark Jones won a corner that relieved the pressure and Ferguson's outswinging cross was perfect for McEvilly. He climbed well at the back post to head the ball down back across goal and into the net.

Oxford then hit the post with 20 minutes left, when Roget connected well with a corner from the left that hit the near post. Hackett missed an absolute sitter from about 10 yards, when he blazed horribly wide, as Oxford failed to make the most of their chances. Wrexham on the other hand were showing their hosts how it should be done and scored a third with 15 minutes left - a contender for goal of the season.

Lee McEvilly received the ball infield from the left and he laid the ball off for Mark Jones. The midfielder then flicked the ball around his man and then went on to unleash an unstoppable shot that bent into the inside of the near post from twenty yards, which drew applause from the home fans as the 400+ Wrexham fans went wild. Game over!

Referee: Ray Oliver (West Midlands)

Oxford United 0 Wrexham 3
Lee McEvilly 39' 58'
Mark Jones 75'

Attendance: 4,491

Williams gets the better of Craig Davies.

Oxford United

Starting XI:

19 Billy Turley
06 Jon Ashton
03 Matthew Robinson
23 Leo Roget
05 Chris Willmott
02 Lee Mansell
04 Barry Quinn 45'
10 Chris Hargreaves
08 Lee Bradbury 45'
18 Eric Sabin 45'
09 Steve Basham

Subs:

01 Christopher Tardif (GK)
07 Chris Hackett 45'
12 Craig Davies 45'
14 Jude Stirling
32 Adam Griffin 45'

Stats:

Shots on Goal: 10
Shots on Target: 5
Shots off Target: 5
Possession: 50%
Fouls Conceded: 13
Corners: 4
Yellow Cards: 4
Red Cards: 0

Wrexham AFC

Starting XI:

01 Michael Ingham
04 Dave Bayliss
08 Danny Williams
25 Mike Williams
15 Lee Roche
16 Matt Crowell
17 Mark Jones
10 Darren Ferguson
12 Dean Bennett
09 Jon Walters
11 Lee McEvilly

Subs:

03 Alex Smith
13 Michael Jones (GK)
14 Robbie Foy
20 Simon Spender
27 Jamie Reed

Stats:

Shots on Goal: 8
Shots on Target: 3
Shots off Target: 5
Possession: 50%
Fouls Conceded: 9
Corners: 4
Yellow Cards: 3
Red Cards: 0

Mark Jones on the ball.

McEvilly battles through the U's defence.

Unchanged from last week, Wrexham started the game brightly and should have been ahead within five minutes. A diagonal pass from Ferguson was headed back across the area by Walters, but the inrushing McEvilly scuffed his shot wide. Mark Jones then dispossessed a Posh midfielder and struck a left footed shot well from the edge of the area, but Mark Tyler made a comfortable save, diving low to his left.

Peterborough's chances were few and far between, with Gain having his shot blocked by Bayliss in the 15th minute. Five minutes later Posh did put together a decent move with Thorpe heading Holden's cross back for Hand, but his volley flew over Ingham's bar and into the Kop.

Ferguson was having a big influence on the game and a ball inside the full back sent Bennett bursting into the box but, despite being on his favoured right foot, the wide man had his shot blocked by a covering tackle from Sagi Burton.

The second-half started in a much slower fashion with Peterborough playing closer attention to Ferguson and, as a result, his influence on the game reduced. It took at least 10 minutes following the restart for the first chance, when Walters cross was cut out by a good save from Tyler with McEvilly waiting for it at the back post.

Four minutes later and Wrexham were behind after they failed to clear the danger from a corner. In the build-up to the goal Peterborough were starting to look dangerous and a corner was conceded by Roche following a good cross from the Peterborough right by Holden. When the corner was delivered, Wrexham failed to clear the danger and Crow prodded the ball past Ingham and into the net.

Wrexham struck back with Mark Jones curling a shot from the edge of the area into the arms of Tyler, but the shot lacked any power to trouble the Posh keeper. Ten minutes after the opening goal Wrexham were on level terms.

Peterborough allowed a Wrexham throw-in on the left to be worked to Ferguson and as he travelled along the edge of the area, he played a perfectly weighted inside pass for Mark Jones. It was brilliant vision from Ferguson and Jones timed his run to perfection. His low shot beat Tyler but struck the near post.

Fortunately for Wrexham the ball rebounded across the face of goal and struck the retreating Burton who could do nothing as the ball ended up in the net.

The two teams exchanged free-kicks at the end, with McEvilly driving the ball into the wall for Wrexham and Hand curled his effort over the bar at the other end.

Referee: Phil Joslin (Nottinghamshire)

Wrexham 1	**Peterboro' United 1**
Sagi Burton (og) 69'	Danny Crow 59'

Attendance: 4,481

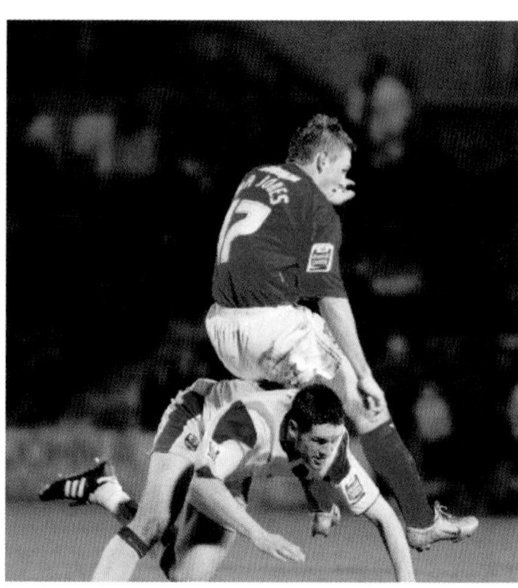

"Oi, will you get off my back!"

Starting XI:

01 Michael Ingham
04 Dave Bayliss
08 Danny Williams
25 Mike Williams
15 Lee Roche
16 Matt Crowell
17 Mark Jones
10 Darren Ferguson
12 Dean Bennett 84'
09 Jon Walters
11 Lee McEvilly

Subs:

03 Alex Smith
13 Michael Jones (GK)
14 Robbie Foy 84'
20 Simon Spender
27 Jamie Reed

Stats:

Shots on Goal: 8
Shots on Target: 6
Shots off Target: 2
Possession: 59%
Fouls Conceded: 12
Corners: 8
Yellow Cards: 2
Red Cards: 0

Starting XI:

01 Mark Tyler
11 Adam Newton
14 Christopher Plummer
05 Sagi Burton
06 Mark Arber
02 Dean Holden
04 Paul Carden
08 Peter Gain
25 Jamie Hand
22 Danny Crow 76'
26 Lee Thorpe

Subs:

09 Trevor Benjamin
10 Calum Willock 76'
12 Sean St. Ledger
20 Ryan Semple
21 Jamie Day

Stats:

Shots on Goal: 6
Shots on Target: 2
Shots off Target: 4
Possession: 41%
Fouls Conceded: 21
Corners: 4
Yellow Cards: 2
Red Cards: 0

Fergie battles in midfield.

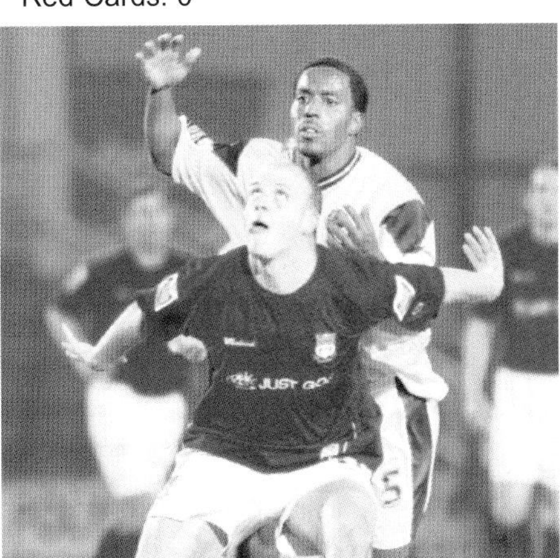
McEvilly keeps his eye on the ball.

Well, there weren't too many incidents as two mediocre sides went at it in an all-round displa,y as depressing as the Fenland afternoon. A general inability to thread more than two passes together, plus an inordinate number of passes going straight into touch, soon became the order of the day.

Dean Bennett showed well in the early stages before fading badly and it wasn't too long before we were behind. A ball over the top saw everyone, fans included, looking for the offside flag, whilst Julian Joachim strolled round Ingham to score. We seemed to be second to every important ball and it's difficult to recall us winning any 50-50 challenges, Danny excepted.

Bayliss and Lawrence were nowhere with crosses, whilst Jones and Roche failed dismally to impose any authority on the game. Evil tried hard, while Jon Walters just tried the patience.

The second period followed much the same pattern, until around the hour mark when we finally seemed to be in the ascendancy. Ferguson, rising out of a trough of ineptitude for the first and only time in the game, played in Evil for carbon copy of Joachim's goal.

Criminally, though, we dropped our guard at the back and within five minutes were trailing again. A little dink over the top, Ingy hesitated before advancing and the man once dubbed "Joe Chim" by an Aussie commentator, scored with a crashing drive.

I felt we should have had a penalty shortly after that, when Kuipers seemed to floor Evil and, when we raised our game toward the end, Evil saw a long-range shot well saved and a Lawrence effort was headed off the line. But a leveller would have been more than our performance deserved.

Denis Smith: "I felt this was another game where we have been the better team, but failed to turn that play into a win. We were not happy about the two goals we conceded, as they came from poor defending in the build up, but to be fair to Julian Joachim he still had plenty to do to beat Michael Ingham on both occasions. He had two chances and he's scored twice! It will be an interesting discussion with the referee when I ask him about the penalty incident. As he must have been one of the few people in the ground who didn't think it was one. The fourth official alongside us was doing his best not to smile at the decision, while the Boston dugout could hardly believe their luck"

Referee: Paul Melin (Surrey)

Boston United 2	**Wrexham 1**
Julian Joachim 14' 66'	Lee McEvilly 60'

Attendance: 1.938

Walters and Bennett make a point.

Starting XI:

25 Michael Kuipers
15 Mark Greaves
06 Alan Whitre
05 Ben Futcher
02 Lee Cannoville
07 Bradley Maylett 90'
12 Simon Rusk
17 Stewart talbot
22 Ian Ross 88'
09 Jason Lee
19 Julian Joachim 90'

Subs:

04 Paul Ellender
10 Francis Green 90'
11 Chris Holland
14 David Galbraith 88'
23 Lawrie Dudfield 90'

Stats:

Shots on Goal: 9
Shots on Target: 5
Shots off Target: 4
Possession: 45%
Fouls Conceded: 20
Corners: 5
Yellow Cards: 3
Red Cards: 0

Starting XI:

01 Michael Ingham
04 Dave Bayliss
08 Danny Williams
06 Dennis Lawrence
15 Lee Roche
16 Matt Crowell 86'
17 Mark Jones
10 Darren Ferguson
12 Dean Bennett 73'
09 Jon Walters
11 Lee McEvilly

Subs:

03 Alex Smith 73'
13 Michael Jones (GK)
20 Simon Spender
25 Mike Williams
27 Jamie Reed 86'

Stats:

Shots on Goal: 9
Shots on Target: 5
Shots off Target: 4
Possession: 55%
Fouls Conceded: 8
Corners: 3
Yellow Cards: 1
Red Cards: 0

Mark Jones on the ball.

Lee McEvilly goes close.

Mansfield looked lively at the start and forced three corners in the opening ten minutes following confusion in the Wrexham defence. Ingham made a good save to deny D'Laryea and then pulled off another close range save from Dawson.

Wrexham were poor and relied too much on the high ball up to the front two, a tactic that the Stags dealt with easily. With six minutes of the half remaining Wrexham conceded a needless penalty, when Danny Williams made a hash of his clearance flicking the ball back over his head into the danger area. Williams tried to redeem himself, but he was penalised for a shirt pull on Richard Barker. Barker took the penalty well sending Ingham the wrong way from 12 yards - 1-0 down at half-time.

The second-half was different story as Wrexham played the ball on the ground and got their just rewards with three goals in the opening 15 minutes. Four minutes after the restart, Wrexham were awarded a corner. Matt Crowell was on set-piece duty for the game and he floated the ball to the penalty area where an unmarked Danny Williams headed home.

Four minutes later and Wrexham turned the game full circle claiming their second goal. It was a good move with Roche picking out McEvilly on the edge of the area and the in-form striker took the ball down well and converted with a well placed shot from 18 yards into the bottom corner.

There was still more to come from Wrexham as they raced into a two-goal lead on the hour mark. Walters and Ferguson played a neat one-two with Ferguson's ball back to Walters inch perfect for the striker and, as he burst into the box, he tucked the ball under Pressman for a well-taken third.

Wrexham were buoyant, but took their foot of the pedal and a better-quality side would have punished them. Both Russell and Day had chances to reduce the deficit for Mansfield, but it was Wrexham who completed the scoring with three minutes to go.

Mark Jones was picked out with a through ball from Walters and with Pressman advancing off his line, Jones calmly lifted the ball over the stranded keeper for a spectacular fourth, which was probably harsh on Mansfield, but welcome nevertheless.

Referee: Andy Hall (West Midlands)

Wrexham 4	**Mansfield Town 1**
Danny Williams 49'	
Lee McEvilly 53'	Richard Barker 41' (p)
Jon Walters 61'	
Mark Jones 87'	

Attendance: 3,421

Danny Williams is swamped after his goal.

Starting XI:

01 Michael Ingham
04 Dave Bayliss
08 Danny Williams
06 Dennis Lawrence
15 Lee Roche
16 Matt Crowell
17 Mark Jones 88'
10 Darren Ferguson
03 Alex Smith
09 Jon Walters
11 Lee McEvilly 84'

Subs:

05 Paul Warhurst 88'
12 Dean Bennett 84'
13 Michael Jones (GK)
20 Simon Spender
25 Mike Williams

Stats:

Shots on Goal: 11
Shots on Target: 8
Shots off Target: 3
Possession: 46%
Fouls Conceded: 14
Corners: 5
Yellow Cards: 2
Red Cards: 0

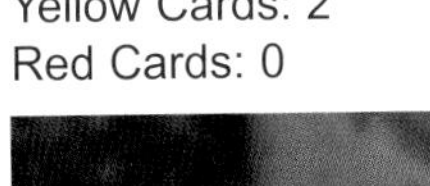

Starting XI:

01 Kevin Pressman
02 Gavin Peers 75'
05 Rhys Day
06 Alex Baptise
03 Gareth Jelleyman
11 Adam Birchall 63'
07 Stephen Dawson 56'
15 Giles Coke
08 Gus Uhlenbeek
27 Jonathon D'Laryea
09 Richard Barker

Subs:

12 Jake Buxton 56'
13 Jason White (GK)
18 Adam Rundle
20 Simon Brown 63'
23 Allan Russell 75'

Stats:

Shots on Goal: 6
Shots on Target: 4
Shots off Target: 2
Possession: 44%
Fouls Conceded: 10
Corners: 7
Yellow Cards: 0
Red Cards: 0

McEvilly and Peers battle it out.

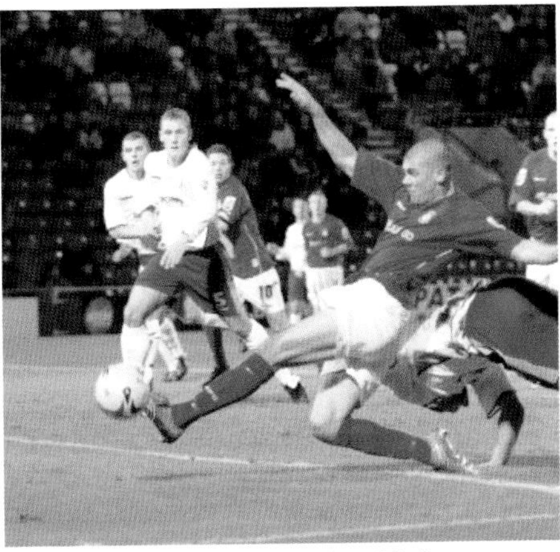

Walters scores the third.

Wrexham started the game brightly and Jon Walters had the ball in the back of the net after five minutes, but this was chalked off by the referee for an earlier foul in the build up to the goal. Wrexham continued to look lively against a well-organised defence, but struggled to create any clear-cut chances. On the other hand Notts County continually found space behind the both wing-backs, but the final ball lacked any quality and Wrexham cleared the danger.

In-form Lee McEvilly had an opportunity to put Wrexham ahead midway through the first-half when the ball broke to him in the box, but Pilkington did well to turn his shot behind for a corner. Wrexham then forced three successive corners to pile the pressure on the County defence but, despite a few nervous moments for the visitors, they held strong and eventually hacked the third corner clear.

As the first-half drew to a close the visitors cleared one header off the line and a diving header took the ball away from Lee McEvilly as the striker was about to pounce. Wrexham also lost the services of Dennis Lawrence a minute before the break, with what looked like a rib injury and he was replaced by youngster Mike Williams, noticeably ahead of Paul Warhurst.

The second-half started with County already time-wasting. Wrexham enjoyed the better of the possession, but clear cut chances were few and far between for the Red Dragons. Darren Ferguson broke into the box to receive a pass from Jon Walters, but his shot on his weaker right foot was blocked behind for a corner by Lewis McMahon.

Lee McEvilly also had a half chance when he was allowed space down the left side of the area, but he fired his low shot into the side netting.

With the game having 0-0 written all over it, Notts County took the lead with six minutes left. The visitors had finally sprung into life and Mike Ingham had to rush off his line to clear for a throw-in down Wrexham's left. This was taken quickly and the ball into the box was inadvertently flicked on by McEvilly and Wrexham lost the second header with substitute Jake Sheridan looping the ball over Ingham from close range.

Denis Smith immediately replaced Crowell with Robbie Foy and this move paid dividends when the on-loan Liverpool striker equalised deep into injury time. It was a perfect through ball from Walters that sent Foy clear on goal and the striker showed no fear curling the ball around the stranded Pilkington for the equaliser.

Referee: Neil Swarbrick (Lancashire)

Wrexham 1	**Notts County 1**
Robbie Foy 90'	Jake Sheridan 84'

Attendance: 4,726

Robbie Foy scores his last gasp equaliser.

Starting XI:

01 Michael Ingham
04 Dave Bayliss
08 Danny Williams
06 Dennis Lawrence 44'
15 Lee Roche
16 Matt Crowell 85'
17 Mark Jones
10 Darren Ferguson
03 Alex Smith 72'
09 Jon Walters
11 Lee McEvilly

Subs:

05 Paul Warhurst
12 Dean Bennett 72'
13 Michael Jones (GK)
14 Robbie Foy 85'
25 Mike Williams 44'

Stats:

Shots on Goal: 8
Shots on Target: 6
Shots off Target: 2
Possession: 52%
Fouls Conceded: 8
Corners: 9
Yellow Cards: 0
Red Cards: 0

Starting XI:

01 Kevin Pilkington
08 Julien Baudet
20 Kelvin Wilson
19 Emmet Friars
02 David Pipe
24 Leis McMahon
04 Mike Edwards
23 Liam Needham
17 Robert Ullathorne
10 Glynn Hurst 45'
28 Mark DeBolla 64'

Subs:

12 Chris Palmer
22 Stacy Long
25 Andy White 64'
27 Jake Skeridan 45'
30 Shaun Marshall (GK)

Stats:

Shots on Goal: 7
Shots on Target: 4
Shots off Target: 3
Possession: 48%
Fouls Conceded: 7
Corners: 3
Yellow Cards: 0
Red Cards: 0

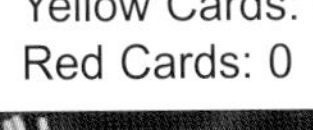

Lee Roche takes to the air.

McEvilly flies into the challenge.

A drab first-half played out on a bumpy pitch saw the Town struggle to create chances. Wrexham almost broke the deadlock with 15 minutes on the clock, when a shot from Matt Crowell struck a Carlisle defender and looped up in the air over a flat-footed Westwood. With the keeper struggling to get back, the ball struck the top of the bar, and bounced across the face of the goal with no Wrexham striker on hand to turn it in.

With Wrexham struggling to make any impact on the Carlisle goal, Denis Smith used the half-time break to replace Alex Smith with Andy Holt and was forced into a tactical change when McEvilly went off injured. He was replaced by Simon Spender who went out on the right wing with Lee Roche moving into midfield and Mark Jones pushing up front.

The move appeared to pay dividends with Wrexham opening the scoring five minutes after the restart. Ferguson also played further forward as a result of the change and it was from his run onto the through ball resulting in the penalty being awarded when he went down under a challenge from Lumsdon who was the last man. Despite denying a clear shot on goal, he only received a yellow card for his misdemeanour. Murphy also ended up in the book for kicking the ball off the spot, but Crowell made no mistake sending the keeper the wrong way to put Wrexham a goal to the good.

With Wrexham looking comfortable and restricting Carlisle to half chances, it was disappointing in the way the equaliser was conceded, as the game entered the final twenty minutes. Carlisle won a corner down their left. This was swung out towards the far post. Ingham came for the cross, but missed and the in-rushing Gray powered a header that rebounded off the bar and struck the unlucky Lawrence on his back before going into the net.

With the game now in the last 10 minutes, Wrexham gave away a soft penalty, but if the initial ball into the box was dealt with correctly, then Ingham would not have been in the position to concede the spot-kick. An easy ball from the right was not challenged by the Wrexham defence and the ball was headed down to the near post by substitute Holmes. Howley reacted the quickest and as he picked up the ball, Ingham rushed off his line and clattered into the striker. The contact was minimal and with the striker on the deck the referee pointed to the spot. Lumsdon, who should have been sent off for Wrexham's penalty, stepped up and sent Ingham the wrong way from the spot.

Robbie Foy was introduced and Lawrence was thrown up front as Wrexham went in search for an equaliser. However, Wrexham were unable to muster a shot, from open play, on target all afternoon.

Referee: Jonathon Moss (West Yorkshire)

Carlisle United 2	**Wrexham 1**
Dennis Lawrence 71' (og)	
Chris Lumsdon 81' (p)	Matt Crowell 50' (p)

Attendance: 6,219

Lee misses out this time.

Starting XI:

20 Kieren Westwood
15 Paul Arnison
05 Danny Livesey
06 Kevin Gray
21 Zigor Aranalde 68'
07 Brendan McGill
04 Chris Billy
08 Chris Lumsdon
03 Peter Murphy
24 Michael Bridges
10 Karl Howley

Subs:

01 Anthony Williams (GK)
09 Derek Holmes 68'
11 Adam Murray
14 Simon Grand
22 Raphael Nade

Stats:

Shots on Goal: 10
Shots on Target: 1
Shots off Target: 9
Possession: 56%
Fouls Conceded: 12
Corners: 9
Yellow Cards: 3
Red Cards: 0

Starting XI:

01 Michael Ingham
04 Dave Bayliss
08 Danny Williams
06 Dennis Lawrence
15 Lee Roche
16 Matt Crowell 86'
17 Mark Jones
10 Darren Ferguson
03 Alex Smith 45'
09 Jon Walters
11 Lee McEvilly 45'

Subs:

07 Andy Holt 45'
13 Michael Jones (GK)
14 Robbie Foy 86'
20 Simon Spender 45'
25 Mike Williams

Stats:

Shots on Goal: 4
Shots on Target: 0
Shots off Target: 4
Possession: 44%
Fouls Conceded: 14
Corners: 5
Yellow Cards: 2
Red Cards: 0

Matty Crowell dispatches the penalty.

Mark Jones foils Chris Billy.

Despite coming into the game on the back of three straight defeats, Rochdale were full of confidence, and were on top for the majority of the first-half. Michael Ingham was called into action early on, when Wrexham could only clear a corner to the edge of the area where Gary Jones fired in a first time shot that Ingham was at full stretch to tip around the post.

Wrexham responded well with Andy Holt picking out Mark Jones in the box. The Welsh under-21 international showed good technique by waiting for the ball to drop over his head, before volleying goal-wards - only to be denied by a covering Rochdale defender.

On 21 minutes, Wrexham were caught in possession in the Rochdale half and, with Andy Holt unable to get back into position, Gary Jones sent over a measured a cross to the back post were Paul Tait strolled in unmarked, planting his header past Ingham. Rochdale noticeably grew in confidence, and they almost extended their lead six minutes later, when Ingham made a spectacular save from a Lambert header.

Wrexham were struggling to test Gilks in the Rochdale goal, and were grateful that referee Garry Sutton awarded a soft penalty with four minutes of the half remaining. The referee noticed a push by Griffiths on Lawrence from a Ferguson delivery.

Despite Crowell scoring a penalty last week, Foy wanted to take it - Crowell won the debate! Crowell kept his cool to send Gilks the wrong way.

The ineffective Foy was replaced at half-time by Bennett, this giving Wrexham more presence up front with Walters testing Gilks almost immediately from the start with a long-range shot that was tipped behind for a corner. Rochdale again controlled the possession and almost regained the lead from a Cooksey corner - Ingham saving well with his feet.

Wrexham then broke quickly up field and when a cross into the Dale box was only headed back out to the edge of the area, Ferguson arrived on-cue to smash in a 25-yard volley into the top left hand corner which, flew past Gilks in the Rochdale goal. A hot contender for goal of the season.

Ferguson's goal lifted Wrexham and they had opportunities to extend their lead with Walters squandering a number of chances. However, it was the visitors who finished stronger and at the end of the game the Dragons were grateful for the final whistle.

Referee: Garry Sutton (Lincolnshire)

Wrexham 2	**Rochdale 1**
Matt Crowell 41' (p)	Paul Tait 21'
Darren Ferguson 65'	

Attendance: 5,167

Fergie salutes his goal.

Starting XI:

01 Michael Ingham
04 Dave Bayliss
08 Danny Williams
06 Dennis Lawrence
15 Lee Roche
16 Matt Crowell
17 Mark Jones
10 Darren Ferguson
07 Andy Holt
09 Jon Walters
14 Robbie Foy 45'

Subs:

02 Jin Whitley
12 Dean Bennett 45'
13 Michael Jones (GK)
18 Shaun Pejic
25 Mike Williams

Stats:

Shots on Goal: 8
Shots on Target: 5
Shots off Target: 3
Possession: 45%
Fouls Conceded: 13
Corners: 3
Yellow Cards: 1
Red Cards: 0

Starting XI:

01 Matthew Gilks
02 Warren Goodhind
05 Gareth Griffiths 55'
04 Tony Gallimore
12 Alan Goodall
04 Ernie Cooksey
11 Gary Jones
08 Neil Brisco
10 Paul Tait
17 Richard Lambert
19 Blair Sturrock

Subs:

06 Jonathon Boardman
07 Lee Cartwright
15 Rory McArdle 55'
16 Tommy Jaszczun
28 Danny Woodhall (GK)

Stats:

Shots on Goal: 11
Shots on Target: 7
Shots off Target: 4
Possession: 55%
Fouls Conceded: 17
Corners: 8
Yellow Cards: 1
Red Cards: 0

The big man climbs the highest.

Lee Roche on the ball.

Wrexham started the first-half where they left off against Rochdale and took the game to the visitors. Despite Grimsby being restricted to a couple of attacks in the opening 15 minutes, Wrexham were unable to create any chances from open-play. The closest they came was when Dennis Lawrence had two free headers, from corners, that both missed the target. The closest Grimsby came to troubling Wrexham was also from a corner, when Ramsden placed a back post header wide.

Wrexham were dominating the midfield with Crowell and Roche breaking down the Grimsby attacks.

Holt broke clear down the left with five minutes of the half left, but his low centre was behind the four advancing Wrexham players. Wrexham did not have to wait long for the opening goal, as Mark Jones broke the deadlock a minute later. It was a simple goal in the end, as Jon Walters headed back Mike Ingham's long clearance into the path of Jones. The Wales under-21 international lashed home into the bottom corner with his left foot from the outside of the area.

Despite this positive start Wrexham, were rocked within five minutes when Michael Reddy was given the freedom of Wrexham's right flank to collect Cohen's pass. The striker advanced 20 yards into the area and, still unchallenged, he finished past Ingham, with a cultured shot.

Wrexham were rocked again with six minutes left, when Grimsby were awarded a soft free kick after Reddy went down on the touchline on the left wing. The free kick was swung into the six-yard box and, with Ingham stuck to his spot, Downey converted the cross with a close range header.

The referee then completely lost the plot. Bollard went down with a head injury following a challenge by Holt. With Bollard rolling around as if he was shot, Holt obviously said some healing words, as all of a sudden a miracle happened as Bollard was back on his feet squaring up to Holt! In the end the referee showed Bollard a second yellow card, and then a red before his linesman informed him that he had not already booked him! Amidst farcical scenes Bollard was then welcomed back on the pitch by the embarrassed referee.

Darren Deadman did have his red card out in injury time, when Danny Williams was fouled by Reddy who then pushed the Wrexham defender. Despite Williams not doing anything wrong, both players ended up in the book. This time Deadman correctly remembered he had booked Williams in the opening 10 minutes, then showed the defender a red card.

Wrexham had a free kick at the death, with Crowell firing over.

There was still more incidents to come after the final whistle as three fans ran on the pitch from the Kop with one of them attacking the Grimsby keeper.

Referee: Darren Deadman (Cheshunt)

Wrexham 1	**Grimsby Town 2**
Mark Jones 42'	Michael Reddy 52'
	Glen Downey 84'

Attendance: 4,527

The red card that wasn't.

Starting XI:

01 Michael Ingham
04 Dave Bayliss
08 Danny Williams
06 Dennis Lawrence
15 Lee Roche
16 Matt Crowell
17 Mark Jones
10 Darren Ferguson
07 Andy Holt
09 Jon Walters
12 Dean Bennett 76'

Subs:

05 Paul Warhurst 76'
13 Michael Jones (GK)
14 Robbie Foy
18 Shaun Pejic
25 Mike Williams

Stats:

Shots on Goal: 13
Shots on Target: 5
Shots off Target: 8
Possession: 53%
Fouls Conceded: 10
Corners: 13
Yellow Cards: 2
Red Cards: 1

Starting XI:

01 Steve Mitchell
20 Gary Croft 75'
04 Simon Ramsden 50'
12 Robert James 45'
03 Tom Newey
15 Gary Cohen
08 Paul Bollard
18 Ciaran Toner
11 Andy Parkinson
19 Gary Jones
09 Michael Reddy

Subs:

07 Jean-Paul Kamudimba Kalala 75'
10 Marton Gritton 45'
17 Glen Downey 50'
22 Andy Taylor
23 Nick Hegarty

Stats:

Shots on Goal: 5
Shots on Target: 2
Shots off Target: 3
Possession: 47%
Fouls Conceded: 14
Corners: 3
Yellow Cards: 3
Red Cards: 0

Dean battles with Andy Parkinson.

No way through for Fergie.

This was an awful game of football contested by two pub teams seemingly unable to control and pass the ball. Wrexham went down to a mediocre Shrewsbury showing little or no passion and although the stats show that we had two shots on goal, I can only remember one!

The fact that we played with just Walters up front, tells you all you need to know about our ambitions on the night. Our only attacking plan seemed to be to pump free kicks into Dennis Lawrence, generally without any success.

The first-half ended goalless, which is no surprise considering that there were no shots on goal from either side.

Wrexham stuck with one man up front for the start of the second-half, which was surprising, as although Walters was winning his share of high balls up to him, there were no players supporting him and Shrewsbury were normally first to the second ball.

Shrewsbury were at least trying to get the ball played down the flanks in the space vacated by Wrexham's wing backs and this ultimately resulted in the only goal of the game in the last 20 minutes.

Ben Herd was allowed far too much time and space on the right, where he measured a cross for new signing Glynn Hurst to steer a header home into the bottom corner from about 10 yards. It was bad enough allowing the cross, but it also appeared that Hurst was unmarked in the box. This can't be confirmed as it was difficult to see the opposite end of the pitch from the away kop, as the mist descended down in the latter part of the second-half.

Despite trailing by a goal, Wrexham failed to create anything from open play. Robbie Foy and Paul Warhurst were introduced up front in an attempt to salvage a point. It was substitute Paul Warhurst who recorded Wrexham's first effort on target, and he came on in the 85th minute! His effort from the edge of the area, was more like a pass into the arms of an under worked Hart in the Shrewsbury goal.

The two minutes of injury time summed up Wrexham's performance, with Foy attempting to prevent conceding a throw-in, blasted the ball out for a goal kick!

This was later topped off when Wrexham had a throw-in deep in their half. This was played to Ingham, only for the keeper to side foot the ball out of play even deeper in our own half!

An awful night for Wrexhams 2,000 travelling fans.

Referee: Tony Leake (Lancashire)

Shrewsbury Town 1 Wrexham 0
Glynn Hurst 72'

Attendance: 6,249

Holty skips down the wing.

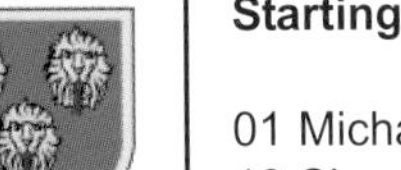

Starting XI:

01 Joe Hart
12 Ben Herd
02 Stuart Whitehead
25 Richard Hope
03 Kevin Sharp
19 David Edwards
04 Jamie Tolley
06 Neil Sorvel
11 Neil Ashton
07 Colin McMenamin
23 Glynn Hurst 83'

Subs:

08 Kelvin Langmead 83'
09 Mark Stallard
16 Gavin Cowan
21 Jay Denny
31 Richard Brush (GK)

Stats:

Shots on Goal:6
Shots on Target:1
Shots off Target:5
Possession:50%
Fouls Conceded:8
Corners: 2
Yellow Cards:0
Red Cards:0

Starting XI:

01 Michael Ingham
18 Shaun Pejic
04 Dave Bayliss 85'
06 Dennis Lawrence
15 Lee Roche
16 Matt Crowell 75'
17 Mark Jones
10 Darren Ferguson
07 Andy Holt
09 Jon Walters
12 Dean Bennett

Subs:

02 Jim Whitley
03 Alex Smith
05 Paul Warhurst 85'
13 Michael Jones (GK)
14 Robbie Foy 75'

Stats:

Shots on Goal:7
Shots on Target:2
Shots off Target:5
Possession:50%
Fouls Conceded:15
Corners: 6
Yellow Cards:0
Red Cards:0

Walters just misses out.

Jon Walters mixes it up.

Just like at Shrewsbury in midweek, the first 30 minutes were a waste of time and it didn't brighten up much after that on a cold and snowy day. Both keepers were spectators as much as the fans. Wrexham continued with one man up front and again Walters looked stranded at times with the midfield offering little support.

The second-half started with a poor back pass to Ingham almost letting in Lincoln for the opening goal. This time it was Dave Bayliss, who was a half-time substitute for Dennis Lawrence, who under hit his back pass and although Yeo reached the ball before Ingham did, he directed the ball wide from the edge of the area.

Lincoln did take the lead in the 63rd minute and although it wasn't against the run of play, it was a break away goal after Wrexham, and Danny Williams in particular, was caught up field in possession of the ball. Taking a quick Fergie free kick he ran into a crowd of Lincoln players who dispossessed him. Lincoln broke quickly down their right and, with every pass into space, the Wrexham defence looked more and more out of position. Eventually a ball was played in from the right and, after it missed the Lincoln attacker in the centre, the ball evaded Lee Roche and broke to Simon Yeo who placed the ball past Ingham.

Robbie Foy was about to come on at this point, but it took over five minutes for the on-loan striker to be introduced along with Jamie Reed, with Matt Crowell and Dean Bennett leaving the field.

Wrexham had half chances at best, and on a number of occasions the Lincoln defence had to make last ditch lunges to block strikes on their goal. Wrexham were awarded a free kick for handball, but Ferguson's effort from 25 yards drifted into the arms of Marriott.

In the second minute of injury time, Wrexham equalised through Mark Jones. Receiving an Andy Holt cross, Jones controlled it with a superb first touch, wrong footing the Lincoln defence. This allowed the midfielder to turn and curl an unstoppable shot past Marriott from 12 yards.

Denis Smith: "I though the first-half we were in control, in fact we were in control for most of the game. They only had two chances, one from a back-pass and the other from our free-kick. In the second-half we played the game more like Lincoln, and we probably played three or four systems today because we haven't got a striker at the moment. In the first-half we were very patient. We created little half chances but once they got the goal we started to get frustrated. The real problem at the moment is that we can't keep a clean sheet and we need to do this if we are going to improve. Mark Jones had an excellent first-half but didn't do so well after the break because we changed the system. In the first 45 minutes we gave him more freedom, which allowed him to get forward more. That said, I'd rather he played poorly and scored! I'm still on the lookout for a striker and I know I can get one in, the important part is making sure that it is the right one. I released Paul Warhurst because it looked as though we were going to get a new player in on Thursday, but that fell through at the last moment. I'll be back on the phone again on Monday."

Referee: Patrick Miller (Bedfordshire)

Wrexham 1	**Lincoln City 1**
Mark Jones 92'	Simon Yeo 63'

Attendance: 3,809

Pejic coping with the snow.

Starting XI:

01 Michael Ingham
18 Shaun Pejic
08 Danny Williams
06 Dennis Lawrence 45'
12 Dean Bennett 69'
15 Lee Roche
16 Matt Crowell 69'
17 Mark Jones
10 Darren Ferguson
07 Andy Holt
09 Jon Walters

Subs:

03 Alex Smith
04 Dave Bayliss 45'
13 Michael Jones (GK)
14 Robbie Foy 69'
27 Jamie Reed 69'

Stats:

Shots on Goal: 10
Shots on Target: 7
Shots off Target: 3
Possession: 50%
Fouls Conceded: 12
Corners: 7
Yellow Cards: 0
Red Cards: 0

Starting XI:

01 Alan Marriott
17 Colin Cryan
04 Gareth McAuley
06 Jamie McCombe
03 Paul Mayo 5'
11 Scott Kerr
21 Luke Foster
22 Dean keates
09 Francis Green 85'
29 Simon Yeo 85'
24 Jeff Hughes

Subs:

08 Gary Birch 85'
15 Steve Robinson
18 Oliver Ryan 85'
23 Nat Brown 5'
27 Leon Mettam

Stats:

Shots on Goal: 5
Shots on Target: 3
Shots off Target: 2
Possession: 50%
Fouls Conceded: 10
Corners: 5
Yellow Cards: 0
Red Cards: 0

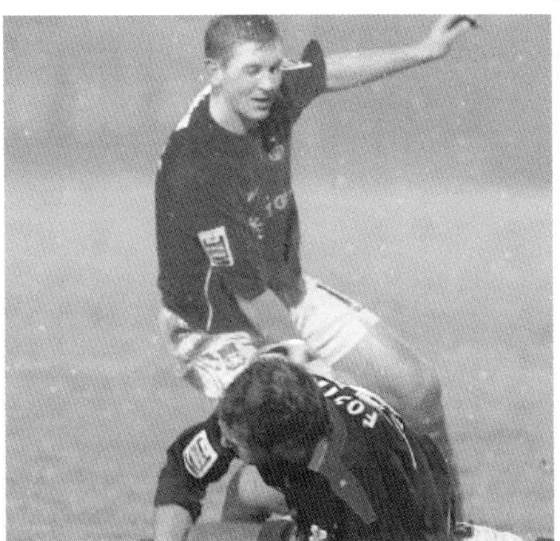

Mark Jones robs Luke Foster.

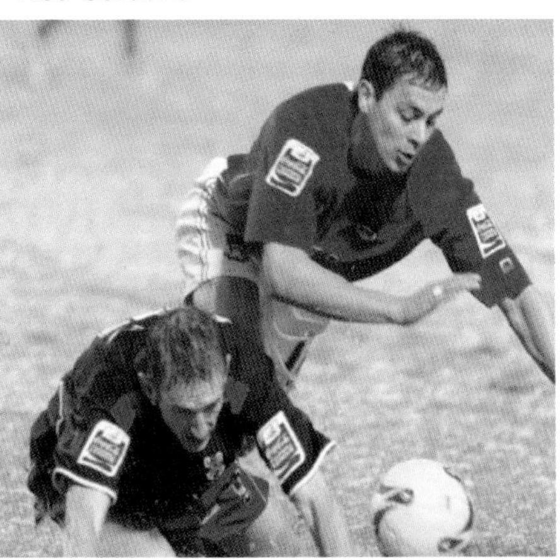

Bennett on his way down.

A bold team selection by Denis Smith saw us take the game to Rushden in the early stages. A free-kick here, a corner there, but no real penetration to hint at the pleasure to come.

Ferguson and Holt were busy as ever and the returning Whitley was a revelation, involved seemingly in just about everything as we moved into the ascendancy. There was brief cause for concern when Shaun Pejic, also back from a lengthy absence, gave us a nightmarish glimpse of the Pej of old with a dreadful back-pass, which fell straight to Diamonds' leading scorer Drewe Broughton, and only a combination of poor finishing and Ingy's presence, prevented a goal.

Otherwise, Danny and Mike Williams dealt fairly competently with most things thrown at them, including the new "boy wonder" Lee Tomlin.

We went ahead on 36 minutes. Mark Jones unleashed an out-of-the-blue 25-yarder, which flashed into the roof of the net. We went in at the break comfortably the better side. Jon Walters came more into the game as the half drew to a close, and with a bit of luck, could have notched himself.

As the rain came down in the second period, the large visiting support was treated to the luxury of their side bossing a game. We had a couple of scares – someone cleared off the line and Ingham needed hands like flypaper to hold onto a Broughton drive – but overall we were as comfortable as you can be at 1-0.

Young Marc Williams had the chance to wrap things up but crashed his shot against the bar, but there wasn't long to wait. Walters, whose close control (for a big man) doesn't get the credit it deserves, could have gone for goal himself, but wisely elected to set up Jonah whose finish was consummate on 67 minutes. That was about it for the action and we moved up to 8th in the table, just a point off the play-offs.

Denis Smith: "It just shows importance of clean sheets! I took a gamble with two YTs in side, but it paid off. Marc did really well on his debut and got better as the game went on. But I thought his brother had a superb match at the back. Mark Jones' goals were fantastic. The first we almost come to expect, but his second was probably better, as he placed it after a good build-up. Now though, we must push on and put a run together, with a very important game next weekend against a side that don't like losing away from home. I expected a tricky match here today and for the first 20 minutes that was just what we got, but as the match wore on, we looked much better when we got going."

Referee: Trevor Parks (West Midlands)

Rushden & D 0 Wrexham 2
Mark Jones 36' 67'

Attendance: 2,617

Mike Williams coped well all afternoon.

Starting XI:

42 Daniel Crane
45 Peter Castle
05 Graham Allen 22'
02 Phillip Gulliver
15 Ashley Nicholls 45'
43 Tony Stokes
07 David Savage
16 Neil McCafferty 70'
21 Ronnie Bull
36 Lee Tomlin
09 Drewe Broughton

Subs:

08 Gregory Pearson
23 Marcus Kelly 70'
24 Magnus Okuonghae 22'
44 John Turner
46 Tyrone Berry 45'

Stats:

Shots on Goal: 14
Shots on Target: 7
Shots off Target: 7
Possession: 51%
Fouls Conceded: 16
Corners: 7
Yellow Cards: 0
Red Cards: 0

Starting XI:

01 Michael Ingham
18 Shaun Pejic
08 Danny Williams
25 Mike Williams
20 Simon Spender
02 Jim Whitley
17 Mark Jones
10 Darren Ferguson
07 Andy Holt
09 Jon Walters
21 Marc Williams 83'

Subs:

03 Alex Smith
04 Dave Bayliss
12 Dean Bennett 83'
13 Michael Jones (GK)
14 Robbie Foy

Stats:

Shots on Goal: 15
Shots on Target: 8
Shots off Target: 7
Possession: 49%
Fouls Conceded: 12
Corners: 7
Yellow Cards: 1
Red Cards: 0

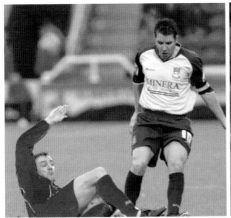

Fergie in the thick of things.

Another one for Mark Jones.

Wrexham got off to the worst possible start finding themselves a goal down after only four minutes. The impressive Shane Tudor was given too much room down the Orient right and he delivered a superb ball in behind the Wrexham defence for Gary Alexander to score. The O's top scorer looked in an offside position, but he made no mistake with the finish, sweeping the ball past Ingham from 12 yards with his first touch.

The goal rocked Wrexham, and Orient played some neat football with balls down the flanks for their wingers and strikers to stretch the Wrexham defence. On a number of occasions Mike Williams was caught on the wrong side of Alexander, but the young defender did well to track back to clear the danger.

At the other end of the pitch, Jon Walters had appeals for a penalty turned down after he appeared to be pushed in the back, although the striker should have done a lot better moments later. Good play from Wrexham down the right opened up the visitors defence and when the ball was played in to Walters, he went on a jinking run, but could only fire tamely with his left foot into the arms of Glyn Garner from the edge of the area.

Orient upped the tempo of the game in the last five minutes, and had opportunities to extend their lead before they were awarded a penalty with two minutes of the half left. The penalty was awarded when the central defenders missed Miller's cross from the right and the ball struck the outstretched arm of Simon Spender with the referee having no hesitation in pointing to the spot. With no complaints coming from Wrexham, left back Matt Lockwood stepped up confidently and sent Ingham the wrong way with a well placed shot.

Wrexham had a lot to do to make the ground back in the second-half and they did at least give it a go. With Wrexham chasing the game, it did leave them exposed at the back, and the O's almost put the game beyond Wrexham six minutes after the restart. McMahon played the ball in behind Mike Williams for Ibehre to latch onto, but he drove his shot low past Ingham and the far post.

Wrexham were offered a lifeline with 10 minutes left, when Danny Williams was pulled down in the box as he tried to turn Alexander. Despite being awarded a penalty, no Wrexham player wanted the ball and when Dean Bennett stepped up with a straight run-up, you could predict that Garner would dive to his left to make the comfortable save.

Wrexham did grab a consolation goal in the last minute, when Mark Jones skipped into the area and after Garner blocked his two shots, Jones played the ball across the box to Marc Williams who also saw his shot blocked. The ball then broke to Bennett and with his shot taking a deflection, it trickled past a wrong footed Garner and into the net.

Referee: Jonathon Moss (West Yorkshire)

Wrexham 1	**Leyton Orient 2**
Dean Bennett 89'	Gary Alexander 4'
	Matt Lockwood 43' (p)

Attendance: 5,031

The lads disagree with Mr.Moss - the ref.

Starting XI:

01 Michael Ingham
18 Shaun Pejic
08 Danny Williams
25 Mike Williams 87'
20 Simon Spender 62'
02 Jim Whitley
17 Mark Jones
10 Darren Ferguson
07 Andy Holt
09 Jon Walters
21 Marc Williams

Subs:

03 Alex Smith 87'
04 Dave Bayliss
12 Dean Bennett 62'
13 Michael Jones (GK)
16 Matt Crowell

Stats:

Shots on Goal: 10
Shots on Target: 4
Shots off Target: 6
Possession: 61%
Fouls Conceded: 4
Corners: 2
Yellow Cards: 2
Red Cards: 0

Starting XI:

01 Glyn Garner
15 Justin Miller
14 Gabriel Zakuani 45'
06 John Mackie
03 Matthew Lockwood
16 Shane Tudor
04 Michael Simpson
17 Daryl McMahon
11 Joe Keith
09 Gary Alexander
19 Jabo Ibehre 90'

Subs:

02 Donny Barnard
10 Lee Steele 90'
12 Glenn Morris (GK)
20 Derek Duncan
21 Brian Saah 45

Stats:

Shots on Goal: 3
Shots on Target: 2
Shots off Target: 1
Possession: 39%
Fouls Conceded: 3
Corners: 6
Yellow Cards: 3
Red Cards: 0

Bennett after scoring his 89' goal.

Who's making all the noise?

Wrexham progressed to the semi-final of this season's Premier Cup courtesy of a second-half brace from striker Jon Walters.

It was a hard fought victory for last season's runners up, but Wrexham did enough in the second-half to secure their spot in the last four against Total Network Solutions, the runaway leaders of the Welsh Premier League.

Wrexham started the game positively and were unlucky to not open the scoring, but their hosts had three clear cut chances before the half had come to an end.

O'Sullivan had two of the chances, the first of which he fired over the bar and the second came after he had beaten Mike Williams, only to see his shot well saved by Mike Ingham in the Wrexham goal.

Newport had one chance on the stroke of half-time when Green found himself clean through on-goal, but Ingham again did well to turn the shot over the bar.

Wrexham started the second-half well and opened the scoring nine minutes after the restart, when Mike Williams and Alex Smith combined well down the left wing. They picked out Jon Walters on the edge of the area and after beating his defender, he fired low past Pennock to give Wrexham the lead.

Wrexham then had a lucky escape before they extended their lead further. With six minutes left, Newport struck the bar with a long range shot that took a deflection in the crowded penalty area. Wrexham kept their composure and a minute later the result was beyond any doubt, when Jon Walters scored from close range after Mark Jones had supplied a cross from the left wing.

Brian Carey: "After the first-half I wasn't too happy. Newport had two good chances to take the lead. These games are never easy and I'm just glad we got through. I've played in many of them before so I know how difficult they can be. The first goal obviously gave us a lift and probably did the opposite to them. I'm pleased for Jon Walters as his work-rate over the season deserves more goals, and I hope he gets more now. Sam Williams did well in his first game but after watching him in training I wasn't surprised at his performance. All he needed was a goal and he had a few chances to score. We enjoy playing in the Welsh Premier Cup and we have done well in the competition over the years. It's important to us to be the best team in Wales and our team selection this evening said it all. The semi final against TNS will be a very difficult game. I saw them play Liverpool earlier in the season and they're flying in their league. We will give them all the respect they deserve."

Referee: M Whitby (Swansea)

Newport County 0 Wrexham 2
Jon Walters 54' 84'

Attendance: 442

Walters - man of the match.

Starting XI:

01 Terry Pennock
02 Terry Evans
03 Geraint Bater 73'
04 Ashley Williams
05 Stuart Edwards
06 Ian Hillier
07 Jason Bowen
08 Nathan Davies
09 Sam O'Sullivan
10 Gary Fisken
11 Matt Green

Subs:

12 Kris Leek 73'
13 Gareth Wharton
14 Dale Evans
15 Mark Griffiths
16 Danny Barton

Stats:

n/a

Starting XI:

01 Michael Ingham
18 Shaun Pejic
08 Danny Williams
25 Mike Williams
20 Simon Spender
02 Jim Whitley
17 Mark Jones
16 Matt Crowell
03 Alex Smith
09 Jon Walters
27 Sam Williams

Subs:

04 Dave Bayliss
12 Dean Bennett
13 Michael Jones (GK)
19 Levi Mackin
21 Marc Jones

Stats:

n/a

Walters getting on the scoresheet.

Sam Williams in action.

The first of six goals came when Dave Bayliss made a defensive mistake, cushioning his header back into the danger area. No Wrexham player reacted and Scott Ruscoe just beat his team mate to the ball to fire past an exposed Ingham from 12 yards.

Due to injury problems, Dennis Lawrence moved up front to forge an unlikely strike partnership with Ugarte, who was on as a sub.

Wrexham's equaliser was in complete contrast to their performance and it was no real surprise that it was a stunning first-time effort from Mark Jones.

TNS had a chance when slack marking allowed Evans a free shot from 10 yards, but he flashed his shot over the bar. TNS were not to be denied, but were helped when the Wrexham midfield, which missed a leader all game, just parted for them. With the Wrexham defence retreating to the 18-yard line, Wilde struck a decent shot from 20 yards which passed Ingham into the left hand corner of the net.

Wrexham looked down and out, but with the game approaching injury time, Juan Ugarte restored parity with a well taken goal. A simple ball from Jones found Ugarte in space, and with Doherty stranded off his line, Ugarte lifted the ball over the keeper from 20 yards for the equaliser.

Wrexham dominated proceedings in extra-time and were worthy of their lead courtesy of a strongly hit shot from Lawrence. Mark Jones played a clever ball in the box to Ugarte, but a TNS defender could only deflect the ball into the path of Lawrence who struck the ball into the roof of the net with his left foot.

Wrexham failed to build on this lead and Ingham was at fault for TNS's equaliser, when he ran off his line and could only partially head the danger clear. The ball fell to central defender Steve Evans, who as a makeshift striker, in one turn, lobbed the ball from 35 yards over the stranded Ingham with the ball bouncing once, before crossing the line into an empty net.

The second period of extra time was a non-event and so followed the drama of the penalty shoot-out.

Alex Smith stepped up first for Wrexham - but his penalty was poor and was easily saved by Doherty, only for John Layer to hit the left hand post with his effort.

Dave Bayliss then blasted Wrexham's second penalty into the left hand corner, with Nicky Ward finding the top right hand corner for TNS.

Mark Jones is okay with long range efforts, but could only send his spot kick straight at Doherty. Ingham dived to his right to deny Steve Evans, as it remained one each after three penalties.

Danny Williams sent Doherty the wrong way for Wrexham's fourth and a well placed penalty from Ruscoe brought the scores level again.

Juan Ugarte made no mistake with a well placed shot and Marc Lloyd Williams put the game into sudden death with his penalty.

Sudden death started with Spender sending Doherty the wrong way with a cool penalty and the game continued when Jamie Wood squeezed the ball past Ingham off the left hand post.

The nerves started when Doherty saved Lawrence's effort but TNS's celebrations were premature as Chris King fired high over the bar.

The drama continued with the eighth set of penalties, when Doherty pulled off a save diving low to his left to a poor Whitley effort. Ingham saved the midfielder's blushes when he dived to his left and pushed Jackson's effort onto the bar with a brilliant save.

Wrexham's ninth penalty of the night was despatched confidently by Pejic and Ingham was the hero for Wrexham when he denied TNS's keeper Doherty to send Wrexham through to the final.

Referee: Mark Whitby (Swansea)

Wrexham 3	**TNS 3**
Mark Jones 79'	Scott Ruscoe 39'
Juan Ugarte 89'	Nicky Ward 86'
D. Lawrence 101'	Steve Evans 105'

Attendance: 1,116

Starting XI:

01 Michael Ingham
04 Dave Bayliss
08 Danny Williams
06 Dennis Lawrence
12 Dean Bennett 52'
02 Jim Whitley
17 Mark Jones
03 Alex Smith
07 Andy Holt
09 Jon Walters 58'
27 Sam Williams 45'

Subs:

13 Michael Jones (GK)
16 Matt Crowell
18 Shaun Pejic 58'
20 Simon Spender 52'
30 Juan Ugarte 45'

Stats:

n/a

Starting XI:

01 Ged Doherty
02 Tommy Holmes 74'
04 Steve Evans
04 Mike Jackson
05 Chris King
06 Scott Ruscoe
07 Barry Hogan
08 Steven Beck
09 Mike Wilde 90'
10 Graham Evans 60'
11 Jamie Wood

Subs:

12 John Leah 74'
13 John Toner
14 Marc Lloyd Williams 90
15 Nicky Ward 60'
16 Lee Williams

Stats:

n/a

Juan Ugarte, our new fly half!

Mike Ingham in penalty action.

A positive start from Wrexham resulted in the opening goal after just 12 minutes from a Crowell corner. Lawrence popping up at the near post to head in unchallenged from six yards out.

Three minutes later, Sam Williams scored on his league debut. Wrexham worked the ball well down the right flank, from where Crowell delivered a superb ball to the far post where Williams had to stretch to guide the ball inside the far post with a well-taken header from 10 yards.

On 18 minutes, Mark Jones was replaced by Levi Mackin, who himself had only just returned from a lengthy lay off. During this spell, Wycombe had their first shot on goal, when the ball fell to Mooney on the edge of the area, but his dipping shot was well caught by Ingham underneath his own bar.

Juan Ugarte went close for Wrexham on the half-hour mark, when a lose header broke to him from 30 yards. Ugarte advanced forward before driving a low shot that Matt Duke had to turn behind for a corner at his near post.

It was all Wrexham now, and a sweeping move five minutes later should have put the game beyond any doubt. Wrexham broke well down the left where Andy Holt again had too much space to measure a cross in the box. This resulted in a melee in the six-yard box and Wycombe only managed to scramble the ball behind for a corner.

Wycombe introduced two substitutes at the break, and a change of formation resulted in them having more of the ball in Wrexham's half, but the visitors failed to test Ingham with any chances of note.

Wrexham lost Ugarte soon after the restart when he was left in a heap on the ground and although the referee waved play on, he failed to book the Wycombe player for the late foul. Marc Williams replaced the on-loan striker, and his endless running kept the pressure on the Wycombe defence.

Wrexham were now content at keeping Wycombe at bay, and remained on top despite Wycombe having more of the ball. The defence, marshalled by Danny Williams was well on top with Ingham having little to do.

The game petered out towards the end, but with the hard work of the two Williamses up front, the Wycombe defence were always under pressure.

Our best performance of the season by a long way.

Referee: D Whitestone (Northamptonshire)

Wrexham 2	**Wycombe Wanderers 0**
D.Lawrence 12'	
Sam Williams 15'	

Attendance: 4,311

Marc Williams - one for the future?

Starting XI:

01 Michael Ingham
18 Shaun Pejic
08 Danny Williams
06 Dennis Lawrence
20 Simon Spender
02 Jim Whitley
17 Mark Jones 20'
16 Matt Crowell
07 Andy Holt
27 Sam Williams
30 Juan Ugarte 52'

Subs:

13 Michael Jones (GK)
19 Levi Mackin 20'
21 Marc Williams 52'
22 Matty Done
25 Mike Williams

Stats:

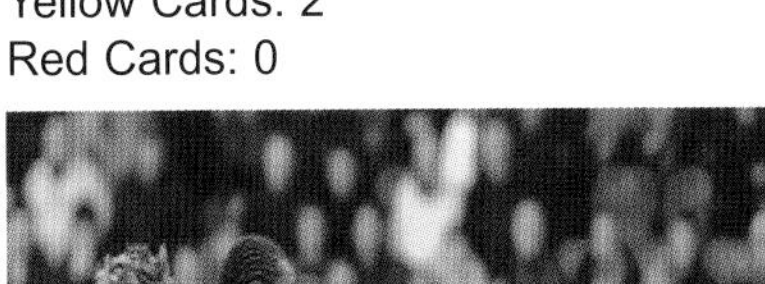

Shots on Goal: 11
Shots on Target: 5
Shots off Target: 6
Possession: 56%
Fouls Conceded: 19
Corners: 7
Yellow Cards: 2
Red Cards: 0

Starting XI:

31 Matt Duke
12 Russell Martin 45'
05 Roger Johnson
06 Mike Williamson
03 Clint Easton 45'
07 Kevin Betsy
08 Joe Burnell
10 Matt Bloomfield 69'
04 Stefan Oakes
16 Tommy Mooney
09 Jermaine Easter

Subs:

11 Ian Stonebridge 69'
21 Steve Williams (GK)
22 Sergio Torres
25 Dean Bowditch 45'
26 Aidan Collins 45'

Stats:

Shots on Goal: 2
Shots on Target: 1
Shots off Target: 1
Possession: 44%
Fouls Conceded: 5
Corners: 4
Yellow Cards: 0
Red Cards: 0

Dennis open's Wrexham's account.

Two of the older members of today's team.

After a weekend off, Wrexham were fresh and up for a game against probably the worst team in the division.

On-loan Matt Derbyshire made his debut, and marked the occasion with two first-half goals. The result left us four points off the play offs with three games in hand. A real platform to mount an assault on the play offs.

Derbyshire failed with his first sight of goal, despite his pace taking him past the defender, he failed to get any decent power on his shot to trouble the visitor's keeper.

Derbyshire had another effort soon after, when Lawrence missed a cross in the box, the on-loan Blackburn striker could not steer his header on target.

Minutes later, Derbyshire opened his account with Wrexham, when he broke the deadlock in the 24th minute. Wrexham were awarded a free-kick on the left touch line that Crowell delivered deep to the far post. Lawrence did well to head the ball downwards and from a tight angle Derbyshire was first to react to turn the ball past Tynan from close range.

Derbyshire was through on goal 12 minutes later and claimed his second of the night with a superb finish. Wrexham had a throw in from in their own half that they worked down the right flank to set Derbyshire free. The striker broke into the area despatching the ball inside of the far post with a sublime finish with the outside of his right foot.

It was 2-0 at the interval. The second-half was in stark contrast to the first with little chances created from both teams. This resulted in a very dull second-half encounter and although the visitors had more of the game, their clear lack of quality in the final-third resulted in the Wrexham defence again having another comfortable 45 minutes.

The best chance that Wrexham could muster in the second-half was when Derbyshire was set clear down the left flank with his centre looking perfect for Spender to race onto, but the covering Bull cleared the ball away to safety.

The rest of the second-half was a real none event as Wrexham did all the damage in the first-half, but towards the end, they did require someone to put their foot on the ball in the midfield in order not to concede too much possession to the opposition.

Referee: Lee Mason (Lancashire)

Wrexham 2 Rushden & Diamonds 0
Derbyshire 24' 36'

Attendance: 3,195

Dennis rises the highest in this tussle.

Starting XI:

01 Michael Ingham
18 Shaun Pejic
08 Danny Williams
06 Dennis Lawrence
20 Simon Spender
02 Jim Whitley
17 Mark Jones
16 Matt Crowell 89'
07 Andy Holt
14 Matt Derbyshire
27 Sam Williams

Subs:

13 Michael Jones (GK)
19 Levi Mackin 89'
21 Marc Williams
22 Matt Done
25 Mike Williams

Stats:

Shots on Goal: 8
Shots on Target: 5
Shots off Target: 3
Possession: 53%
Fouls Conceded: 9
Corners: 2
Yellow Cards: 0
Red Cards: 0

Starting XI:

47 Scott Tyan
06 Rob Gier
14 Wayne Hatswell
02 Philip Gulliver
21 Ronnie Bull
46 Tyrone Berry
11 Darren Caskey
43 Tony Stokes 55'
23 Marcus Kelly
09 Drewe Broughton
10 Petr Mikolanda 45'

Subs:

04 Gary Mills
07 David Savage 55'
15 Ashley Nicholls
36 Lee Tomlin 45'
42 Daniel Crane (GK)

Stats:

Shots on Goal: 7
Shots on Target: 1
Shots off Target: 6
Possession: 47%
Fouls Conceded: 13
Corners: 9
Yellow Cards: 3
Red Cards: 0

Matt Derbyshire rides the tackle.

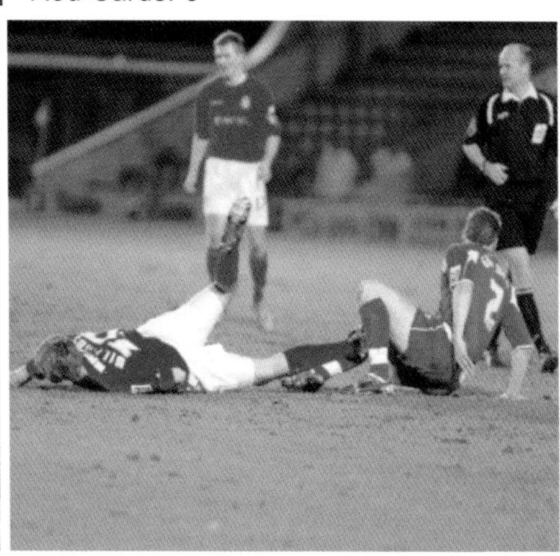

Sam Williams is flattened by Phil Gulliver.

There were some early nerves on show as we struggled to get out of our own half for the first five minutes, but thereafter the first period developed (or rather didn't) into a humdrum, incident-free hotchpotch.

The pitch did neither side any favours, with a number of Wrexham's long balls almost finding Derbyshire (the nearby county, that is, not our loan striker of that name).

The game did, however, burst into life five minutes from the break. A home forward burst through from halfway and skipped past several challenges only to be expertly dispossessed in the act of shooting by the chasing Spender. A minute later Spends was in the thick of the action at the other end, his textbook volley comprehensively beating home 'keeper Pressman, only to cannon back off a post.

Seven minutes into the second-half we were ahead. Stags defender Buxton, blissfully unaware of Derbyshire's predatory instincts, sold Pressman short with a back-pass and the goal was a formality for Mr. Derbyshire. Wrexham were in the ascendancy now and 11 comfortable minutes later, Derbyshire doubled our lead, outpacing the home defence to fire under Pressman, who will feel he should have done better.

So, two up, controlling the game and the visiting choir in full voice. What could go wrong? Within six minutes the score was two each and we were hanging on for dear life as Mansfield looked like scoring every time they poured forward, which for the last 20 minutes was pretty much constantly.

Danny Williams tripped the home side's Brown for a clear penalty, clinically despatched by Richie Barker, and two minutes later the same player headed in firmly at the far post as the entire Reds side seemed to have joined the League Against Cruel Sports – that's to say, giving the Stags a sporting chance. Our defence was a pub-league mess, and we were grateful more than once for Big Kick Ingy's safe hands.

Three minutes of injury time, all of it spent in our half, did little to calm the nerves as ultimately we claimed the point. A team with serious promotion aspirations should and would have brought home the three points. Disappointing to say the least!

Denis Smith: "It was a mad five minutes that cost us dear today. We have defended well for the last three games, apart from that brief spell here and it has cost us two points. In the previous two games I have had half-time to chat to them, not today."

Referee: Gary Lewis (Cambridgeshire)

Mansfield Town 2 **Wrexham 2**
R.Barker 64' (p) 67' M.Derbyshire 51' 62'

Attendance: 3,139

Mark Jones going in hard.

Starting XI:

01 Kevin Pressman
27 Laurence Wilson
22 Jon Olav Hjelde
12 Jake Buxton
06 Alex Baptiste
18 Adam Rundle 63'
04 Jonathon D'Laryea
15 Giles Coke 79'
07 Stephen Dawson
09 Richard Barker
31 Danny Reet 58'

Subs:

08 Gus Uhlenbeek 63'
13 Jason White (GK)
17 Callum Lloyd 79'
20 Simon Brown 58'
21 Kyle Jacobs

Stats:

Shots on Goal: 15
Shots on Target: 8
Shots off Target: 7
Possession: 53%
Fouls Conceded: 10
Corners: 7
Yellow Cards: 0
Red Cards: 0

Starting XI:

01 Michael Ingham
18 Shaun Pejic
08 Danny Williams
06 Dennis Lawrence
20 Simon Spender
02 Jim Whitley
17 Mark Jones
16 Matt Crowell
07 Andy Holt
27 Sam Williams
14 Matt Derbyshire

Subs:

13 Michael Jones (GK)
19 Levi Mackin
21 Marc Williams
22 Matt Done
25 Mike Williams

Stats:

Shots on Goal: 19
Shots on Target: 9
Shots off Target: 7
Possession: 47%
Fouls Conceded: 17
Corners: 4
Yellow Cards: 1
Red Cards: 0

Sam Williams celebrates Derbyshires goal.

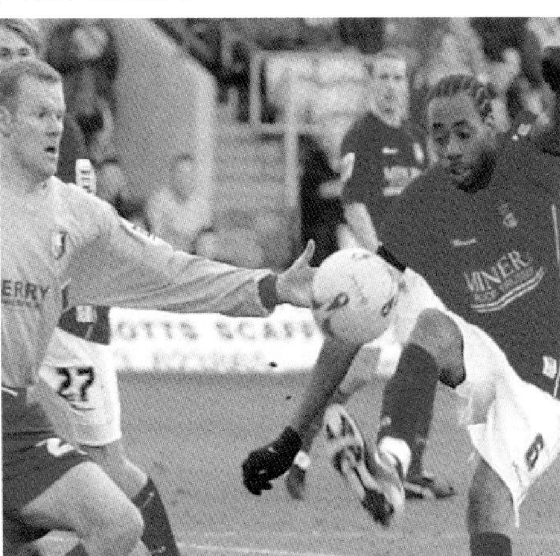

Dennis up in attack.

Northampton started the strongest with Wrexham finding it difficult to gain any possession in the opposition's half.

Northampton's best chance fell to Kirk when he was played in on the edge of the area and Ingham did well to block the shot at the feet of the striker. The ball broke kindly for Crowe after it escaped the clutches of Ingham, but Dennis Lawrence tracked back well to clear his shot off the line.

The best Wrexham could muster was a mazy run from Mark Jones that started just inside his own half. The midfielder, who joined up with the Wales squad after the game, advanced to the edge of the Northampton area, but his toe poked effort lacked any power to trouble Harper in the visitor's goal.

The first-half lacked any clear-cut chances of note, with Wrexham only creating one chance for Derbyshire. A ball was played down the left channel with the pace of the on-loan Blackburn striker taking him away from the Northampton defence. Derbyshire collected the ball on the corner of the area, but he rushed his shot with the ball travelling harmlessly across the face of goal.

The second-half continued in a similar pattern to the first and it became obvious that the first goal of the game would prove to be the winner, as both defences remained on top.

This duly came midway through the second-half when hesitancy from Danny Williams resulted in the Cobblers' winner.

A ball was played over the top of Williams, on the edge of the area, and with McGleish chasing him down, Ingham retreated back to his six-yard line. Williams allowed the ball to bounce and this was enough for Gilligan to nip in ahead of him and he lobbed the ball past Ingham into an empty net.

If anything this goal galvanised Northampton and Ingham had to pull off two good saves to keep Wrexham in the game. Danny Williams was again the culprit, failing to cut out Jess' through ball with Ingham doing well to deny McGleish by diving at the feet of the striker. Within a couple of minutes a ball was delivered in from the right wing to the far post where McGleish stooped low ahead of Pejic, but his header lacked any power and Ingham smothered the ball at the back post.

Wrexham introduced Done and Mackin and although Done did well with some decent crosses from the left wing, Wrexham failed to carve out any openings of note.

Referee: Lee Probert (Gloucestershire)

Wrexham 0	**Northampton Town 1**
	Ryan Gilligan 68'

Attendance: 5,012

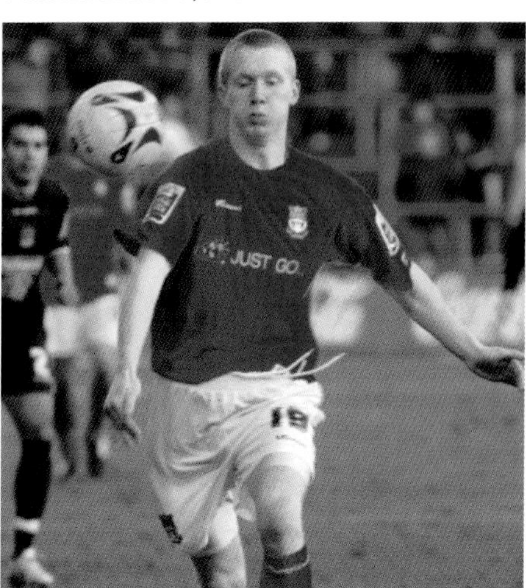

Levi Mackin in full flow.

Starting XI:

01 Michael Ingham
18 Shaun Pejic
08 Danny Williams 83'
06 Dennis Lawrence
20 Simon Spender
02 Jim Whitley
17 Mark Jones
16 Matt Crowell 74'
07 Andy Holt
14 Matt Derbyshire
27 Sam Williams

Subs:

13 Michael Jones (GK)
19 Levi Mackin 83'
21 Marc Williams
22 Matty Done 74'
25 Mike Williams

Stats:

Shots on Goal: 9
Shots on Target: 3
Shots off Target: 6
Possession: 59%
Fouls Conceded: 8
Corners: 4
Yellow Cards: 0
Red Cards: 0

Starting XI:

01 Lee Harper
05 Luke Chambers
16 Sean Dyche
06 Chris Doig
02 Jason Crowe
11 Eoin Jess 90'
12 David Hunt 78'
21 Jamie Hand
18 Gavin Johnson
08 Andy Kirk 25'
09 Scott McGleish

Subs:

04 Ashley Westwood 90'
13 Martin Bunn (GK)
20 Pedj Bojic 78'
25 Scott Cross
28 Ryan Gilligan 25'

Stats:

Shots on Goal: 5
Shots on Target: 4
Shots off Target: 1
Possession: 41%
Fouls Conceded: 6
Corners: 6
Yellow Cards: 0
Red Cards: 0

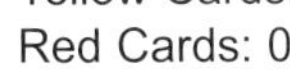

Jim Whitley in action.

Dennis and Sean Dyche about to battle.

Our first visit to Barnet for a few years saw a game played in a freezing wind on a rutted meadow of a pitch. The conditions ensured that there was no shortage of incident, and with both sides looking very committed there were more than the usual number of miskicks and sliced clearances. The Bees, kicking down the hill with the wind behind them, were in Wrexham faces from the word go and really should have been at least two up before they actually scored.

Ingham, whose kicking against the wind was perversely better than usual, spilled a routine cross and in the ensuing melee a shot crashed against our bar. Minutes later the home side's Kandol headed over when it seemed easier to notch. A home goal looked increasingly likely and it duly arrived on the half-hour. The pacy striker Norville bursting into our area to absolutely spank his shot past Ingham at the near-post. Our keeper then saved smartly from Kandol, but the big-peroxided striker was not to be denied, when Ingham was hesitant leaving his line, Kandol's shot hit him and looped just under the bar.

Things were looking grim, but we were thrown a lifeline a minute before half-time when the ball broke to Jonah, 20-yards out, his superbly struck drive gave home goalie Reed no chance.

The second-half saw the ineffective Spender and Whitley replaced by Bennett and Ferguson, and the latter's contribution was immediate, his through ball giving Sam Williams to score. Sadly, this proved beyond the young striker, but a minute or two later Ferguson played in Derbyshire who expertly drew the keeper to shoot just inside the post. And that, you felt, was that. Surely now we'd push on to win comfortably....but Ferguson faded as suddenly as he'd bloomed, and we found ourselves pinned in our own half as Barnet stormed onto the offensive, forcing a worrying number of free-kicks and corners, as well as having a goal disallowed. A trip by Jonah saw the ref flourish a yellow card.

When Wrexham pressed it was only sporadically. Young Reed fumbled an innocuous cross just past the post and Jonah headed over from six yards as Holty's long throws caused occasional havoc, while Ferguson, forgivably, and Derbyshire, less so, saw lobs beat Reed, but sail over the bar. A winner for either side, though, would have been an injustice

Referee: Brian Curson (Leicestershire)

Barnet 2	**Wrexham 2**
Jason Norville 30'	Mark Jones 44'
Tresor Kandol 37	Matt Derbyshire 51'

Attendance: 2,127

Matt Derbyshire celebrates.

Starting XI:

28 Matthew Reed
04 Ian Hendon
06 Anthony Charles
14 Ismail Yakubu
16 Simon Clist
10 Ben Strevens 73'
23 Barry Fuller
25 Andy Hessenthaler 62'
02 Nick Bailey 73'
18 Tresor Kandol
20 Jason Norville

Subs:

07 Liam Hatch 73'
08 Dean Sinclair 73'
13 Ryan Jones (GK)
17 Dwane Lee 62'
24 Paolo Vernazza

Stats:

Shots on Goal: 11
Shots on Target: 7
Shots off Target: 4
Possession: 48%
Fouls Conceded: 18
Corners: 4
Yellow Cards: 1
Red Cards: 0

Starting XI:

01 Michael Ingham
18 Shaun Pejic
08 Danny Williams
06 Dennis Lawrence
20 Simon Spender 45'
02 Jim Whitley 45'
17 Mark Jones
16 Matt Crowell
07 Andy Holt
27 Sam Williams
14 Matt Derbyshire

Subs:

10 Darren Ferguson 45'
12 Dean Bennett 45'
13 Michael Jones (GK)
22 Matty Done
25 Mike Williams

Stats:

Shots on Goal: 11
Shots on Target: 7
Shots off Target: 4
Possession: 52%
Fouls Conceded: 11
Corners: 5
Yellow Cards: 1
Red Cards: 0

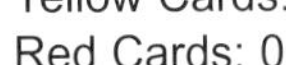

Sam Williams battles with the Barent defence.

Mark Jones pulls the first goal back.

Bury came to the Racecourse on the back of nine games without a win and desperate for points to save their League status. We had not won for three games and were really looking for maximum points against one of the poorer teams in the division.

It was a bright opening to the game with Bury enjoying a lot of possession down the Wrexham left. Despite Bury looking dangerous they failed to create any chances and it was Wrexham who had the first shot on goal and it was no real surprise that it came from Mark Jones. The midfielder picked up the lose ball midway in Bury's half and he advanced to 25 yards from goal from where his well struck left footed drive was superbly turned around the post by a full stretch Schmeichel (yes, son of).

Matt Derbyshire went in the book after 25 minutes for diving when he went to ground, after rounding Schmeichel in the box. If it was a dive, then it was a stupid decision, as he would have had an open goal to role the ball into. This was probably our best opportunity of the match.

Chances were few and far between, with the Bury midfield working hard to close down their counterparts. This resulted in Wrexham having to play the ball back to the three central defenders and their inevitable lumps forward failed to pick out a red shirt.

Half-time could not come quickly enough as the quality of the game dropped minute-by-minute, but the half-time team talks did nothing to brighten up an uninspiring game.

The second-half continued in the same dreary fashion and there were no chances of note. Bury looked far too organised to be relegated and once again our lack of a cutting edge let us down.

Denis Smith: "I am sure that everyone who looked at today's game beforehand would have known what to expect. Anyone who expected anything else would have been very disappointed. If you look at Bury's recent League form and their results, they are all either 0-0 or 1-0; there are very few goals in their games. They are set up to be difficult to break down and they aim to frustrate teams. Even when they push forward, they ensure that they have players covering at the back and their system is designed to deny you any scoring chances

Referee: Mick Fletcher (Worcestershire)

Wrexham 0 Bury 0

Attendance: 4,134

Derbyshire rises the highest.

Starting XI:

01 Michael Ingham
18 Shaun Pejic
08 Danny Williams
06 Dennis Lawrence
12 Dean Bennett
02 Jim Whitley 56'
17 Mark Jones
16 Matt Crowell 79'
07 Andy Holt
27 Sam Williams
14 Matt Derbyshire

Subs:

13 Michael Jones (GK)
19 Levi Mackin 56'
21 Marc Williams
22 Matt Done 79'
25 Mike Williams

Stats:

Shots on Goal: 8
Shots on Target: 4
Shots off Target: 4
Possession: 50%
Fouls Conceded: 14
Corners: 7
Yellow Cards: 2
Red Cards: 0

Starting XI:

25 Kasper Schmeichel
12 Paul Scott
05 David Challinor
04 John Fitzgerald
06 Colin Woodthorpe
07 David Flitcroft 81'
08 Dwayne Mattis
11 Brian Barry-Murphy
17 David Buchanan
33 Colin Marrison
10 Tom Youngs 79'

Subs:

15 Chris Bass
20 Nick Adams 81'
22 Matthew Tipton
24 Jake Speight 79'
30 Aaron Grundy (GK)

Stats:

Shots on Goal: 4
Shots on Target: 1
Shots off Target: 3
Possession: 50%
Fouls Conceded: 17
Corners: 2
Yellow Cards: 3
Red Cards: 0

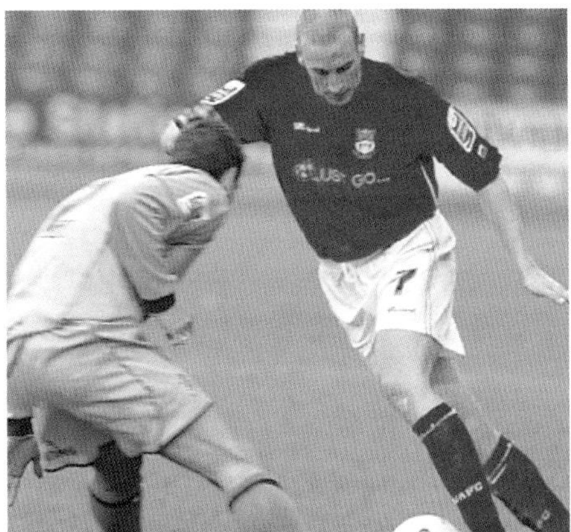

Holty trying to unlock the Bury defence.

Mark Jones in hot persuit.

On the day our victory in the court battle was announced, around a 600 fans made the short journey to Moss Rose.

We did not have to wait long for the opening goal, when Derbyshire played Mark Jones in down the right and he picked out Sam Williams on the edge of the area. After controlling the ball Sam Williams' shot took a deflection off a defender and went in over the keeper.

Macclesfield looked decent going forward without ever troubling Ingham, apart from routine saves. The closest they came was when the lively Whitaker fired his shot over the bar from the edge of the area.

Wrexham built on their advantage with a well taken header from Andy Holt after 33 minutes. Shaun Pejic picked up the ball on the touch-line, delivered a high looping cross to the centre of the area from where Holt stormed in unmarked to bury his header past Lee inside of the near post.

Wrexham were dominant, but just before half-time disaster struck as a Holt headed own goal from a Macc corner, which allowed them back into the game.

Macclesfield were boosted by this gift, and Wrexham fell apart after the break. It was no surprise when the equaliser arrived with 15 minutes left when McNeil managed to fend off the weak challenge from Lawrence on the edge of the area and the impressive Whittaker made no mistake by firing the loose ball past Ingham to bring the scores level.

Worse was to follow seven minutes later as Macclesfield took the lead just as Denis was lining up a triple substitution. Wrexham had plenty of opportunities to clear the ball from open play, but when the cross finally came in from the right, Lawrence had to scramble it behind for a corner. With the substitutes lining up to come on, the corner was delivered to the edge of the six-yard area, from where Briscoe arrived unmarked to power his header past Ingham to complete Macclesfield's comeback. It was well deserved.

Shortly after this we created our only chance of the second-half, as a Lawrence shot from a Done cross was easily saved by Lee. A 2-0 lead squandered again and in truth a very poor end to what will always be a great day in our club's history.

Denis Smith: "This is as low as I have felt since coming to Wrexham - on a footballing front."

Referee: G Laws (Tyne & Wear)

Macclesfield Town 3	**Wrexham 2**
Andy Holt 43' (og)	Sam Williams 9'
Danny Whitaker 74'	Andy Holt 33'
Andrew Teague 82'	

Attendance: 1,616

Andy Holt celebrates his goal.

Starting XI:

13 Tommy Lee
04 David Moreley
05 Danny Swailes
06 Martin Bullock
07 Paul Harsley 45'
12 Danny Whitaker
14 Kevin McIntyre
18 Andrew Teague
24 Ian Brightwell
26 Alan Navarro
28 Matty McNeil

Subs:

01 Alan Fettis (GK)
09 Kevin Townson
10 John Miles
19 Michael Briscoe 45'
23 Andrew Smart

Stats:

Shots on Goal: 14
Shots on Target: 6
Shots off Target: 8
Possession: 50%
Fouls Conceded: 10
Corners: 10
Yellow Cards: 2
Red Cards: 0

Starting XI:

01 Michael Ingham
18 Shaun Pejic
08 Danny Williams
06 Dennis Lawrence
12 Dean Bennett
02 Jim Whitley 83'
17 Mark Jones
19 Levi Mackin 83'
07 Andy Holt
27 Sam Williams 83'
14 Matt Derbyshire

Subs:

09 Jon Walters 83'
13 Michael Jones (GK)
16 Matt Crowell 83'
22 Matt Done 83'
25 Mike Williams

Stats:

Shots on Goal: 8
Shots on Target: 5
Shots off Target: 3
Possession: 50%
Fouls Conceded: 11
Corners: 4
Yellow Cards: 1
Red Cards: 0

Matt Derbyshire tries to round Lee.

Fans happy at the court result.

On a difficult pitch both sides struggled early on and Wrexham were not helped when Jim Whitley limped off after seven minutes to be replaced by Levi Mackin, on the bench after Matt Crowell was recalled to the first team.

We had to wait 15 minutes for the first effort on goal, when Cooksey headed wide from a right wing cross. Up to this point Wrexham's performance had been controlled without threatening the Rochdale goal and the opening, after 20 minutes, came as a surprise.

It was a simple goal in the end, with Sam Williams heading Ingham's long clearance to Andy Holt on the left. Holt swung in a deep cross that evaded the last defender and although the ball took an awkward bounce off the pitch, Derbyshire kept his composure to fire the ball through the legs of Gilks.

Wrexham were almost caught out moments later when the ball was lost in midfield and with no player offering a tackle, Dagnall was allowed to progress to the edge of the area, from where he curled a shot narrowly wide of the post.

The Wrexham defence looked comfortable and the Dragons had an opportunity to double their advantage before half-time. A clever through ball from Bennett set Derbyshire free and from a tight angle his shot from 10 yards was expertly tipped over by Gilks to keep Rochdale in the game.

Dale enjoyed a lot of possession in the second-half without creating any chances. Ingham was a spectator for the first 15 minutes before saving a Christie header.

Moments later and Dave Bayliss was heading for an early bath for his second foul on Matt Derbyshire, who had given him a torrid afternoon. There were no complaints from Bayliss, booked earlier for an elbow on Derbyshire, and that was the end of Rochdale's challenge. Three easy points for the Dragons.

Brian Carey: "This was a big result for us, after throwing away points in the past week. Indeed, I would go as far as saying this was a massive result for us. It might not have repaired the damage we did to our play-off hopes recently, but it is a help. Now we have to do our best to get as many points as possible and see if we can push ourselves back into play-off contention. This was a character test for the players, as for 70 minutes they had to make sure they defended that 1-0 goal lead. It was a test and one that we passed. We have shown that we can get in front and go on to win, which was important after some recent results."

Referee: Mick Russell (Hertfordshire)

Rochdale 0	**Wrexham 1**
	Matt Derbyshire 20'

Attendance: 2,856

Mike and Dennis comisserate with Bayliss.

Starting XI:

01 Matthew Gilks
18 Simon Ramsden
15 Rory McArdle
25 Dave Bayliss
03 Tony Gallimore
11 Gary Jones 82'
22 John Dolan 73'
04 Ernie Cooksey 37'
09 Chris Dagnall
17 Richard Lambert
10 Ivseden Christie

Subs:

06 Jonathon Boardman
07 Lee Cartwright
14 Scott Warner 37'
21 Ben Kitchen 83'
27 Gary Brown 73'

Stats:

Shots on Goal: 12
Shots on Target: 6
Shots off Target: 6
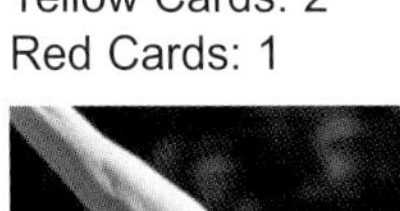
Possession: 54%
Fouls Conceded: 15
Corners: 5
Yellow Cards: 2
Red Cards: 1

Starting XI:

01 Michael Ingham
18 Shaun Pejic
08 Danny Williams 69'
06 Dennis Lawrence
12 Dean Bennett
02 Jim Whitley 7'
17 Mark Jones
16 Matt Crowell
07 Andy Holt
27 Sam Williams
14 Matt Derbyshire

Subs:

09 Jon Walters
13 Michael Jones (GK)
19 Levi Mackin 7'
22 Matty Done
25 Mike Williams 69'

Stats:

Shots on Goal: 7
Shots on Target: 4
Shots off Target: 3
Possession: 46%
Fouls Conceded: 10
Corners: 6
Yellow Cards: 2
Red Cards: 0

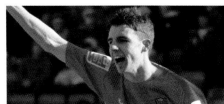

Derbyshire with his 20 minute winner.

Bayliss (of Rochdale) sees red.

Wrexham made one change from the team that defeated Rochdale at the weekend with Levi Mackin replacing the injured Jim Whitley. It was the Red Dragons who opened the scoring within 90 seconds after Cheltenham had already hit the post.

In a frantic opening couple of minutes Townsend planted his header from a free-kick against the woodwork with Michael Ingham rooted to his spot. Wrexham broke quickly from this with Derbyshire breaking the offside-trap to latch onto the long clearance from Bennett. Derbyshire capitalised on hesitancy from the full-back, advancing into the area and finished clinically after rounding the keeper.

Wrexham suffered a blow when Dennis Lawrence limped off the pitch just after the half hour mark and within two minutes Cheltenham were back on level terms, although substitute Mike Williams was not responsible for the equaliser. A high ball was delivered in from the Cheltenham right and Wilson got in ahead of Bennett at the far post. Wilson picked out McCann on the edge of the area and he gave Ingham no chance with a shot from 18-yards.

With Darren Ferguson replacing Mackin at half-time, Wrexham started the second period brightly with Derbyshire's pace again exposing the Cheltenham defence. A through-ball from Ferguson set him clear and after Derbyshire knocked the ball past the keeper he went to ground, but the referee waved play on.

Wilson floated in a ball in from the left that hung in the air and as Ingham came for the ball, he spilled it whilst under pressure from Odejayi, and Guinan had the simple task to score from 10-yards out.

Cheltenham should have been out of sight when Odejayi timed his run well to break the offside-trap. With the striker clean through on goal, he attempted to bend the ball around Ingham from just inside of the area, but his shot went a couple of yards wide of the post.

This miss proved costly as Derbyshire grabbed his and Wrexham's second of the night. A clever through ball from Ferguson sent Derbyshire clear, and with the offside-flag this time staying down, Derbyshire coolly lifted the ball over Higgs and one bounce later it ended up in the back of the empty net.

Denis Smith: "It was frustrating not to win, but in the end it was a game that could have gone either way."

Referee: Trevor Parkes (West Midlands)

Cheltenham Town 2	**Wrexham 2**
Grant McCann 35'	M.Derbyshire 1' 64'
Stephen Guinan 56'	

Attendance: 2,737

Holt wins the challenge.

Starting XI:

01 Shane Higgs
02 Jeremy Gill
05 Gavin Caines
15 Michael Townsend
19 Craig Armstrong
22 John Melligan 88'
08 John Finnigan
11 Grant McCann
07 Brian Wilson
17 Kayode Odejayi 81'
09 Stephen Guinan

Subs:

10 Damian Spencer 81'
12 Scott Brown (GK)
14 David Bird 88'
26 Michael Wylde
33 Mickey Bell

Stats:

Shots on Goal: 11
Shots on Target: 5
Shots off Target: 6
Possession: 49%
Fouls Conceded: 10
Corners: 3
Yellow Cards: 1
Red Cards: 0

Starting XI:

01 Michael Ingham
18 Shaun Pejic
08 Danny Williams
06 Dennis Lawrence 33'
12 Dean Bennett
16 Matt Crowell
17 Mark Jones
19 Levi Mackin 45'
07 Andy Holt
27 Sam Williams 87'
14 Matt Derbyshire

Subs:

09 Jon Walters 87'
10 Darren Ferguson 45'
13 Michael Jones (GK)
20 Simon Spender
25 Mike Williams 33'

Stats:

Shots on Goal: 9
Shots on Target: 6
Shots off Target: 3
Possession: 51%
Fouls Conceded: 10
Corners: 5
Yellow Cards: 0
Red Cards: 0

Matt Derbyshire is foiled this time.

Derbyshire coolly chips the keeper and scores.

The first visit from Chester since the infamous "nine-men out" debacle saw the Dragons sweep into a two-goal lead. Danny Williams putting the Reds in front after 11 minutes - heading home a Crowell corner unchallenged.

Wrexham had a perfect opportunity to double their advantage only minutes later, when they were awarded a penalty after Sam Williams was brought down in the box. The challenge came following a scramble in the City area, but Harrison guessed correctly with his save, diving to his right to smother Crowell's poorly hit penalty.

With the first-half entering the last 10 minutes, Wrexham got the crucial second goal and what a goal it was. Mark Jones collected the lose ball 25 yards from goal, from where he delivered a shot with the outside of his right foot, that bent around Harrison and inside of the near post.

Chester looked a different team come the start of the second-half, but if was Wrexham who had the chance to put the game beyond City's reach. Derbyshire was played in down the right channel and after he burst into the area, he flashed a shot come cross that travelled across the six yard box that Sam Williams almost turned in at the far post.

Chester looked particularly dangerous from corners and Wrexham had too many lucky escapes in the second-half, as Chester upped the pressure. Despite the chances they created, Chester failed to test Michael Ingham and any save he made were routine. Branch was particularly the culprit often directing headers wide as Wrexham maintained their two goal advantage.

Chester flashed more crosses in across the six-yard box, but got the goal their second-half efforts deserved with a minute remaining. Edwards managed to get the better of two Wrexham players on the edge of the area, before despatching the ball past Ingham and inside of the near post from 18 yards.

With four minutes of injury time, Chester missed the perfect chance to grab an unlikely point. The ball was delivered in from the right and Ellender controlled the ball on the edge of the six-yard box, but Bennett somehow managed to get in a last ditch challenger to block the shot on Ingham's goal. The full time whistle went with much relief to the majority of the Racecourse crowd, but the game should have been put beyond any doubt long before Edwards had pulled a goal back.

Referee: Anthony Leake (Lancashire)

Wrexham 2	**Chester City 1**
Danny Williams 11'	Jake Edwards 89'
Mark Jones 36'	

Attendance: 7,240

Sir Mark celebrates his cracker.

Starting XI:

01 Michael Ingham
18 Shaun Pejic
08 Danny Williams
06 Dennis Lawrence
12 Dean Bennett
16 Matt Crowell
17 Mark Jones
10 Darren Ferguson
07 Andy Holt
27 Sam Williams
14 Matt Derbyshire

Subs:

09 Jon Walters
13 Michael Jones (GK)
20 Simon Spender
22 Matty Done
25 Mike Williams

Stats:

Shots on Goal: 10
Shots on Target: 3
Shots off Target: 7
Possession: 55%
Fouls Conceded: 11
Corners: 6
Yellow Cards: 2
Red Cards: 0

Starting XI:

36 Paul Harrison
34 Mark Albrighton
15 David Artell
35 Paul Ellender
22 Scott McNiven
07 Stuart Drummond
14 Ben Davies
21 Abdelhalim El Khoti 72'
03 Carl Regan 62'
08 Michael Branch
28 Jake Edwards

Subs:

01 Chris MacKenzie (GK)
04 Sean Hessey
10 Ryan Lowe 62'
29 Paul Rutherford 75'
32 Paul Tait

Stats:

Shots on Goal: 10
Shots on Target: 6
Shots off Target: 4
Possession: 45%
Fouls Conceded: 14
Corners: 8
Yellow Cards: 3
Red Cards: 0

The girls enjoyed that one!

The passion carries on after the final whistle.

Swansea reclaimed their Premier Cup crown and £100,000 prize money with a repeat of last season's final victory over Wrexham.

The Swans dominated the first period and got the vital goals when they were on top. Wrexham looked down at out at half-time, but the introduction of Simon Spender pegged Swansea back after the break and Wrexham had opportunities to equalise long before substitute Spender's goal made it a nervous ending for the defending champions.

Swansea then turned up the pressure and overran the Wrexham midfield and deservedly took the lead midway through the first-half. Dean Bennett was struggling to contain Andy Robinson down the Swansea left, and the visitors opened the scoring with a move down the opposite flank. Leon Britton was played in behind Lawrence and after he reached the touch-line, his cut back was turned in at the near post by Wrexham's Danny Williams.

Swansea soon doubled their advantage when Lee Trundle was allowed time to fire in a shot from the left side of the area, that Ingham could only parry into the path of Fallon. Despite only being in the six-yard box, the former Swindon striker made a meal of his first goal for the club by only just scrambling the ball into the empty net.

Spender's introduction at half-time helped Wrexham back into the game. He stemmed the attacks down the Wrexham right and he was always an option in attack to deliver crosses in from the flank. Danny Williams had the first opportunity after the break, but he could only steer his header off target. Wrexham introduced Walters for Ferguson, with Sam Williams dropping back into midfield and it was the presence of Walters that forced the throw that Wrexham pulled a goal back from. All players in the crowded area missed Holt's long throw and the ball arrived for Spender. He made no mistake with a low volley that fired past Gueret at his near post.

Wrexham continued to press in the final 10 minutes, but their only chance came in stoppage time when Danny Williams headed wide from a cross by Spender from the right wing.

Swansea retained their trophy, but Wrexham at least put up a fight in the second-half and it all could have been different if Wrexham had scored early on in the second-half.

Referee: Ceri Richards (Llanelli)

Wrexham 1	**Swansea City 2**
Simon Spender 71'	Danny Williams (og) 37', Rory Fallon 41'

Attendance: 3,032

The two Sams tussle for the ball.

Starting XI:

01 Michael Ingham
18 Shaun Pejic
08 Danny Williams
06 Dennis Lawrence
12 Dean Bennett 45'
16 Matt Crowell
17 Mark Jones 76'
10 Darren Ferguson 70'
07 Andy Holt
27 Sam Williams
14 Matt Derbyshire

Subs:

09 Jon Walters 70'
13 Michael Jones (GK)
19 Levi Mackin 76'
20 Simon Spender 45'
25 Mike Williams

Stats:

n/a

Starting XI:

27 Willy Gueret
05 Alan Tate
17 Keith Lowe
16 Gary Monk
02 Sam Ricketts
04 Kristian O'Leary
23 Owain Tudor Jones
07 Leon Britton
10 Lee Trundle
29 Rory Fallon
18 Andy Robinson 82'

Subs:

06 Roberto Martinez 82'
09 Adebayo Akinfenwa
11 Adrian Forbes
15 Tom Williams
24 Leon Knight

Stats:

n/a

Holt and Tate battle it out.

Spender's goal lifts the team.

No joy at for the Dragons at Grimsby, where a lack of bite up-front meant that the Grimsby keeper had just one save to make all afternoon.

The absence of Matt Derbyshire limited Wrexham's options up-front, with both Jon Walters and Sam Williams lacking the pace to trouble the defence. Grimsby were not much better and this resulted in a drab opening 20 minutes of the game.

The game turned with 25 minutes gone, when Grimsby were awarded a free-kick on the halfway line. The first ball towards the edge of the area was headed back by Reddy into the path of Whittle. The midfielder lifted the ball over the top of the Wrexham defence, who stood on the edge of the 18-yard line appealing for offside. Gary Jones looked yards off, but with the flag staying down, he made no mistake with his shot past Ingham from 12 yards.

Grimsby were buoyant following the goal and dominated the remainder of the first-half and went close to extending their lead when 6ft 7inch defender Rob Jones headed over from Woodhouse's corner. Michael Ingham was called into action again with five minutes of the half remaining, when the ball was crossed in from the wing and Ingham had to dive down at his near post to keep Gary Jones' header out.

Wrexham's display picked up after the break, but for all their efforts in midfield, we lacked the creativity to open up the stubborn Grimsby defence. Wrexham's best chance came when they were awarded a free-kick on the edge of the area that Crowell fired through the wall, only to see Mildenhall punch it away to safety.

Wrexham changed formation to 4-4-2 for the last 10 minutes, with Sam Williams being replaced by Alex Smith. The substitute went onto the left wing and this allowed Wrexham to put Dennis Lawrence up front.

This left Wrexham exposed at the back and the game was put beyond them with two minutes left on the clock. Shaun Pejic allowed the ball to bounce and this was the only incentive Reddy needed as he battled past Pejic and made no mistake with a neat finish past Ingham from the edge of the area.

Referee: Trevor Kettle (Berkshire)

Grimsby Town 2 Wrexham 0
Gary Jones 25'
Michael Reddy 88'

Attendance: 6,058

Alex Smith challenges.

Starting XI:

01 Steve Mildenhall
02 John McDermott
06 Justin Whittle
12 Robert Jones
03 Tom Newey
15 Gary Cohen 58'
08 Paul Bolland
32 Curtis Woodhouse
10 Marc Goodfellow
09 Michael Reddy
19 Gary Jones

Subs:

05 Ben Futcher
07 Jean-Paul Kamudimba
11 Andy Parkinson 58'
20 Gary Croft
31 Junior Mendes

Stats:

Shots on Goal: 6
Shots on Target: 3
Shots off Target: 3
Possession: 50%
Fouls Conceded: 15
Corners: 2
Yellow Cards: 2
Red Cards: 0

Starting XI:

01 Michael Ingham
18 Shaun Pejic
08 Danny Williams
06 Dennis Lawrence
20 Simon Spender
16 Matt Crowell
17 Mark Jones
10 Darren Ferguson
07 Andy Holt
09 Jon Walters
27 Sam Williams 81'

Subs:

03 Alex Smith 81'
04 Dave Bayliss
13 Michael Jones (GK)
21 Marc Williams
25 Mike Williams

Stats:

Shots on Goal: 6
Shots on Target: 2
Shots off Target: 4
Possession: 50%
Fouls Conceded: 9
Corners: 6
Yellow Cards: 1
Red Cards: 0

Jon Walters working tirelessly.

Rooster's not happy with the decision.

Shrewsbury came to the Racecourse after a week of tub-thumping by manager Peters and played three up front and as if their lives depended on it. You have to say that they deserved the points for their first-half efforts.

Wrexham got off to a disastrous start that left them two down and a man down after only 15 minutes

After just two minutes Shaun Pejic was harshly adjudged to have brought down a Shrewsbury player on the touchline. The free-kick was swung in from the left where Dennis Lawrence got the only touch on the ball to divert it inside of the near post for the opening goal of the game.

Worse was to follow on 15 minutes as they found themselves a man and two goals down. A hopeful free kick towards the six-yard box that the Wrexham defence failed to deal with. Bennett stopped the goal bound effort by hand balling on the line. The inevitable red card followed and McMenamin sent Ingham the wrong way from the spot.

Wrexham were in disarray and the game was really there for Shrewsbury's taking, but they failed to press home their advantage. In fact Shrewsbury were lucky not to be reduced to 10 men when Steve Hogg escaped a second yellow card for a foul on Ferguson. Gary Peters did not wait long before replacing the midfielder with Tolley to keep Shrewsbury's one man advantage.

Danny Williams was lucky to escape red on half-time as he launched a hapless Shrewsbury player into orbit with a ferocious tackle.

McEvilly's introduction at half-time unsettled the Shrews and Wrexham started to take the game to their neighbours and Lee was unlucky to just hit the post with a 30-yard free kick.

With 12 minutes left, Derbyshire "poked" home from close range after Shrewsbury failed to clear a Ferguson corner. The annoying McMenamin then saw red for a rash challenge on Walters after he was clear on goal.

Wrexham threw everything at Shrewsbury, with Ingham coming up for corners and Derbyshire skying a great chance just before the end. Its fair to say that 2,000 Shrewsbury fans enjoyed their day out a bit more than we did.

Referee: Richard Beeby (Nottinghamshire)

Wrexham 1	**Shrewsbury Town 2**
M. Derbyshire 78'	D.Lawrence 3'(og)
	K. McMenamin 15' (p)

Attendance 6,310

Dean Bennett sees red.

Starting XI:

01 Michael Ingham
18 Shaun Pejic
08 Danny Williams
06 Dennis Lawrence
12 Dean Bennett
16 Matt Crowell 45'
17 Mark Jones
10 Darren Ferguson
07 Andy Holt
14 Matt Derbyshire
27 Sam Williams 73'

Subs:

09 Jon Walters 73'
11 Lee McEvilly 45'
13 Michael Jones (GK)
20 Simon Spender
25 Mike Williams

Stats:

Shots on Goal: 10
Shots on Target: 3
Shots off Target: 7
Possession: 48%
Fouls Conceded: 15
Corners: 7
Yellow Cards: 4
Red Cards: 1

Starting XI:

01 Joe Hart
12 Ben Herd
28 Sagi Burton
25 Richard Hope
11 Neil Ashton
19 David Edwards
06 Neil Sorvel
17 Steven Hogg 40'
07 Colin McMenamin
08 Kelvin Langmead
23 Glynn Hurst 60'

Subs:

02 Stuart Whitehead
04 Jamie Tolley 40'
09 Mark Stallard 60'
16 Gavin Cowan
31 Lance Cronin (GK)

Stats:

Shots on Goal: 7
Shots on Target: 3
Shots off Target: 4
Possession: 52%
Fouls Conceded: 15
Corners: 4
Yellow Cards: 3
Red Cards: 1

Matt Derbyshire gives the Town hope.

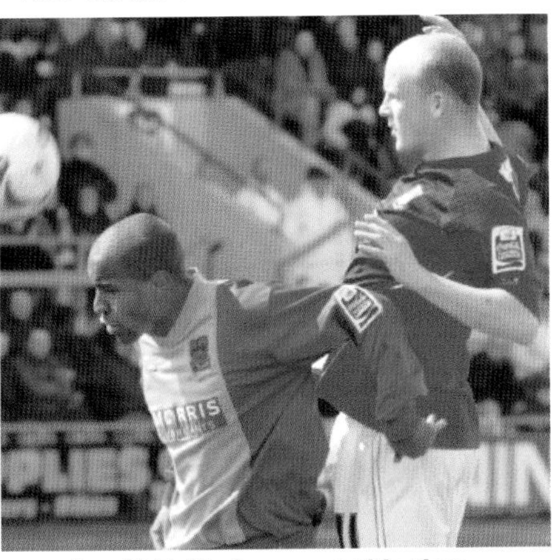

Lee McEvilly loses out this time.

Our fourth league defeat on the trot just about topped off the worst possible week in a Wrexham fan's life. Should you be unfortunate enough to end up in hell it will probably feel just like this.

A fairly even first-half saw few chances with only the pace of Derbyshire and Asdamoah troubling the defences and Pejic showing up strong for the Welshmen. Neither keeper was called on to make a save.

Ten minutes after the break and the game came to life. Stockport based official Scott Mathieson gave Chester the worst penalty I have ever seen when penalising Danny Williams for a pin-point tackle on Chester forward Blundell. I was yards closer to the incident than he was and I was also closer to bringing down Blundell than Williams was. An awful decision! The ref didn't even book Danny for his challenge, which showed that at least he had some doubts about it. Ben Davies converted the penalty and sparked mad celebrations in a very small corner of North East Wales.

Ten minutes later, and Ingham kept Wrexham in the game by diving low to his right to save from a threatening Asamoah.

This miss proved costly, as Wrexham equalised a minute later when our best move of the night saw Ferguson advance in from the left touch line and his pin-point cross picked out McEvilly at the back post. The Wrexham striker, who was making his first start since an injury in December, made no mistake by heading the ball down past MacKenzie to bring the scores level.

Wrexham failed to build on this and Chester struck back six minutes later following an awful mistake by Matt Crowell. His pass along the half way line was behind Mark Jones and one pass later Deadly Derek was clean through on goal, tucking the ball past Ingham with a cool finish from 15 yards.

Needing at least a point to keep the play offs a possibility, we ended the game with four strikers on the pitch, but failed to put a shot on target. For the second time in four days we were "lucky" enough to witness delirious scenes of joy from our normally downtrodden neighbours. Small comfort to Wrexham fans that this victory virtually guaranteed survival for Chester.

Denis Smith: "Was it a penalty? Not from my position or that of our fans behind that goal, but the referee has given it!"

Referee: Scott Mathieson (Stockport)

Chester City 2	**Wrexham 1**
B. Davies 56' (p)	Lee McEvilly 69'
D. Asamoah 75'	

Attendance: 4,801

"It is in Wales matey!"

Starting XI:

01 Chris MacKenzie
15 David Artell
22 Scott McNiven
34 Mark Albrighton
11 Tom Curtis
07 Stewart Drummond
09 Gregg Blundell 71'
14 Ben Davies
04 Sean Hessey 85'
19 Derek Asamoah
28 Jake Edwards 90'

Subs:

02 Stephen Vaughan
03 Carl Regan 71'
21 Abdelhalim El Kholti 85'
32 Paul Tait 90'
36 Paul Harrison (GK)

Stats:

Shots on Goal: 4
Shots on Target: 2
Shots off Target: 2
Possession: 43%
Fouls Conceded: 13
Corners: 5
Yellow Cards: 2
Red Cards: 0

Starting XI:

01 Michael Ingham
18 Shaun Pejic
08 Danny Williams
06 Dennis Lawrence
20 Simon Spender 78'
16 Matt Crowell 83'
17 Mark Jones
10 Dennis Lawrence
07 Andy Holt
14 Matt Derbyshire
11 Lee McEvilly

Subs:

03 Alex Smith
09 Jon Walters 78'
13 Michael Jones (GK)
25 Mike Williams
27 Sam Williams 83'

Stats:

Shots on Goal: 2
Shots on Target: 1
Shots off Target: 1
Possession: 57%
Fouls Conceded: 10
Corners: 5
Yellow Cards: 2
Red Cards: 0

Lee McEvilly celebrates the equaliser.

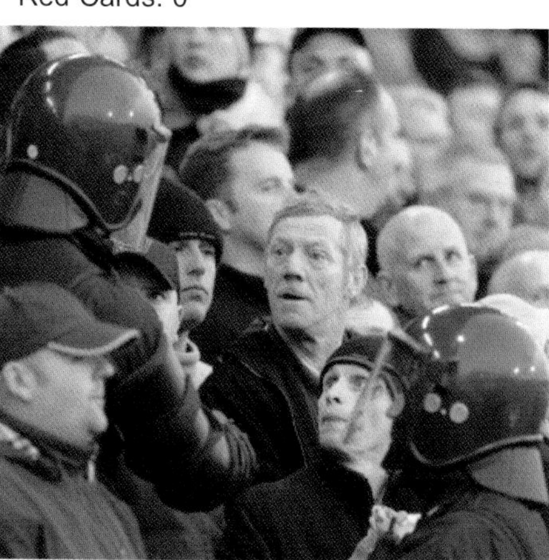

"Do you have a cold sore constable?"

The nightmare continued at Stockport. I could probably put anything in this report because most of you will skip over to something a little more attractive. This was an awful performance from a team with realistic play off chances.

Denis Smith made changes to personnel, but not the system, in an attempt to end Wrexham's run of four straight defeats. Danny Williams was moved into midfield with Mike Williams recalled to defence and Sam Williams also started in midfield. This meant Matt Crowell was on the bench and you can only assume Mark Jones was injured, as he was sitting in the stands. In one final change, Jon Walters replaced Lee McEvilly up-front.

However, just six minutes into the game and Wrexham were a goal down from a free-kick on the left delivered to the edge of the area. Bramble was unchallenged and his knock-down into the box was pounced on by Ashley Williams, who headed past Ingham from 12-yards out.

Wrexham now looked disorganised at the back with Lawrence particularly uncomfortable playing in the middle of the back three. County had several penalty appeals turned down in this period.

However, just after the half hour mark, a period of Wrexham pressure paid dividends. Ferguson delivered a set play into the box that Jon Walters managed to head downwards and Spender reacted the quickest to hammer the ball past Spencer from roughly 15 yards - 1-1!

What happened four minutes later was just inexcusable, as Wrexham were again undone by a routine free-kick into the box. Danny Williams was penalised for hand ball, but the free-kick was delayed as Lawrence and Bramble ended up in the book for taking their personal feud too far. This delay must have unsettled Wrexham, as they completely switched off because Michael Raynes rose unchallenged to find the corner of the net with Ingham having no chance of making the save.

The second-half was a total non-event for Wrexham, with James Spencer having so little to do in the Stockport goal he was able to banter with the Wrexham fans behind him. What was his verdict on the Town? Easiest game that he had all season. I can believe it as well.

Denis Smith: "I was embarrassed by our defending in the first 35 minutes! No one took responsibility at set pieces and I had the Land of the Giants out there today."

Referee: Phil Joslin (Nottinghamshire)

Stockport County 2	**Wrexham 1**
Ashley Williams 6'	Simon Spender 38'
Michael Raynes 42'	

Attendance: 4,750

Simon Spender celebrates his goal.

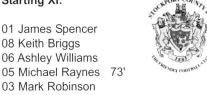

Starting XI:

01 James Spencer
08 Keith Briggs
06 Ashley Williams
05 Michael Raynes 73'
03 Mark Robinson
34 Jason Taylor
32 Kevin O'Connor
21 Jamie Ward
22 Adam Griffin
23 Michael Malcolm 68'
09 Tesfaye Bramble 45'

Subs:

07 Matthew Hamshaw
10 David Beharall 73'
16 Benjamin Smith (GK)
19 Danny Boshell 68'
20 Liam Dickinson 45'

Stats:

Shots on Goal: 14
Shots on Target: 8
Shots off Target: 6
Possession: 43%
Fouls Conceded: 10
Corners: 3
Yellow Cards: 1
Red Cards: 0

Starting XI:

01 Michael Ingham
18 Shaun Pejic
06 Dennis Lawrence
25 Mike Williams 79'
20 Simon Spender
08 Danny Williams
10 Darren Ferguson
27 Sam Williams 79'
07 Andy Holt
09 Jon Walters
14 Matt Derbyshire 61'

Subs:

03 Alex Smith 79'
11 Lee McEvilly 61'
13 Michael Jones (GK)
15 Lee Roche
16 Matt Crowell 79'

Stats:

Shots on Goal: 16
Shots on Target: 7
Shots off Target: 9
Possession: 57%
Fouls Conceded: 12
Corners: 6
Yellow Cards: 2
Red Cards: 0

Matt Derbyshire shoots.

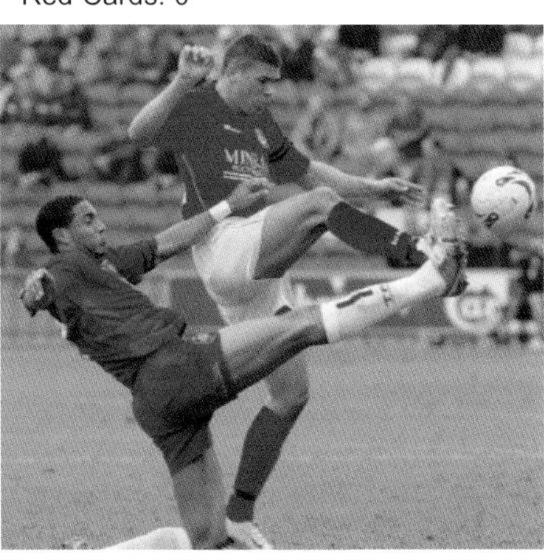

Jon Walters battles with the County defence.

After five straight defeats we still had an outside chance of the play-offs, as did our visitors from Bristol. How this was possible was not apparent in a drab encounter, fought out in wet and slippery conditions?

Wrexham showed four changes from the weekend defeat at Stockport, with Danny Williams restored to his defensive role and Matt Crowell recalled into midfield. Michael Jones replaced the injured Michael Ingham in goal and it was no real surprise to see Lee McEvilly starting at the expense of Jon Walters.

These changes had a quick reward for manager Denis Smith, with Wrexham opening the scoring within five minutes after a positive start to the game. The goal came courtesy of a superb through ball from Ferguson, when he picked out the run of Derbyshire behind the defence and the on-loan striker finished with a strike through the legs of Scott Shearer.

Wrexham's next best chance of the half came from a McEvilly free-kick that he curled over from 25 yards. This was the start of a lull in the game with the tempo from Wrexham's play fizzing out, but they made half-time comfortably maintaining their 1-0 lead.

Rovers enjoyed a lot more of the possession after the break, but the Wrexham defence held strong, with the challenge often enough for the opposition attackers to direct their efforts off target. Junior Agogo had their best chance when he headed wide a Carruthers' centre.

There were more nervous moments in the Wrexham defence as the game went on, but due to the slippery conditions, the ball frequently escaped both teams when it skipped off the ground. Wrexham did get lucky when they could only clear a corner to the edge of the area, from where a drive by Carruthers was deflected into the arms of a grateful Michael Jones via the foot of Rovers' top scorer Richard Walker.

Wrexham were now relying on the counter attack and substitute Bennett, who replaced Darren Ferguson, should have done better when he got in down the left, but his cross could only pick out goalkeeper Scott Shearer.

So the run of defeats came to an end and we are four points off the play offs with three games to play

Denis Smith: "We kept a clean sheet and that is just what we needed especially with a young goalkeeper."

Referee: Lee Mason (Lancashire)

Wrexham 1 **Bristol Rovers 0**
Matt Derbyshire 5'

Attendance: 3,749

"You're not going anywhere!"

Starting XI:

13 Michael Jones
18 Shaun Pejic
08 Danny Williams
06 Dennis Lawrence
20 Simon Spender
16 Matt Crowell
10 Darren Ferguson 82'
27 Sam Williams
07 Andy Holt 44'
14 Matt Derbyshire
11 Lee McEvilly 67'

Subs:

03 Alex Smith 44'
09 Jon Walters 67'
12 Dean Bennett 82'
22 Matty Done
25 Mike Williams

Stats:

Shots on Goal: 6
Shots on Target: 3
Shots off Target: 3
Possession: 40%
Fouls Conceded: 11
Corners: 2
Yellow Cards: 0
Red Cards: 0

Starting XI:

23 Scott Shearer
32 Aaron Lescott
02 Craig Hinton
06 Steve Elliott
11 Chris Carruthers
26 Lewis Haldene 62'
08 James Hunt
20 Craig Disley
07 Stuart Campbell 85'
09 Junior Agogo
10 Richard Walker

Subs:

05 Christian Edwards
19 Alistair Gibb 62'
22 Chris Lines 85'
33 Martin Horsell (GK)
39 Darren Mullings

Stats:

Shots on Goal: 6
Shots on Target: 1
Shots off Target: 5
Possession: 60%
Fouls Conceded: 9
Corners: 10
Yellow Cards: 0
Red Cards: 0

The young strike force are thwarted.

Matt Derbyshire nips in

Wrexham started this game with play off hopes but the game followed the dismal pattern of the last month with Wrexham making a slow start to the game, conceding an early goal and never looked like fighting themselves back into the game.

Michael Jones continued in goal for Wrexham in the absence of Michael Ingham and the team showed more changes with Mark Jones and Jon Walters back in the team and Alex Smith replacing the injured Andy Holt down the left. The absence of Holt proved to be crucial as Wrexham's wing backs never looked like getting in behind the Torquay defence, until the introduction of teenager Matty Done in the second-half.

Torquay started the game with a decent tempo and forced a couple of early saves from Jones. They got the goal they needed in the ninth minute, but it was again bad defending from Wrexham as they failed to clear the ball in the box. Pejic, Spender and Ferguson all had opportunities to clear the danger but they just stood there as Martin Phillips found himself in space down the left channel and he placed his shot through the legs of Carrots.

The goal did spark Wrexham into life and Andy Marriott made easy saves from long range efforts from Crowell and Walters. What did come across during the quiet spell is that you could not hear any of the Wrexham outfield players talking, as if there was no leader on the pitch. The only voices were coming from teenager Michael Jones and he made it clear to Lawrence on one occasion that when he calls for the ball it is his!

The second-half saw Wrexham step-up the tempo somewhat, but in truth this was a very poor performance against a struggling side.

Andy Marriott received a hero's welcome from the 200 Wrexham fans who had made the long and expensive trip, but unfortunately for Wrexham, the performance was overshadowed by an incident at the end when stewards had to intervene to pull Darren Ferguson away from Wrexham fans after they traded insults with one another. A miserable finale to a weekend best forgotten.

Denis Smith: "Two weeks ago we were cast iron play off certainties, now I'm glad we have points on board or we'd be looking at relegation. Why? You have to speak to the players. I've run out of things to say to them and out of ideas to get them going. I'm not happy. If people want to give me stick I'll be glad to talk to them, but they'd better be brave."

Referee: Andy Penn (West Midlands)

Torquay United 1 **Wrexham 0**
Martin Phillips 9'

Attendance: 2,623

Big Den challenges in this attack

Starting XI:

01 Andy Marriott
25 Steven Reed
28 Lee Andrews
18 Steve Woods
05 Craig Taylor
14 Martin Phillips
24 Danny Hollands
06 Darren Garner
11 Kevin Hill
09 Lee Thorpe
10 Jo Kuffour 84'

Subs:

02 Matthew Hockley 84'
08 Alan Connell
16 Paul D Robinson
19 Anthony Lloyd
26 Morike Sako

Stats:

Shots on Goal: 6
Shots on Target: 3
Shots off Target: 3
Possession: 54%
Fouls Conceded: 12
Corners: 6
Yellow Cards: 1
Red Cards: 0

Starting XI:

13 Michael Jones
18 Shaun Pejic
08 Danny Williams
06 Dennis Lawrence
20 Simon Spender
16 Matt Crowell 63'
17 Mark Jones 78'
10 Darren Ferguson
03 Alex Smith 90'
09 Jon Walters
14 Matt Derbyshire

Subs:

12 Dean Bennett 78'
15 Lee Roche
22 Matty Done 63'
25 Mike Williams 90'
27 Sam Williams

Stats:

Shots on Goal: 12
Shots on Target: 2
Shots off Target: 10
Possession: 46%
Fouls Conceded: 11
Corners: 8
Yellow Cards: 1
Red Cards: 0

Alex Smith threads another pass.

"The dressing rooms are over there Sir"

Relegation threatened Oxford came to the Racecourse knowing that only a win would really suffice to keep them in the League. They started the game in sprightly fashion and Michael Jones was forced to make a succession of early saves from both Burgess and N'Toya.

However, it was Wrexham who scored first. After 28 minutes, a Roche cross from the right was dropped by keeper Guatelli under pressure from Walters. Matt Crowell pounced on the loose ball and drove it into an unguarded net. Guatelli was then carried off on a stretcher and Oxford's players were furious about the goal, although, the reasons for this were unclear as there was nothing wrong with it.

With the half drawing to a close, substitute keeper Tardiff pulled off two decent saves to deny Walters and Derbyshire, when a second goal would have killed Oxford off. At the other end Sabin curled a shot around the post and Burgess wasted a good chance, shooting over from a good opening.

Oxford responded well and prompted by Sabin, the best player on the pitch, stepped up the pressure on Wrexham. They got their rewards when they were awarded a penalty after 63 minutes. Sabin skipped into the box where an outstretched leg from Shaun Pejic brought the striker down. Although Michael Jones dived the right way, N'Toya's spot kick squirmed underneath the body of the Wrexham keeper and into the corner of the net.

Done replaced Ferguson as we changed to 4-4-2 and Wrexham went looking for a winner. Young Matty gave Wrexham that extra dimension and from one run, when he beat three Oxford defenders to burst into the box, a defender's leg managed to deflect the ball away from Derbyshire and Walters at the far post who were waiting for a tap in.

Holt and Done combined well down the left and from Holt's cross Derbyshire narrowly floated a header wide of the near post with the keeper stuck on his line. Wrexham did not manufacture anything after that, but there was still time for Burgess to miss yet another sitter from six yards out after smart work by Sabin. It ended 1-1 and Oxford all but relegated.

Denis Smith: "I wouldn't say it wasn't a fair result, and the game swung from end-to-end, both sides were really going for it. We finished the game with three scholars on the pitch and the future looks good."

Referee: Steve Tanner (Somerset)

Wrexham 1	**Oxford United 1**
Matt Crowell 28'	Tcham N'Toya 64' (p)

Attendance: 4,575

Holty foils N'Toya.

Starting XI:

13 Michael Jones
18 Shaun Pejic
08 Danny Williams
25 Mike Williams
15 Lee Roche
16 Matt Crowell
17 Mark Jones 45'
10 Darren Ferguson 56'
07 Andy Holt
09 Jon Walters 85'
14 Matt Derbyshire

Subs:

01 Michael Ingham (GK)
03 Alex Smith
06 Dennis Lawrence 85'
12 Dean Bennett 45'
22 Matt Done 56'

Stats:

Shots on Goal: 10
Shots on Target: 4
Shots off Target: 6
Possession: 54%
Fouls Conceded: 15
Corners: 4
Yellow Cards: 0
Red Cards: 0

Starting XI:

27 Andrea Guatelli 32'
02 Lee Mansell
15 John Dempster
05 Chris Willmott
03 Matthew Robinson
04 Barry Quinn
10 Chris Hargreaves 45'
17 Andrew Burgess
09 Steve Basham 62'
33 Tcham N'Toya
18 Eric Sabin

Subs:

01 Christopher Tardiff (GK) 32'
07 Yemi Odubade
08 Jay Smith 45'
14 Tim Sills 62'
20 Jamie Brooks

Stats:

Shots on Goal: 11
Shots on Target: 2
Shots off Target: 9
Possession: 46%
Fouls Conceded: 9
Corners: 3
Yellow Cards: 1
Red Cards: 0

Matty after scoring the game's opener.

Walters having close attention.

Wrexham started the game with a new look of 4-4-2 with Darren Ferguson on the bench. This meant Matty Done featured on the left flank, but in honesty he did not receive much of the ball to make an impact.

Darlington, who still had a slim outside chance of a play off spot, made a poor start and the response from Wrexham was not much better with a Done effort, clearing the cross-bar, the only shot on goal in the opening exchanges.

The first half hour resembled a game where both teams had nothing to play for and with little efforts on target, both keepers enjoyed an easy opening to the game. Despite this, the goal on the half hour mark was in complete contrast to the proceeding 30 minutes. Wrexham broke well down the right wing with Jon Walters getting the better of his marker on the touchline. The ball was well worked inside via Dean Bennett and Danny Williams thumped the ball almost through keeper Sam Russell from 25 yards.

Wrexham were buoyant after the goal and it was difficult to understand how Darlington had an outside chance of a play off spot, whereas Wrexham had blown their opportunity weeks-a-go.

Darlington were awarded a free-kick following a foul by Mike Williams that Logan curled in, but he was unlucky to see his effort rebound off Ingham's far post with the Wrexham keeper routed to the spot. From the rebound, Bates collected the ball on the left flank and cut into the box. With the Wrexham defence standing off him, he cracked in a right-footed shot that Ingham expertly tipped over the bar for a corner.

Darlington replied with former Wrexham winger Neil Wainwright threatening down the right and Simon Johnson curled another effort over after cutting in down the left, but despite this pressure, Wrexham looked confident in defence.

Darren Ferguson was introduced for Done for the last 10 minutes, as Wrexham reverted back to 3-5-2, and he had an opportunity when he was picked out by a right wing cross, but was unable to steer his left footed shot on target.

In the 92nd minute Wrexham conceded an unlikely equaliser that summed up our whole season. It was no surprise that it came from an uncontested set play with Andy Cooke on hand to smash in the corner.

Denis Smith: "We have had enough chances in the second half to have killed the game off."

Referee: Kevin Friend (Leicestershire)

Darlington 1	**Wrexham 1**
Andrew Cooke 90'	Danny Williams 31'

Attendance: 4,648

Derbyshire is brought down.

Starting XI:

23 Sam Russell
02 Ryan Valentine
12 Shelton Martis
14 David McGurk
17 David Duke
11 Simon Johnson
16 Clark Keltie
10 Jonjo Dickman 63'
25 Carlos Logan 63'
09 Gut Bates 63'
20 Akpo Sodje

Subs:

01 Nathan Wright (GK)
07 Neil Wainwright 63'
15 Andrew Cooke 63'
22 Neil Maddison
28 Mark McLeod 63'

Stats:

Shots on Goal: 15
Shots on Target: 4
Shots off Target: 11
Possession: 53%
Fouls Conceded: 5
Corners: 3
Yellow Cards: 0
Red Cards: 0

Starting XI:

01 Michael Ingham
15 Lee Roche
18 Shaun Pejic
25 Mike Williams
07 Andy Holt
12 Dean Bennett
08 Danny Williams
16 Matt Crowell
22 Matt Done 82'
09 Jon Walters 87'
14 Matt Derbyshire

Subs:

10 Darren Ferguson 82'
13 Michael Jones (GK)
20 Simon Spender
21 Marc Williams 87'
23 Gareth Evans

Stats:

Shots on Goal: 11
Shots on Target: 3
Shots off Target: 8
Possession: 47%
Fouls Conceded: 14
Corners: 4
Yellow Cards: 1
Red Cards: 0

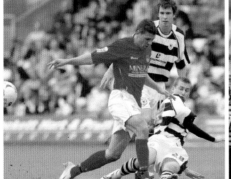

"Walters thwarted."

"Matt, can I have your telephone number?"

Danny Williams 2005-2006 winner.

The following is a list of players that have received the Wrexham A.F.C. Player of the Year Winner award "The Jack Williams' Trophy":

1975/76 Brian Lloyd
1976/77 Graham Whittle
1977/78 Gareth Davies
1978/79 John Roberts
1979/80 Dixie McNeil
1980/81 Steve Fox
1981/82 Eddie Niedzwiecki
1982/83 Robbie Savage
1983/84 David Gregory
1984/85 Jack Keay
1985/86 Mike Williams
1986/87 Mike Williams
1987/88 Kevin Russell
1988/89 Kevin Russell
1989/90 Nigel Beaumont
1990/91 Mark Morris
1991/92 Andy Thackeray
1992/93 Tony Humes
1993/94 Gary Bennett
1994/95 Gary Bennett
1995/96 Wayne Phillips
1996/97 Andy Marriott
1997/98 Brian Carey
1998/99 Dean Spink
1999/00 Darren Ferguson
2000/01 Mark McGregor
2001/02 Jim Whitley
2002/03 Andy Morrell
2003/04 Dennis Lawrence
2004/05 Andy Holt
2005/06 Danny Williams

Mark Jones 2005-2006 winner.

The following is a list of players that have received the Wrexham A.F.C. Young Player of the Year Winner award:

1983/84 Shaun Cunnington
1984/85 Andy Edwards
1985/86 Shaun Cunnington
1986/87 Roger Preece
1987/88 Darren Wright
1988/89 Darren Wright
1989/90 Gareth Owen
1990/91 Gareth Owen
1991/92 Phil Hardy
1992/93 Jonathan Cross
1993/94 David Brammer
1994/95 Bryan Hughes
1995/96 Mark McGregor
1996/97 Mark McGregor
1997/98 Neil Roberts
1998/99 Robin Gibson
1999/00 Robin Gibson
2000/01 Lee Roche
2001/02 Shaun Pejic
2002/03 Craig Morgan
2003/04 Craig Morgan
2004/05 Mark Jones
2005/06 Mark Jones

No	Date		Att	Pos	Pt	F-A	H-T	Scorers, Times, and Referees	1	2	3	4	5	6	7	8	9	10	11	subs used
1	H	BOSTON		-	W	2-0	1-0	Jones Ma 23, Roche 83	**Ingham**	**Roche**	Holt	**Bayliss**	Pejic	Lawrence	Jones Ma	Williams D	**Walters**	**McEvilly***	Ferguson	Bennett
	6/8		4,503	-	3				*Abbey*	*Canoville*	*Greaves*	*Futcher*	*McCann^*	*Maylett*	*Talbot*	*Holland*	*Joachim*	*Whelan"*	*Johnson**	*Rusk/Thomas/Norris*
								Ref: G Lewis	Wrexham got off to a flying start against ambitious Boston. Jones hit home an unstoppable 25-yard strike. Lee Roche, one of five new signings finished off good work by Dean Bennett. The Pilgrims new attack of Julian Joachim & Noel Whelan offered little, & had just one shot on goal.											
2	A	NOTTS CO		12	L	0-1	0-0		Ingham	Roche	Holt	Bayliss	Pejic	Lawrence^	Jones Ma	Williams D	Walters	McEvilly*	Ferguson	Bennett/Mackin
	9/8		*4,382*	*11*	3			*Long 90*	*Pilkington*	*O'Call'ghan*	*Baudet*	*Wilson*	*Ullathorne*	*Pipe*	*Edwards*	*McMahon*	*Palmer**	*White"*	*Scoffman^*	*Long/Hurst/Gill*
								Ref: M Thorpe	Stacy Long made a dream debut for the Magpies having only just signed non-contract terms from non-league Chorlton. The Dragons defence argued Lawrence had been fouled as Mike Edwards ran on to set up Long to coolly round Mike Ingham who seemed destined to deny County.											
3	A	NORTHAMPTON		12	D	0-0	0-0		Ingham	Roche	Holt	Bayliss	Pejic	Lawrence	Jones Ma	Williams D	Walters	McEvilly*	Ferguson	Bennett
	13/8		*5,075*	*17*	4				*Harper*	*Crowe*	*Bojic**	*Dyche*	*Chambers*	*Hunt*	*Taylor*	*Dudfield*	*Sabin^*	*Low"*	*Jess*	*Johnson/Kirk/Gilligan*
								Ref: C Boyeson	The Dragons battled to a hard-earned point at Sixfields. Andy Kirk almost broke the deadlock for the bookies League Two favourites with two minutes left when he lobbed a right-foot shot on to the crossbar. Mark Jones made two goal-line clearances, one from the profligate Josh Low.											
4	H	CARLISLE		16	L	0-1	0-0		Ingham	Roche*	Holt	Bayliss	Pejic	Lawrence	Jones Ma	Wil'ams D"	Walters	McEvilly^	Ferguson	Sp'der !/Bennett/Mackin
	20/8		4,239	*8*	4			*McGill 63*	*Williams*	*Arnison**	*Livesey*	*Gray*	*Aranalde*	*McGill*	*Murray A*	*Billy*	*Simpson*	*Hawley*	*Holmes^*	*Murphy/Nade*
								Ref: D Drysdale	Anthony Williams saved Jon Walters last-minute penalty kick to ensure the Cumbrians victory after Kevin Gray had pulled down Lawrence. Spender was sent off for an over the top challenge & Brendan McGill fired in from the resulting free-kick, as the ref left the home fans fuming.											
5	A	BURY		17	D	2-2	2-1	McEvilly 11, Flitcroft 24 (og)	Ingham	**Warhurst**	Holt	Bayliss !	**Linwood**	Lawrence	Jones Ma	Williams D	Walters	McEvilly*	Ferguson^	**Foy**/Mackin
	27/8		*2,468*	*20*	5			*Barry-Murphy 13, Tipton 52*	*Edwards*	*Scott*	*Challinor*	*Hardiker*	*Whaley*	*Mattis*	*Flitcroft^*	*B-Murphy**	*Kennedy*	*Newby"*	*Tipton*	*U'worth/Se'more/Barlow*
								Ref: P Robinson	Wrexham remain unbeaten at Gigg Lane since 1993 after McEvilly ran on to Walters through ball to fire in. Barry-Murphy. Dave Flitcroft's attempted clearance ended up in his own net. Matt Tipton fired home to level from 25 yards. Bayliss was shown red (89) for elbowing Tipton.											
6	H	BARNET		11	W	3-1	2-1	Jones Ma 1, Warhurst 32, Foy 59	Ingham	Warhurst	Smith	Holt	Linwood	Lawrence	Jones Ma*	Williams D	Walters	Foy	Ferguson	Mackin
	29/8		3,768	*7*	8			*Hendon 45p*	*Tynan*	*Hendon*	*King*	*Charles*	*Gross*	*Strevens**	*Bailey*	*Lee*	*Sinclair*	*Graham^*	*Grazioli*	*Soares/Roache*
								Ref: T Parkes	Jon Walters' incisive pass saw Jones fire across Scott Tynan for the perfect start. A Ferguson corner found Paul Warhurst who turned to fire in. The 'Bee's hit back when Lawrence fouled Dean Sinclair to let Ian Hendon score from the spot. Rob Foy's curling left-foot shot wrapped it up.											
7	H	CHELTENHAM		9	W	2-0	1-0	Holt 8. Walters 69	Ingham	Bennett	Smith	Holt	Linwood'	Warhurst	Jones Ma^	Williams D	Walters	Foy"	Ferguson	Sp'der/Mackin/McEv'ly
	10/9		3,671	10	11				*Higgs*	*Gill*	*Townsend"*	*Taylor*	*Victory*	*Wilson*	*Finnigan'*	*McCann*	*Melligan*	*Spencer^*	*Odejayi*	*Bird/Vincent/Caines*
								Ref: R Booth	Wrexham made light of a spate of injuries to dominate John Ward's side. Andy Holt charged into the box to powerfully head home Ferguson's in-swinging corner. Ingham tipped Kayode Odejayi's shot round the post. Mark Jones set up Jonathan Walters to volley into the top corner.											
8	A	LINCOLN		11	L	0-2	0-0		Ingham	Bennett	Smith	Holt'	Warhurst	Lawrence	Jones Ma	Williams D	Walters	Foy^	Ferguson	Linwood/McEvilly
	13/9		*2,956*	*10*	11			Brown 64, Keates 90	Marriott	*Cryan*	*Morgan*	*McCombe*	*Beevers*	*Kerr*	*Keates*	*Brown*	*Asamoah**	*Birch^*	*Mayo*	*Green/McAuley*
								Ref: A Penn	The Dragons were out-muscled by Keith Alexander's Red Imps. Both goalkeepers were tested during a goalless first half, but a half-cleared corner saw Nat Brown slide in to convert Scott Kerr's cross. Wrexham battled back, but Dean Keates' late left-foot strike secured the points.											
9	A	LEYTON ORIENT		11	D	1-1	0-0	Ferguson 53	Jones Mi	Bennett	Smith	Bayliss	Linwood	Lawrence	Jones Ma*	Wil'ams D"	Walters	Foy^	Ferguson	Mackin/McE'ly/W'hurst
	17/9		*3,733*	*9*	12			*Alexander 80*	*Garner*	*Miller*	*Zakuani*	*Mackie*	*Lockwood*	*Easton*	*Simpson*	*McMahon*	*Carlisle**	*Alexander*	*Ibehre^*	*Tudor/Echanomi*
								Ref: B Desmond	The Dragons were forced to play 17-yr-old 'keeper Michael Jones, but at the other end they failed to test Glyn Garner once in the opening half. Smith set-up Ferguson to fire in from just outside the box, but the O's hit back when Matt Lockwood's cross was headed in by Gary Alexander.											
10	H	MACCLESFIELD		13	D	1-1	0-0	Williams 65	Ingham*	Bennett	Smith	Linwood	Warhurst	Lawrence	Jones Ma	Williams D	Walters	Foy^	Ferguson	Jones Mi/Spender
	24/9		3,830	*21*	13			*Russell 72*	*Fettis*	*Morley*	*Briscoe*	*Barras^*	*Swailes*	*Whitaker*	*Harsley*	*McIntyre*	*Sandwith**	*Bullock*	*Townson*	*Smart/Russell*
								Ref: D Gallagher	Wrexham's injury woes continued when 'keeper Mike Ingham was taken off after 25 minutes with a groin strain. Williams drove a powerful header into the bottom corner from Ferguson's in-swinging corner. Brian Horton's side levelled when Allan Russell blasted in his first goal.											
11	A	WYCOMBE		16	L	**1-4**	0-2	Jones Ma 54	Jones Mi	Bennett	Smith	Linwood*	Bayliss	Lawrence	Jones Ma	Williams D	Walters^	Foy	Ferguson	**Williams Mi/Reed**
	27/9		*4,166*	*2*	13			*Tyson 16, 81 Betsy 22, Mooney 58*	*Talia*	*Senda*	*Johnson*	*Willmson*	*Easton*	*Torres**	*Blo'mfield*	*Oakes*	*Betsy*	*Mooney^*	*Tyson"*	*Burnell/Dixon/St'Bridge*
								Ref: G Lewis	John Gorman's side remained the only unbeaten side in the league. The bounce beat 'keeper Mike Jones as Nathan Tyson ran in to score with ease. A slip by Bayliss saw Kevin Betsy fire in. Mark Jones reduced the arrears with a fine shot. Tom Mooney fired in before Tyson struck.											

Coca-Cola League 2 - Summary

No	Date	Att	Pos	Pt	F-A	H-T	Scorers, Times, and Referees	1	2	3	4	5	6	7	8	9	10	11	subs used
12	H	STOCKPORT	12	W	3-0	1-0	Walters 21, Jones Ma 51, 57	Jones Mi	Spender	Smith	Linwood	Bayliss	Lawrence	Jones Ma	Williams D	Walters"	Bennett*	Ferguson^	Foy/Mackin/McEvilly
	1/10	4,153	*22*	16				*Ikeme*	*Clare"*	*Raunes*	*Vaughan*	*Gr'nwood*	*Hamshaw*	*Briggs**	*Will'ms A*	*Robinson*	*Dje !*	*Malcolm^*	*Crowe/B'mble/W'ms C*
							Ref: N Miller	It all went wrong for County when French defender Ludodic Dje elbowed Paul Linwood to receive his marching orders (7). A rocket shot into the top corner, saw Jon Walters deservedly extend the lead. Mark Jones rifled in a poor clearance home, and then drilled in Alex Smith's cross.											
13	H	TORQUAY	10	W	4-2	2-0	Walters 17, 76 B'nett 44, Sp'der 49	Ingham	Spender	Smith	Linwood	Bayliss	Holt*	Jones Ma	Williams D	Walters	Bennett"	Ferguson	Warhurst^/Mackin/McEvilly
	15/10	4,301	*22*	19			*Connell 66, Bedeau 90*	*Marriott*	*Woods*	*Taylor*	*Sharp*	*Hill*	*Sow**	*Garner*	*Hewlett*	*Kuffour*	*Bedeau*	*Connell^*	*Constantine/Coleman*
							Ref: N Swarbrick	Andy Marriott was given a welcome return. Jon Walters tapped in a Holt cross. Bennett fired in Jones' through ball. Spender blasted in his first goal. Ingham gifted Alan Connell a goal, after he dropped the ball at his feet. Walters hit home his 2nd. Bedeau headed in Garner's free kick.											
14	A	BRISTOL ROV	13	L	1-2	0-0	Lawrence 57	Ingham	Spender	Smith	Holt	Bayliss	Lawrence	Jones Ma	Williams D	Walters^	**Ugarte***	Ferguson	Foy/McEvilly
	22/10	*5,730*	*14*	19			*Walker 88, 90*	*Shearer*	*Lescott*	*Hinton*	*Elliott*	*Ryan*	*Gibb"*	*Hunt*	*Disley*	*Car'thers**	*Walker*	*Agogo^*	*For'ster/H'dane/C'bell*
							Ref: P Miller	Richard Walker headed a brace of goals in the dying minutes to give the 'Pirates' all three points. Wrexham led when Williams headed down for Lawrence to shoot home. Walker headed in Jamie Forrester's cross at the far post, and in injury time he climbed unmarked to head in again.											
15	A	PETERBOROUGH	11	D	1-1	0-1	Holt 88	Ingham	Warhurst	Smith*	Holt	Bayliss	Lawrence	Jones Ma	Wil'ams D^	Walters	McEvilly	Ferguson	Foy/Mackin
	25/10	*4,014*	*8*	20			*Farrell 30*	*Tyler*	*Newton*	*Burton*	*Arber*	*St.Ledger*	*Holden*	*Hand*	*Carden*	*Farrell**	*Crow^*	*Thorpe*	*Kennedy/Willock*
							Ref: M Russell	Mark Wright's side were denied a win when Andy Holt rose to head home Ferguson's corner. The Posh led when on-loan Lee Thorpe crossed for David Farrell to slot in. The lively Danny Crow slammed the bar twice, while both McEvilly and Walters wasted chances for the Dragons.											
16	H	DARLINGTON	7	W	1-0	0-0	McEvilly 89p	Ingham	Roche	Smith^	Holt	Bayliss	Lawrence	Mackin*	Williams D	Walters	McEvilly	Ferguson	Foy/Crowell
	29/10	4,881	*13*	23				*Russell*	*Martis*	*Hutc'ison!*	*Clarke*	*Duke**	*Wai'right*	*Peacock^*	*Dickman*	*Valentine*	*Johnson*	*Sodje*	*Thomas/Nd'bu-Nsungu*
							Ref: G Sutton	A drab game exploded into life when a penalty was given after Joey Hutchinson brought down Foy. The decision incensed the visitors, who believed the incident was outside the box. McEvilly hit in the penalty after earlier hitting a post. Hutchinson was sent-off after the final whistle.											
17	A	OXFORD	7	W	3-0	1-0	McEvilly 39, 58 Jones Ma 75	Ingham	Roche	Bennett	Williams M	Bayliss	Williams D	Jones Ma	Crowell	Walters	McEvilly	Ferguson	
	12/11	*4,491*	*14*	26				*Turley*	*Ashton*	*Robinson*	*Roget*	*Willmott*	*Mansell*	*Quinn**	*Bradbury*	*Harg'ves^*	*Sabin"*	*Basham*	*Griffin/Hackett/Davies*
							Ref: R Olivier	Brian Talbot's side suffered their first home defeat, while Wrexham won their first away game. McEvilly pounced on Walters' cross to shoot into the corner of the net. He rose highest to head in Ferguson's out swinging corner. Jones hit a stunning 25-yd shot that flew past Billy Turley											
18	H	PETERBOROUGH	8	D	1-1	0-0	Burton (og) 69	Ingham	Roche	Bennett	Williams M	Bayliss	Williams D	Jones Ma	Crowell	Walters	McEvilly	Ferguson	Foy
	19/11	4,480	*11*	27			*Crow 59*	*Tyler*	*Newton*	*Plummer*	*Burton*	*Arber*	*Holden*	*Carden*	*Gain*	*Hand*	*Crow**	*Thorpe*	*Willock*
							Ref: P Joslin	Wrexham dominated the first half with in-form McEvilly the tormentor-in-chief. It was Mark Wright's side who led when Peter Gain's corner was bundled home by Danny Crow after a goalmouth melee. The Dragons levelled when Jones' shot hit a post and Sagi Burton ran the ball in.											
19	A	BOSTON	9	L	1-2	0-1	McEvilly 60	Ingham	Roche	Bennett	Williams D	Bayliss	Lawrence	Jones Ma	Crowell^	Walters	McEvilly	Ferguson	Smith/Reed
	26/11	*1,938*	*10*	27			*Joachim 14, 66*	*Kuipers*	*Greaves*	*White*	*Futcher*	*Canoville*	*Maylett^*	*Rusk*	*Talbot*	*Ross**	*Lee*	*Joachim"*	*Galbrith/Green/Dudfield*
							Ref: P Melin	The class of Julian Joachim saw him hit home low from 20-yds. Ferguson set up McEvilly to fire home from 12-yds. Canoville fed Joachim to round Ingham. Michel Kuipers felled McEvilly (71), but appeals were waved away. Two goal-line clearances denied McEvilly & Lawrence.											
20	H	MANSFIELD	7	W	**4-1**	0-1	Williams 49, McEvilly 53, Walters	Ingham	Roche	Smith	Williams D	Bayliss	Lawrence	Jones Ma^	Crowell	Walters	McEvilly*	Ferguson	Bennett/Warhurst
	6/12	3,421	*21*	30			*Barker 41p* [61, Jones 87]	*Pressman*	*Peers"*	*Day*	*J-Baptiste*	*Jellyman*	*Dawson**	*Uhlenbeek*	*Coke*	*D'Laryea*	*Birchal^*	*Barker*	*Buxton/Brown/Russell*
							Ref: A Hall	The Stags led when Richard Barker was fouled by Williams & converted the penalty. Williams levelled with a header from Crowell's corner. McEvilly fired in a great left-footer. Walters ran onto a Ferguson pass to net. The striker then fed Jones who cheekily chipped over Pressman.											
21	H	NOTTS CO	8	D	1-1	0-0	Foy 90	Ingham	Roche	Smith	Williams D	Bayliss	Lawrence	Jones Ma	Crowell	Walters	McEvilly	Ferguson	Williams Mi/Bennett/Foy
	10/12	4,726	*13*	31			*Sheridan 84*	*Pilkington*	*Pipe*	*Baudet*	*Wilson*	*Friars*	*McMahon*	*Edwards*	*Needham*	*Ullathorne*	*Hurst**	*De Bolla^*	*Sheridan/White*
							Ref: N Swarbrick	Walters had an effort disallowed after 5 mins, which was followed by Rob Ullathorne clearing off his own line. A dull game came to life with a late flourish. Andy White's cross saw Jake Sheridan's looping header give the Magpies the lead, but Foy raced through to level from 20-yards.											
22	A	CARLISLE	8	L	1-2	0-0	Crowell 50p	Ingham	Roche	Smith*	Williams D	Bayliss	Lawrence	Jones Ma	Crowell"	Walters	McEvilly^	Ferguson	Holt/McEvilly/Foy
	17/12	*6,213*	*3*	31			*Gray 71, Lumsdon 81p*	*Westwood*	*Arnison*	*Livesey*	*Gray*	*Arandale**	*McGill*	*Billy*	*Lumsdon*	*Bridges*	*Murphy*	*Hawley*	*Holmes*
							Ref: J Moss	Controversy surrounded the Cumbrians when Ingham was harshly adjudged to have fouled Arnison. Chris Lumsdon blasted in the spot-kick. Wrexham led when Lumsdon tripped Ferguson & Crowell netted the spot. Kevin Gray levelled after his first header rebounded off the bar.											
23	H	ROCHDALE	6	W	2-1	1-1	Crowell 41p, Ferguson 65	Ingham	Roche	Holt	Williams D	Bayliss	Lawrence	Jones Ma	Crowell	Walters	Foy*	Ferguson	Bennett
	26/12	5,127	*9*	34			*Tait 21*	*Gilks*	*Goodhind*	*Griffiths**	*Gallimore*	*Goodall*	*Cooksey*	*Jones*	*Brisco*	*Tait*	*Lambert*	*Sturrock*	*McArdle*
							Ref: G Sutton	'Dale' led when Paul Tait headed home at the back post from Gary Jones' right-wing cross. Gareth Griffiths shoved Lawrence for Crowell to smash home the penalty. Steve Parkin's side were eventually beaten when Ferguson took a pass and fired in an unstoppable 25-yds half-volley.											

No	Date	Att	Pos	Pt	F-A	H-T	Scorers, Times, and Referees	1	2	3	4	5	6	7	8	9	10	11	subs used
24	H	GRIMSBY	7	L	1-2	1-0	Jones Ma 42	Ingham	Roche	Holt	Wil'iams D!	Bayliss	Lawrence	Jones Ma	Crowell	Walters	Bennett*	Ferguson	Warhurst
	31/12	4,527	*2*	34			*Reddy 52, Downey 84*	*Mildenhall*	*Croft"*	*Ramsden^*	*Jones R**	*Newey*	*Cohen*	*Toner*	*Bolland*	*Parkinson*	*Reddy*	*Jones G*	*Gritton/Downey/Kalala*
							Ref: D Deadman	Glen Downey headed in Tom Newey's free-kick to snatch victory for the Mariners. Wrexham only had a 25-yard cracker from Mark Jones to show for their first half dominance. Michael Reddy capitalised on a mix-up to fire past Ingham. A Williams 2nd caution (90) saw him dismissed											
25	A	SHREWSBURY	8	L	0-1	0-0		Ingham	Roche	Holt	Pejic	Bayliss^	Lawrence	Jones Ma	Crowell*	Walters	Bennett	Ferguson	Foy/Warhurst
	3/1	***6,249***	*19*	34			*Hurst 72*	*Hart*	*Herd*	*Whitehead*	*Hope*	*Sharp*	*Edwards*	*Tolley*	*Sorvel*	*Ashton*	*Hurst**	*McManim*	*Langmead*
							Ref: T Leake	Debutant Glynn Hurst ended Wrexham's record of 26 years without defeat at Gay Meadow, and also ended the Shrews run of three consecutive defeats, when he headed in Ben Herd's right flank cross. Walters missed two good first-half chances, and was off target again after the break.											
26	H	LINCOLN	9	D	1-1	0-0	Jones Ma 90	Ingham	Roche	Holt	Williams D	Pejic	Lawrence*	Jones Ma	Crowell^	Walters	Bennett"	Ferguson	Bayliss/Reed/Foy
	7/1	3,809	*16*	35			*Yeo 63*	*Marriott*	*Cryan*	*McAuley*	*McCombe*	*Mayo**	*Kerr*	*Foster*	*Keates*	*Green^*	*Yeo"*	*Birch*	*Brown/Birch/Ryan*
							Ref: P Miller	A late strike from Mark Jones salvaged a point for Wrexham. Lincoln showed superior battling skills in atrocious conditions. Simon Yeo fired the Imps in front when he knocked in Colin Cryan's cross from short range. But Holt's run saw him square for Jones to rifle into the top corner.											
27	A	RUSHDEN	8	W	2-0	1-0	Jones Ma 36, 67	Ingham	Spender	Holt	Williams D	Pejic	W'iams Mi	Jones Ma	Whitley	Walters	**W'ams Ma***	Ferguson	Bennett
	14/1	*2,617*	*23*	38				*Crane*	*Castle*	*Allen**	*Gulliver*	*Nicholls^*	*Stokes*	*Savage*	*McCaffy"*	*Bull*	*Tomlin*	*Broughton*	*Okuonghae/Berry/Kelly*
							Ref: T Parks	A Mark Jones double earned the Dragons their second away win. He broke down the left and curled a 30-yard shot into the far top corner for his first. He then took Jon Walters' pass to thrash the ball home, to condemn ex-Dragon, Barry Hunter's side, to their sixth successive defeat.											
28	H	LEYTON ORIENT	12	L	1-2	0-2	Bennett 89	Ingham	Spender^	Holt	Williams D	Pejic	W'iams Mi*	Jones Ma	Whitley	Walters	W'iams Ma	Ferguson	Bennett/Smith
	21/1	5,031	*4*	38			*Alexander 4, Lockwood 43p*	*Garner*	*Miller*	*Lockwood*	*Zakuani**	*Mackie*	*Tudor*	*Simpson*	*McMahon*	*Keith*	*Alexander*	*Ibehre^*	*Saah/Steele*
							Ref: J Moss	Martin Ling's side continued their promotion push. Wrexham screamed for offside when Justin Miller set up Gary Alexander to fire in. Matt Lockwood hit in a penalty after Spender handled. Williams was floored, but Bennett missed (80). He then prodded in after a fine Jones run.											
29	H	WYCOMBE	12	W	2-0	2-0	Lawrence 12, Williams S 15	Ingham	Spender	Holt	Williams D	Pejic	Lawrence	Jones Ma*	Whitley	Williams S	Ugarte^	Crowell	Mackin/Williams Ma
	4/2	4,311	*2*	41				*Duke*	*Martin**	*Johnson*	*Will'mson*	*Easton^*	*Betsy*	*Burnell*	*Blo'mfield**	*Oakes*	*Mooney*	*Easter*	*Collins/B'ditch/S'bridge*
							Ref: D Whitestone	Denis Smith was on the touchline after his hip op to watch the Dragons overcome John Gorman's League Two leaders in style. Lawrence rose highest to head in Crowell's corner. Sam Williams doubled the lead when he raced in at the far post to nod in Matt Crowell's right-wing cross.											
30	H	RUSHDEN	11	W	2-0	2-0	Derbyshire 24, 36	Ingham	Spender	Holt	Williams D	Pejic	Lawrence	Jones Ma	Whitley	Williams S	**Derbyshire**	Crowell*	Mackin
	14/2	**3,195**	*24*	44				*Tynan*	*Gier*	*Hatswell*	*Gulliver*	*Bull*	*Berry*	*Caskey*	*Stokes^*	*Kelly*	*Broughton*	*Mikolanda**	*Tomlin/Savage*
							Ref: L Mason	Barry Hunter's side were beaten by loan signing Matt Derbyshire, who made an immediate impact. The 19 year-old striker from Blackburn poked home Crowell's left-wing cross, and his second was all his own work, driving forward and curling the ball into the top left of the net.											
31	A	MANSFIELD	11	D	2-2	0-0	Derbyshire 51, 62	Ingham	Spender	Holt	Williams D	Pejic	Lawrence	Jones Ma	Whitley	Williams S	Derbyshire	Crowell	
	18/2	*3,139*	*17*	45			*Barker 64p, 67*	*Pressman*	*Baptiste*	*Buxton*	*Hjelde*	*Wilson*	*Coke"*	*D'Laryea*	*Dawson*	*Rundle^*	*Barker*	*Reet**	*Brown/Uhlenbeek/Lloyd*
							Ref: G Lewis	Matt Derbyshire again struck twice, pouncing on Jake Buxton's poor back pass for the opener, then showed great pace to outstrip the defence to fire in. A foul by Danny Williams on Simon Brown saw Richard Barker calmly hit home the spot-kick. Barker powered in a header to level.											
32	H	NORTHAMPTON	11	L	0-1	0-0		Ingham	Spender	Holt	Wil'ams D^	Pejic	Lawrence	Jones Ma	Whitley	Williams S	Derbyshire	Crowell*	Done/Mackin
	25/2	5,012	*3*	45			*Gilligan 68*	*Harper*	*Crowe*	*Chambers*	*Dyche*	*Doig*	*Johnson*	*Hunt^*	*Jess"*	*Hand*	*Kirk**	*McGleish*	*Gilligan/Bojic/W'wood*
							Ref: L Probert	Mike Ingham was by far the busier goalkeeper in the first half, diving full stretch to deny Andy Kirk. But Ingham undid his good work when he and Danny Williams left a bouncing ball to each other, allowing Ryan Gilligan to nip in and win it for the Cobblers in a hard fought game.											
33	A	BARNET	10	D	2-2	1-2	Jones Ma 44, Derbyshire 51	Ingham	Spender^	Holt	Williams D	Pejic	Lawrence	Jones Ma	Whitley	Williams S	Derbyshire	Crowell*	Ferguson/Bennett
	4/3	*2,127*	*18*	46			*Norville 30, Kandol 37*	*Reed*	*Hendon*	*Charles*	*Yakubu*	*Clist*	*Strevens"*	*Fuller*	*Hes'haler**	*Bailey^*	*Kandol*	*Norville*	*Lee/Sinclair/Hatch*
							Ref: B Curson	The Bee's Jason Norville hit in an unstoppable drive from the edge of the penalty area. Tresor Kandol beat the offside trap to fire in, but a Mark Jones cracker gave Wrexham a lifeline. Ferguson set up Derbyshire to level, and Norville had an effort ruled offside in a frantic finish.											
34	H	BURY	11	D	0-0	0-0		Ingham	Bennett	Holt	Williams D	Pejic	Lawrence	Jones Ma	Whitley*	Williams S	Derbyshire	Crowell^	Mackin/Done
	11/3	4,134	*19*	47				*Schm'hel*	*Scott*	*Challinor*	*Fitzgerald*	*W'dthorpe*	*Flitcroft^*	*Mattis*	*B-Murphy*	*Buchanan*	*Marrison*	*Youngs**	*Speight/Adams*
							Ref: M Fletcher	A deserved draw gave Bury a boost in their relegation fight. On-loan keeper Kasper Schmeichel, brought down Derbyshire, who the ref judged had dived despite strong appeals for a penalty. Danny Williams cleared Youngs shot off the line & Mattis fired over. Williams also went close.											

No	Date	Att	Pos	Pt	F-A	H-T	Scorers, Times, and Referees	1	2	3	4	5	6	7	8	9	10	11	subs used
35	A	MACCLESFIELD	11	L	2-3	2-1	Williams S 9, Holt 33 [82]	Ingham	Bennett	Holt	Williams D	Pejic	Lawrence	Jones Ma	Whitley*	W'iams S"	Derbyshire	Mackin^	Crowell/Done/Walters
	14/3	***1,616***	*17*	47			*Holt (og) 43, Whitaker 74, Teague*	*Lee*	*Morley*	*Swailes*	*Bullock*	*Harsley**	*Whitaker*	*McIntyre*	*Teague*	*Brightwell*	*Navarro*	*McNeil*	*Briscoe*
							Ref: G Laws	The Dragons looked good for three points when Sam Williams' deflected strike & Holt's header put them two goals up, but Holt inexplicably headed into his own net, and Danny Whitaker smashed the Silkmen level. Macc's joy was complete when Andy Teague headed in the winner.											
36	A	ROCHDALE	9	W	1-0	1-0	Derbyshire 20	Ingham	Bennett	Holt	Wi'ams D^	Pejic	Lawrence	Jones Ma	Whitley*	W'iams S	Derbyshire	Crowell	Mackin/Williams Mi
	18/3	*2,856*	*16*	50				*Gilks*	*Ramsden*	*McArdle*	*Bayliss !*	*Gallimore*	*Jones"*	*Doolan^*	*Cooksey**	*Dagnall*	*Lambert*	*Christie*	*Warner/Brown/Kitchen*
							Ref: M Russell	Matt Derbyshire slotted home Holt's cross after having enough time to let the ball bounce. Dale struggled on a difficult pitch & suffered a blow when Dave Bayliss (on loan from Wrexham) was sent off (62) for a second caution. Derbyshire had a shot cleared off the line & hit the post.											
37	A	CHELTENHAM	9	D	2-2	1-1	Derbyshire 1, 64	Ingham	Bennett	Holt	Williams D	Pejic	Lawrence*	Jones Ma	Mackin^	W'iams S"	Derbyshire	Crowell	Wil'ms Mi/Fe'son/W'lters
	21/3	*2,737*	*6*	51			*McCann 35, Guinan 56*	*Higgs*	*Gill*	*Caines*	*Townsend*	*Armstrong*	*Melligan**	*Finnigan*	*McCann*	*Wilson*	*Odejayi^*	*Guinan*	*Bird/Spencer*
							Ref: T Parks	Two teams chasing a play-off place battled tooth and nail. Derbyshire scored with a low drive, but Northern Irish international Grant McCann levelled, converting Brian Wilson's header from 15-yds. Steve Guinan volleyed the Robins ahead, but Derbyshire lobbed Shane Higgs to level.											
38	H	CHESTER	9	W	2-1	2-0	Williams D 11, Jones Ma 36	Ingham	Bennett	Holt	Williams D	Pejic	Lawrence	Jones Ma	Crowell	Williams S	Derbyshire	Ferguson	
	26/3	**7,240**	*24*	54			*Edwards 89*	*Harrison*	*Albrighton*	*Artell*	*Ellender*	*McNiven*	*Drummond*	*Davies*	*El Kholti^*	*Regan**	*Branch*	*Edwards*	*Lowe/Rutherford*
							Ref: A Leake	Danny Williams' header beat Paul Harrison. Crowell was felled, but got up to fire a weak penalty at Harrison. Mark Jones smashed in a 20-yd a cracker. Chester fought back with ex-Dragon Jake Edwards firing in before Paul Ellender missed a great chance to equalise from six-yards.											
39	A	GRIMSBY	10	L	0-2	0-1		Ingham	Spender	Holt	Williams D	Pejic	Lawrence	Jones Ma	Crowell	W'iams S*	Walters	Ferguson	Smith
	1/4	*6,058*	*2*	54			*Jones G 25, Reddy 88*	*Mildenhall*	*McDermott*	*Whittle*	*Jones R*	*Newey*	*W'dhouse*	*G'dfellow*	*Bolland*	*Cohen**	*Reddy*	*Jones G*	*Parkinson*
							Ref: T Kettle	Denis Smith was left fuming over Gary Jones' opener, as it looked off-side. Jones ran on to lash in a right foot volley off Marc Goodfellow's pass. Wrexham rallied after the break, Crowell threatened with a free kick & Jones fired over, but Michael Reddy broke to fire in a left footer.											
40	H	SHREWSBURY	11	L	1-2	0-2	Derbyshire 78	Ingham	Bennett !	Holt	Williams D	Pejic	Lawrence	Jones Ma	Crowell*	W'iams S^	Derbyshire	Ferguson	McEvilly/Walters
	9/4	6,310	*12*	54			*L'wrence 3 (og), McMenamin 15p*	*Hart*	*Herd*	*Burton*	*Hope*	*Ashton*	*Edwards*	*Sorvel*	*Hogg**	*Langmead*	*Hurst^*	*McM'amin!*	*Tolley/Stallard*
							Ref: R Beeby	Gary Peters side were handed a perfect start when Lawrence glanced a header into his own net. Bennett was sent off for handling on the line, & McMenamin converted. Derbyshire headed in Ferguson's corner, but the Shrews held on despite McMenamin's red-card for a foul on Walters.											
41	A	CHESTER	11	L	1-2	0-0	McEvilly 69	Ingham	Spender*	Holt	Williams D	Pejic	Lawrence	Jones Ma	Crowell^	McEvilly	Derbyshire	Ferguson	Walters/Williams S
	12/4	*4,801*	*15*	54			*Davies 56p, Asamoah 75*	*MacKenzie*	*Artell*	*McNiven*	*Albrighton*	*Curtis*	*Drummond*	*Blundell**	*Davies*	*Hessey^*	*Edwards"*	*Asamoah*	*Regan/El Kholti/Tait*
							Ref: S Matthieson	Derek Asamoah struck for his 7th goal in four games to give Chester their 4th win in a row. Mark Wright's side led with a Ben Davies penalty after Danny Williams was adjudged to have tripped Gregg Blundell. Lee McEvilly levelled with a well-placed header from a Ferguson cross.											
42	A	STOCKPORT	12	L	1-2	1-2	Spender 38	Ingham	Spender	Holt	Wil'ms Mi^	Pejic	Lawrence	Williams D	D'byshire*	W'iams S"	Walters	Ferguson	McEvilly/Smith/Crowell
	15/4	*4,750*	*21*	54			*Williams 6, Raynes 42*	*Spencer*	*Briggs*	*Williams*	*Raynes"*	*Robinson*	*Taylor*	*O'Connor*	*Ward*	*Griffin*	*Malcolm^*	*Bramble**	*Dick'son/Bos'll/Beherall*
							Ref: P Joslin	County secured a priceless win in their battle to avoid the drop from the F.L. Tes Bramble nodded the ball into the path of Ashley Williams to head in. Michael Raynes failed to clear & Simon Spender finished clinically. But Raynes made amends when he headed County back in front.											
43	H	BRISTOL ROV	10	W	1-0	1-0	Derbyshire 5	Jones Mi	Spender	Holt*	Williams D	Pejic	Lawrence	Crowell	Derbyshire	Williams S	McEvilly^	Ferguson"	Smith/Walters/Bennett
	17/4	3,749	*11*	57				*Shearer*	*Lescott*	*Hinton*	*Elliott*	*Carruthers*	*Haldane**	*Hunt*	*Disley*	*Campbell^*	*Agogo*	*Walker*	*Gibb/Lines*
							Ref: L Mason	On-loan Matt Derbyshire ended a run of four successive League Two defeats after converting a precise Ferguson pass. Rovers turned the screw in the second half, with Richard Walker heading over the bar and having an effort well saved by Dragons rookie goalkeeper Michael Jones.											
44	A	TORQUAY	12	L	0-1	0-1		Jones Mi	Spender	Smith	Williams D	Pejic	Lawrence	Jones Ma	Crowell	Walters	Derbyshire	Ferguson	Done/Bennett/W'ams Mi
	22/4	*2,623*	*23*	57			*Phillips 9*	*Marriott*	*Reed*	*Andrews*	*Wood*	*Taylor*	*Phillips*	*Hollands*	*Garner*	*Hill*	*Thorpe*	*Kuffour**	*Hockley*
							Ref: A Penn	Martin Phillips kept the 'Gulls' survival hopes alive & ended the Dragons play-off dream. He fired in a left-foot strike from 12-yds out. The league's bottom club then got men behind the ball to absorb Wrexham pressure. Derbyshire, Ferguson and Walters all went close to equalising.											
45	H	OXFORD	12	D	1-1	1-0	Crowell 28	Jones Mi	Roche	Smith	Williams D	Pejic	W'ams Mi	Jones Ma*	Crowell	Walters^	Derbyshire	Ferguson"	Bennett/Done/Lawrence
	29/4	4,575	*23*	58			*N'Toya 64p*	*Guatelli**	*Mansell*	*Dempster*	*Willmott*	*Robinson*	*Quinn*	*H'greaves^*	*Burgess*	*Basham"*	*N'Toya*	*Sabin*	*Tardiff/Smith/Sills*
							Ref: S Tanner	Boostered by the news that a sale had been agreed with Dickens & Moss, the Dragons led when Andreas Guatelli dropped the ball at Crowell's feet to tap in. The U's levelled when Pejic impeded Eric Sabin & Tcham N'Toya netted the penalty. The U's must now beat Orient to stay up.											
46	A	DARLINGTON	13	D	1-1	1-0	Williams D 31	Ingham	Roche	Holt	Williams D	Pejic	W'ams Mi	Done*	Crowell	Walters^	Derbyshire	Bennett	Ferguson/Williams Ma
	6/5	*4,648*	*8*	59			*Cooke 90*	*Russell*	*Valentine*	*McGurk*	*Martis*	*Duke*	*Keltie*	*Johnson S*	*Dickman**	*Logan^*	*Sodje*	*Bates"*	*McLeod/W'wright/Cooke*
		Home / Away					Ref: K Friend	David Hodgson's side needed to beat the Dragons by a large margin to reach the play-off's. The Quakers appeared to be heading for defeat after a long range strike by Danny Williams.. But at the last gasp Andy Cooke headed in from close range after a scramble from a corner kick.											
Average		4,521 / 3,886																	

Carling Cup	Attt		F-A	H-T	Scorers, Times, and Referees	1	2	3	4	5	6	7	8	9	10	11	subs used
1 H DONCASTER	16	L	0-1	0-0		Ingham	Bennett^	Smith	Bayliss	Pejic*	Holt	Jones Ma	Williams	Walters	**Foy**"	Ferguson	**Warhurst**/Mackin/Done
23/8	2,177	*1:13*			*Hughes 86*	*W'rington*	*McGuire*	*Fenton*	*Foster*	*Ryan*	*Cop'nger"*	*Mulligan*	*Ravenhill**	*McIndoe*	*Guy*	*Fort-West*	*Hughes/Offiong*
					Ref: J Moss	Dennis Lawrence pulled a muscle in the warm-up & Pejic was carried off with ligament damage after the break. Andy Warrington made fine saves from Ferguson, Jones & Walters, but Dave Mulligan's cross failed to be cleared and Australian Adam Hughes blasted in from six yards.											

LDV Trophy	Attt		F-A	H-T	Scorers, Times, and Referees	1	2	3	4	5	6	7	8	9	10	11	subs used
1 A BLACKPOOL	10	L	3-4	0-1	Jones Ma 77, 78 Ferguson 96	Ingham	Spender*	Smith	Holt	Bayliss^	Lawrence"	Jones Ma	Williams	Walters	Bennett	Ferguson	McEvilly/Foy/Mackin
18/10	*3,239*	*1:19*			*Bl'horn 2, McGregor 84, Southern*	*Pogliacomi*	*McGregor*	*Coid**	*Clarke*	*Armst'ng*	*Wiles*	*Southern*	*Doolan*	*Burns^*	*Blinkhorn*	*Wright"*	*Grayson/Pr'gast/Vernon*
					Ref: C Oliver *[99, Vernon 104]* (After Extra Time 2-2)	The LDV holders crashed out when Matt Blinkhorn capitalised on Lawrence's header over Ingham. Jones rifled in low & fired in, only for Mark McGregor to volley in. Ferguson powerfully hit home. Keith Southern slotted in & Scott Vernon turned Smith to ensure a dramatic win.											

FA Cup	Attt		F-A	H-T	Scorers, Times, and Referees	1	2	3	4	5	6	7	8	9	10	11	subs used
1 A PORT VALE	7	L	1-2	0-1	McEvilly 63	Ingham	Roche	Smith	Spender*	Bayliss	Lawrence	Jones Ma	Williams	Walters^	McEvilly	Ferguson	Foy/Bennett
5/11	*5,046*	*1:8*			*Husbands 20, Constantine 65*	*Goodlad*	*Rowland*	*Pilkington*	*Dinning*	*Bell*	*Birchall*	*Innes^*	*James*	*Husbands**	*Lowndes*	*Const'tine*	*Smith/Porter*
					Ref: D Deadman	Mark Goodlad heroics denied the Dragons as they were unfortunate to go out of the FA Cup. Vale led when Mick Husbands diverted in Chris Birchall's shot. Walters headed on for McEvilly to run on and fire in from 12-yds. Loan signing Leon Constantine finished from close range.											

Welsh Premier Cup	Attt		F-A	H-T	Scorers, Times, and Referees	1	2	3	4	5	6	7	8	9	10	11	subs used
QF A NEWPORT	12	W	2-0	0-0	Walters 54, 84	Ingham	Spender	Smith	Wiams Mi	Pejic	Williams D	Jones Ma	Crowell	Walters	**Williams S**	Whitley	
24/1	*442*	*NS20*				*Pennock*	*Evans*	*Bater**	*Williams*	*Edwards*	*Hillier*	*Bowen*	*Davies*	*O'Sullivan*	*Fisken*	*Green*	*Leek*
					Ref: M Whitby	The Dragons struggled against Peter Beadle's side at Spytty Park. Newport failed to take their chances, but after the break the Dragons took the lead following good work from Smith & Mike Williams. County put up a real fight, but Walters killed the game with a close-range goal.											
SF H TNS	13	W	3-3	0-1	Jones 79, Ugarte 89, L'wrence 101	Ingham	Bennett^	Holt	Bayliss	Lawrence	Williams D	Jones Ma	Whitley	Walters"	Wil'iams S*	Smith	Ugarte/Spender/Pejic
1/2	1,116	*WP1*			*Ruscoe 39, Ward 86, Evans S 105*	*Doherty*	*Holmes^*	*King*	*Jackson*	*Evans S*	*Ruscoe*	*Hogan*	*Beck*	*Wilde"*	*Wood*	*Evans G**	*Ward/Leah/L-Williams*
After Extra Time Won 5-4 on pens					Ref: M Whitby	Wrexham survived a huge scare before clinching a 5-4 win on penalties. Ingham saving Doherty's spot kick. Bayliss let in Scott Ruscoe. Jones hit in a stunning 25-yard volley. Ward hit in from 20-yds. Ugarte lobbed Doherty. Lawrence drilled in, but Evans lobbed Ingham from 30-yds.											
F H SWANSEA	9	L	1-2	0-2	Spender 71	Ingham	Bennett*	Holt	Williams D	Pejic	Lawrence	Jones Ma"	Ferguson^	Williams S	Derbyshire	Crowell	S'der/Walters/Mackin
29/3	3,032	*1:4*			*Williams (og) 37, Fallon 41*	*Guerut*	*Tate*	*Ricketts*	*Lowe*	*Monk*	*O'Leary*	*Jones*	*Britton*	*Trundle*	*Fallon*	*Parkinson**	*Martinez*
					Ref: C Richards	Kenny Jackett's 'Swans' retained the FAW trophy as Danny Williams turned Leon Britton's cross into his own goal. Ex-Dragon Lee Trundle then worked himself clear; his cross was parried by Ingham only for Rory Fallon to scrape the ball home. Spender hammered in a consolation.											

! Sent off * 1st Sub ^ 2nd Sub " 3rd Sub

		P	W	D	L	F	A	W	D	L	F	A	Pts
			Home					Away					
1	Carlisle	46	14	3	6	47	23	11	8	4	37	19	86
2	Northampton	46	11	8	4	30	15	11	9	3	33	22	83
3	Leyton Orient	46	11	6	6	29	21	11	9	3	38	30	81
4	Grimsby	46	13	3	7	37	18	9	9	5	27	26	78
5	Cheltenham*	46	10	7	6	39	31	9	8	6	26	22	72
6	Wycombe	46	9	9	5	41	29	9	8	6	31	27	71
7	Lincoln	46	9	11	3	37	21	6	10	7	28	32	66
8	Darlington	46	10	7	6	32	26	6	8	9	26	26	63
9	Peterborough	46	9	7	7	28	21	8	4	11	29	28	62
10	Shrewsbury	46	10	9	4	33	20	6	4	13	22	35	61
11	Boston	46	11	7	5	34	28	4	9	10	16	32	61
12	Bristol Rov	46	8	6	9	30	29	9	3	11	29	38	60
13	Wrexham	46	12	6	5	36	19	3	8	12	25	35	59
14	Rochdale	46	8	7	8	34	30	6	7	10	32	39	56
15	Chester	46	7	6	10	30	29	7	6	10	23	30	54
16	Mansfield	46	9	7	7	37	29	4	8	11	22	37	54
17	Macclesfield	46	10	9	4	35	27	2	9	12	25	44	54
18	Barnet	46	9	8	6	24	22	3	10	10	20	35	54
19	Bury	46	6	9	8	22	25	6	8	9	23	32	53
20	Torquay	46	7	9	7	33	31	6	4	13	20	35	52
21	Notts County	46	7	11	5	30	26	5	5	13	18	37	52
22	Stockport	46	7	11	5	34	29	4	8	11	23	49	52
23	Oxford	46	7	7	9	25	30	4	9	10	18	27	49
24	Rushden	46	8	5	10	25	31	3	7	13	19	45	45

* Promoted After play-offs

Odds & ends

Double Wins: (2) Rochdale & Rushden.
Double Defeats: (3) Carlisle, Grimsby & Shrewsbury.

Won from behind: (2) Mansfield (h), Rochdale (h),.
Lost from in front: (3) Bristol Rov (a), Macclesfield (a), Carlisle (a).

High Spots: Winning the court battle to have the Racecourse Ground handed back from Alex Hamilton's company Crucial Move Ltd;
Nev Dickens & Geoff Moss agreeing the deal to buy club.
Mark Jones selection for the PFA League Two Team of the Year.
Dennis Lawrence scoring the winning goal for Trinidad & Tobago against Bahrain to become the first Wrexham player To ever play in a World Cup finals whilst on the club's books.
Mike Williams, Mark Williams, Simon Spender, Matt Crowell & Levi Mackin all winning Welsh under-21 caps.
Mark Jones selection for full Welsh squad.

Low spots: The Club being in Administration which Restricted Manager Denis Smith's options.
Missing out on League Two Play-Offs
Losing FAW Premier Cup Final to Swansea City
Losing to both Shrewsbury (h) & Chester (a) in four days!

Ever Presents: (0)
Player of the Season: Danny Williams
Young Player of the Season: Mark Jones
Hat-tricks: (0)
Leading scorer: (13) Mark Jones

	Appearances						Goals					
	Lge	LC	FAC	LDV	PC	Tot	Lge	LC	FAC	LDV	PC	Tot
Bayliss, David	21	1	1	1	1	25						
Bennett, Dean	20/13	1	0/1	1	2	24/14	2					2
Crowell, Matt	26/3				2	28/3	3					3
Derbyshire, Matt	16				1	17	10					10
Done, Matty	1/5	0/1				1/6						
Ferguson, Darren	36/3	1	1	1	1	40/3	2			1		3
Foy, Robbie	7/10	1	0/1	0/1		8/12	2					2
Holt, Andy	34/1	1		1	2	38/1	3					3
Ingham, Mike	41	1	1	1	3	47						
Jones, Mark	42	1	1	1	3	48	13			2	1	16
Jones, Michael	5/1					5/1						
Lawrence, Dennis	38/1		1	1	2	42/1	2				1	3
Linwood, Paul	8/1					8/1						
Mackin, Levi	3/13	0/1		0/1	0/1	3/16						
McEvilly, Lee	14/9		1	0/1		15/10	7		1			8
Pejic, Shaun	26	1			2/1	29/1						
Reed, Jamie	0/3					0/3						
Roche, Lee	17/1		1			18/1	1					1
Smith, Alex	16/5	1	1	1	2	21/5						
Spender, Simon	15/3		1	1	1/2	18/5	2				1	3
Ugarte, Juan	2				0/1	2/1					1	1
Walters, Jon	30/5	1	1	1	2/1	35/6	5				2	7
Warhurst, Paul	6/5	0/1				6/6	1					1
Whitley, Jim	10				2	12						
Williams, Danny	45	1	1	1	3	51	4					4
Williams, Marc	2/2					2/2						
Williams, Mike	7/5				1	8/5						
Williams, Sam	6/1				3	9/1	2					2
(own-goals)							2					2
28 Players Used												

The 2005-2006 Pontin's Holiday's League season can be split into three distinct parts: a decent start to the season, and a good end to the season, but an extremely disappointing run in between. Unfortunately, the disappointing run consisted of a 15-game spell without a win between September and April!

The season began in promising fashion though with a 3-0 victory at Rochdale thanks to goals from Jamie Reed, Matty Done and Levi Mackin. This was followed by two draws, a 1-1 draw with Bury at Buckley Town's Globe Way ground (Reed on target again before the visitors equalised late on) and a 3-3 draw at Shrewsbury in our opening League Cup-tie (Reed netting a brace at Gay Meadow).

Reed's goals were a common feature of the opening six months of the season, the young striker netting nine times before finishing the season at Northern Irish side Glentoran. But his goals weren't enough to halt the slide and bring an end to the winless run, though three draws in the group stage of the League Cup competition did see us incredibly qualify for the Quarter-Finals on goal difference as every game in the group was drawn.

The 15-game winless run yielded just three draws but the majority of the games were close, with only 5-0 and 5-2 League defeats by Carlisle and a 5-0 home defeat by Tranmere Rovers in the Quarter-Final of the League Cup bucking that particular trend.

A 2-1 defeat at Chester City on April 3rd - Lee McEvilly grabbing a second half equaliser - not only proved (unfortunately) to be a dress rehearsal for the first team game at the same venue the following week, but would also be our last defeat of the season. Two days later Blackpool were beaten 2-1 at Bloomfield Road before Tranmere Rovers, who'd managed nine goals against us in two earlier meetings during the course of the season, were held 0-0 in a competitive clash at Globe Way. The final home game of the season then finally brought that elusive first Globe Way victory of the season, as Shrewsbury Town were emphatically dispatched 3-0.

The last game of the season saw us come from 2-0 down to draw 2-2 at Bury thanks to late goals from Alex Darlington and Matty Done, but the four game unbeaten run to end the season came too late to lift us off the foot of the table.

I don't think it would be an unfair assessment to say that the reserves have underachieved during the course of the season. But it must be remembered that the pitfalls inherent with being in administration, i.e. only being allowed a 20-strong first team squad, has had a significant impact at this level, just as it has with the youth side.

For example, many of the club's youngsters have been required to double–up, playing Youth Alliance games on Saturday's and Pontin's League games in the midweek. And if you add

Pontin's League 1 West

			Res	1	2	3	4	5	6	7	8	9	10	11	Sub	Sub	Sub	Sub	Sub
AUGUST																			
17	Rochdale	A	3-0	Mi Jones	Spender	C Evans	G Roche	G Evans	Warhurst	**Mackin**[1]	K Williams	**Reed**[1]	Ma Williams	**Done**[1]	Gray	Mullock	Braisdell	Harris	Fleming
24	**Bury**	**H**	1-1	Mi Jones	Harris	Taylor	G Roche	G Evans	Fleming	Gray	S Edwards	Braisdell	Ma Williams	Done	**Reed(9)**[1]	Mullock	Darlington(10)	Baynes	
31	Shrewsbury Town (LC)	A	3-3	Mi Jones	Spender	C Evans	G Roche	G Evans	Mi Williams	Fleming	Ma Williams	**Reed**[2]	Braisdell	**Done**[1]	S Edwards	Mullock	Harris	Gray(8)	K Williams
SEPTEMBER																			
7	Burnley	A	1-2	Mi Jones	Harris	Done	Spender	G Evans	Mi Williams	Fleming	Bennett	Ma Williams	**Reed**[1]	C Evans	Darlington(10)	Mullock	S Edwards(11)	Braisdell(8)	
21	Carlisle United	A	0-5	Mullock	Harris	Done	Spender	G Evans	Mi Williams	Fleming	Mackin	Reed	Ma Williams	C Evans	G Roche(2)	S Edwards(11)			
OCTOBER																			
5	**Chester City**	**H**	1-1	Mi Jones	Harris	Done	G Roche	G Evans	Mi Williams	Fleming	Mackin	McEvilly	Reed	C Evans	**Ma Williams(10)**[1]	Darlington	Gray	S Edwards(3)	Taylor
26	Tranmere Rovers	A	2-4	Mullock	**L Roche**[1]	Done	G Evans	Spender	Mi Williams	Crowell	Mackin	**Reed**[1]	Ma Williams	Foy	C Evans(8)	G Roche(5)	S Edwards	Fleming	Gray(11)
NOVEMBER																			
14	Shrewsbury Town	A	1-3	Mi Jones	Whitley	C Evans	G Roche	Marriott	Fleming	Gray	S Edwards	Ma Williams	**Reed**[1]	Done	Darlington	Braisdell(2)	Darlington		
23	**Rochdale (LC)**	**H**	1-1	Mullock	Spender	Smith	Pejic	Warhurst	Mi Williams	Gray	Whitley	Reed	**Foy**[1]	C Evans	S Edwards	Harris	Ben Ward		
28	Preston North End	A	0-2	Mi Jones	Spender	Smith	Pejic	Warhurst	Mi Williams	Harris	Whitley	Reed	Ma Williams	C Evans	G Evans(4)	Fleming	Darlington(10)	S Edwards	Braisdell(7)
DECEMBER																			
7	Bradford City (LC)	A	1-1	Mi Jones	Spender	Mi Williams	Roche	G Evans	C Evans	Braisdell	**Ma Williams**[1]	Reed	Darlington	Done	Baynes				
14	**Rochdale**	**H**	1-2	Mi Jones	Spender	Holt	Pejic	Warhurst	G Evans	Bennett	Whitley	**Reed**[1]	Ma Williams	C Evans	Edwards(3)	Taylor	Fleming(7)	Braisdell(10)	Darlington
JANUARY																			
18	**Blackpool**	**H**	2-3	Mi Jones	Gray	Smith	G Evans	Bayliss	G Roche	Mackin	Crowell	**Reed**[1]	**Braisdell**[1]	Foy	C Evans	Baynes	Fleming(7)	Harris	Darlington
FEBRUARY																			
8	**Preston North End**	**H**	0-2	Mi Jones	Harris	Done	Bayliss	G Evans	Mi Williams	Gray	Smith	Ma Williams	Braisdell	C Evans	Fleming(2)	Darlington	S Edwards	G Roche	Baynes
22	**Burnley**	**H**	0-2	Mi Jones	Gray	Done	G Roche	G Evans	Mi Williams	Mackin	Fleming	Ma Williams	Braisdell	C Evans	Darlington(10)	Maxwell	Marriott(4)	Harris(2)	Stewart
27	**Tranmere R. (LCQF)**	**H**	0-5	Mi Jones	Harris	Taylor	G Roche	G Evans	C Evans	Gray	Fleming	Braisdell	Smith	Done	Darlington	Maxwell	Edwards	Marriott(4)	Baynes(6)
MARCH																			
22	**Carlisle United**	**H**	2-5	Mi Jones	Gray	Done	Spender	G Evans	G Roche	Ma Williams	C Evans	**Walters**[1]	**McEvilly**[1]	Smith	Fleming	Edwards(8)	Braisdell(10)	Darlington(2)	Baynes
APRIL																			
3	Chester City	A	1-2	Mi Jones	G Evans	Mi Williams	Bayliss	C Evans	Mackin	Gray	Smith	**McEvilly**[1]	Ma Williams	Done	Fleming(5)	G Roche	Edwards	Taylor	Braisdell(7)
5	Blackpool	A	2-1	Mi Jones	G Evans	Mi Williams	Bayliss	L Roche	Mackin	Braisdell	C Evans	**Walters**[1]	**Ma Williams**[1]	Done	Fleming(5)	Darlington(9)	Edwards	G Roche	
10	**Tranmere Rovers**	**H**	0-0	Mi Jones	L Roche	Taylor	G Roche	G Evans	Fleming	Braisdell	C Evans	Ma Williams	Thomas	Edwards	Darlington	Baynes(7)	Marriott	Lee Jones	
19	**Shrewsbury Town**	**H**	3-0	Mullock	L Roche	**Mi Williams**[1]	G Evans	Bayliss	**Mackin**[1]	Gray	C Evans	**Thomas**[1]	Ma Williams	Done	Fleming	Edwards(8)	Darlington	G Roche	Taylor
26	Bury	A	2-2	Mullock	L Roche	Mi Williams	G Evans	Bayliss	Mackin	Gray	C Evans	Ma Williams	**Darlington**[1]	**Done**[1]	Fleming	Baynes	Taylor	G Roche	

~DENOTES OWN GOAL

the impact that injuries have had on Denis Smith's plans during the campaign, then the Reserve side has pretty much resembled the Youth side for much of the season. Results on the pitch will therefore, almost inevitably, suffer as a consequence.

But remember, the Pontin's League isn't just a stage for First Team squad players to either enjoy some much-needed match practice, or get some games under their belts whilst returning from an injury lay-off. It's also a stepping-stone between the Youth set-up and the First Team. Therefore, given that several players did rise through the Youth and Reserve ranks to make their First Team debuts during the campaign, maybe it wasn't such a disastrous season after all!

Pontin's Holidays League Division One West
Final Table 2005-2006

	P	W	D	L	F	A	GD	PTS
Carlisle United	18	11	4	3	39	16	+23	37
Bury	18	9	4	5	31	25	+6	31
Preston North End	18	7	8	3	32	22	+10	29
Tranmere Rovers	18	7	7	4	30	26	+4	28
Blackpool	18	8	1	9	31	31	0	25
Shrewsbury Town	18	6	6	6	23	25	-2	24
Rochdale	18	7	1	10	23	35	-12	22
Chester City	18	4	6	8	21	30	-9	18
Burnley	18	5	5	8	26	31	-5	17
WREXHAM	**18**	**3**	**4**	**11**	**22**	**37**	**-15**	**13**

Note: Burnley deducted 3 points for breach of Competition Rule 16.

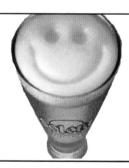

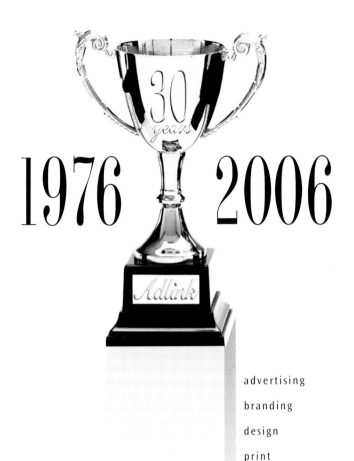

There's simply no denying the fact that football is a results-orientated business. Whichever way you want to look at it, at the end of the day it's results above all that count. I mean, let's fact it, most fans aren't really interested in what goes on behind the scenes, or what happens on the training ground in the week leading up to a game, are they? It's just that ninety minutes of action on the football pitch once or twice a week that really matters.

But, when it comes to youth football, what do we mean by results? Success on the pitch in terms of winning football matches, or successfully nurturing and developing a young player so that he eventually breaks through into the professional ranks and the First Team? I think it's fair to say, ultimately, that it's the latter that defines whether a club's youth set-up is successful or not. Indeed this was acknowledged by Dragons' boss Denis Smith at the end of the season when he praised the club's Centre of Excellence for the number of players that have pushed their way into First Team reckoning in the last twelve months or so.

It just goes to show that not being successful on the pitch at youth level doesn't necessarily mean that you're not functioning properly. Seven wins and twenty-three defeats in the Football League Youth Alliance will suggest that it's been a tough season for Steve Weaver's under-19s, which it undoubtedly has. Mind you, that hasn't come as too much of a shock to Steve, who predicted a tough season ahead when I spoke to him last August: "I think it will be a tough season and a tough League," he said. "We'll have to expose a lot of young lads into the League as others have proved themselves and pushed themselves towards Reserve team football instead. It should be a great year for us in terms of getting kids into the First Team, but Saturday's youth games are going to have to take second fiddle to the First Team during the week in build-up to the games. But it'll be great if a couple of lads break into the first team during the season."

How prophetic his words turned out to be, for it certainly did prove to be a tough season results-wise but, as he predicted, it has proven to be a great year for getting players into the First Team. Admittedly Michael Jones did make his League debut during 2004-2005, but it was during the last campaign that he established himself as a reliable and important member of the First Team squad. Add brothers Mike and Marc Williams, and Matty Done, to the list of scholars that broke into the First Team and you understand why Denis is quick to highlight the success of the club's youth set-up. The four mentioned above have all been offered a professional contract, as has striker Jamie Reed who, after featuring in the youth side early on quickly established himself as a regular scorer in the Reserves before spending the final three months of the season with Northern Irish Premier Division side Glentoran.

On the playing side it has, just as Steve Weaver predicted, been tough. This has, in no small part, been due to the knock-on effect that being in administration has had. The small First Team squad - and not forgetting the number of injuries - has meant that youth players have regularly been required to train with the First Team squad in preparation for a forthcoming match. This has meant that Steve and his

Youth - North & Midlands West Conference

			Res	1	2	3	4	5	6	7	8	9	10	11	Sub	Sub	Sub	Sub	Sub
AUGUST																			
13	**Tranmere Rovers**	H	2-4	Mullock	Baynes	C Evans	Roche	G Evans	Fleming	Gray	Edwards	**Ma Williams[1]**	**Braisdell[1]**	Done	Darlington(8)	Maxwell	Marriott	Taylor	
20	Wigan Athletic	A	2-4	Mullock	Baynes	Taylor	Roche	G Evans	Fleming	Gray	K Williams	**Ma Williams[1]**	Reed	**Done[1]**	Darlington(10)	Maxwell	P Williams(3)	Marriott(8)	
SEPTEMBER							Roche												
3	**Bury**	H	2-1	Mullock	Harris	Marriott	**Roche[1]**	G Evans	Fleming	Gray	Edwards	**Ma Williams[1]**	Braisdell	Done	Darlington(4)	P Williams(9)	Stewart(7)	Mi Jones	
10	**Rochdale**	H	1-3	Mullock	Harris	Taylor	Baynes	G Evans	Fleming	Braisdell	C Evans	Ma Williams	Reed	**Done[1]**	Darlington(7)	Marriott (4)	Stewart(8)		
17	**Oldham Athletic**	H	1-4	Mullock	Baynes	Taylor	Roche	G Evans	Fleming	Gray	Edwards	Ma Williams	**Braisdell[1]**	Done	Reed(10)	Maxwell(1)	Darlington(9)		
24	**York City** (LC1)	H	4-0	Mullock	Baynes	Marriott	Roche	G Evans	Fleming	Gray	C Evans	**Darlington[3]**	Braisdell	Edwards	**Ma Williams(10)[1]**	Lee Jones(4)			
OCTOBER																			
1	**Macclesfield Town**	H	4-2	Mullock	Baynes	Marriott	Roche	G Evans	C Evans	**Gray[1]**	Edwards	**Darlington[1]**	**Ma Williams[1]**	**Done[1]**	Taylor	Lee Jones(2)	Braisdell(9)	Fleming(6)	
8	Carlisle United	A	0-2	Mi Jones	Baynes	Taylor	Roche	Mi Williams	Fleming	Gray	Edwards	Darlington	Ma Williams	Done	Matschok(11)	Mullock	Harris(2)		
15	**Port Vale**	H	0-1	Mullock	Baynes	Taylor	G Evans	Mi Williams	Fleming	Gray	C Evans	Ma Williams	Braisdell	Done	Darlington(10)	Roche(2)			
22	**Stockport County** (LC2)	H	1-4	Mullock	Harris	Marriott	Roche	G Evans	Fleming	Braisdell	Taylor	Ma Williams	Reed	Edwards	**Done(11)[1]**	P Williams(6)	Darlington(10)	Lee Jones	
29	Shrewsbury Town	A	2-1	Maxwell	Baynes	Taylor	Roche	G Evans	C Evans	**Darlington[1]**	Fleming	Ma Williams	**Braisdell[1]**	Edwards	Marriott(11)	Mullock	Lee Jones(5)		
NOVEMBER																			
7	**Skelmersdale** (FAYC1)	H	3-0	Mi Jones	Baynes	Taylor	Roche	Marriott	Fleming	Stewart	P Williams	Darlington	**Ma Williams[3]**	Done	Braisdell(7)	Lee Jones(11)	Backhouse(8)	Matischok	Matischok
12	**Blackpool**	H	1-2	Maxwell	P Williams	Lee Jones	Marriott	Taylor	Edwards	Gray	C Evans	Fleming	**Darlington[1]**	Braisdell	Stewart(11)	D Hughes(2)	Backhouse(10)	Matischok	
21	Oldham Athletic (FAYC2)	A	1-1*	Mi Jones	Baynes	Taylor	Roche	Marriott	Fleming	Braisdell	P Williams	**Darlington[1]**	Ma Williams	Done	Vickers(2)	Maxwell	Stewart	Matischok	Hunt
26	Chester City	A	0-3	Mullock	Harris	C Evans	Baynes	Marriott	Gray	Edwards	Fleming	Ma Williams	Braisdell	Darlington	Roche	Cronshaw(10)	Done		
DECEMBER																			
3	**Walsall**	H	1-3	Mullock	Roche	Marriott	Vickers	G Evans	Fleming	Baynes	C Evans	Ma Williams	**Darlington[1]**	Braisdell	Edwards(3)	Maxwell	P Williams(8)	Stewart	
10	Macclesfield Town	A	0-2	Maxwell	Roche	Lee Jones	G Evans	Marriott	Baynes	Taylor	Backhouse	Darlington	Braisdell	Ma Williams	P Williams(3)	Stewart(6)			
16	**Carlisle United**	H	0-1	Mullock	W Roberts	G Evans	Vickers	Lee Jones	Matischok	Edwards	C Evans	Stewart	Lee Price	A Williams	P Williams	Backhouse	Ben Ward		
20	**Southampton (FAYC3)**	H	2-5	Mi Jones	Baynes	Taylor	Roche	Marriott	P Williams	Darlington	Fleming	Ma Williams	**Braisdell[1]**	**Done[1]**	Lee Jones	Maxwell	Stewart(7)	Backhouse(6)	Matischok
JANUARY																			
7	Port Vale	A	1-2	Mullock	Baynes	Taylor	Roche	G Evans	Edwards	Darlington	Fleming	Ma Williams	Braisdell	**Done[1]**	S Kehide(7)				
14	**Burnley**	H	1-2	Mullock	Harris	Taylor	Roche	G Evans	Fleming	C Evans	Done	**Baynes[1]**	Gray	Braisdell	Darlington(8)	Marriott(3)			
21	**Shrewsbury Town**	H	3-0	Mullock	Harris	Marriott	Roche	G Evans	C Evans	**Baynes[1]**	Fleming	Gray	**Braisdell[1]**	**Darlington[1]**	Matischok(10)	Lee Jones			
28	Burnley	A	1-4	Mullock	Lee Jones	Taylor	Roche	G Evans	Fleming	Baynes	C Evans	Braisdell	Gray	Darlington	Marriott(4)	**Stewart(9)[1]**	Maxwell(1)		
FEBRUARY																			
4	Stockport County	A	0-1	Mullock	Harris	Taylor	Marriott	G Evans	Stewart	Fleming	C Evans	Darlington	Gray	Braisdell	Maxwell(1)	Backhouse(10)	Roche(9)		
11	Blackpool	A	1-0	Maxwell	Baynes	Marriott	Lee Jones	**Roche[1]**	P Williams	Backhouse	Fleming	Edwards	Braisdell	Darlington	Stewart(11)	Matischok(6)	Hunt(9)		
18	**Preston North End**	H	1-5	Maxwell	Roche	Marriott	Lee Jones	G Evans	Baynes	Edwards	Fleming	Backhouse	Gray	**Braisdell[1]**	Stewart(5)	Darlington(7)	Matischok(9)		
MARCH																			
11	Walsall	A	2-0	Maxwell	P Williams	Taylor	Lee Jones	Marriott	Fleming	**Baynes[1]**	Matischok	**Stewart[1]**	Darlington	Edwards	Mullock(1)	Backhouse(8)	Hunt(11)		
18	Tranmere Rovers	A	0-1	Maxwell	Baynes	Taylor	Marriott	Lee Jones	Matischok	Stewart	Backhouse	Darlington	Fleming	Edwards	Mullock(1)	Cronshaw(6)	Hunt(11)	Vickers	
25	**Wigan Athletic**	H	1-0	Mullock	P Williams	Marriott	Vickers	Lee Jones	Fleming	Baynes	Backhouse	**Darlington[1]**	Braisdell	Edwards	Gray(10)	Matischok(8)	Hunt(11)		
APRIL																			
8	Rochdale	A#	1-2	Maxwell	Roche	Marriott	Lee Jones	Vickers	Fleming	Baynes	Edwards	Stewart	**Darlington[1]**	Taylor	Braisdell(9)	Backhouse(5)	Matischok(2)		
15	Oldham Athletic	A	0-3	Maxwell	Price	Lee Jones	Marriott	Taylor	Fleming	Gray	Matischok	Baynes	Darlington	Stewart	Hunt()	Backhouse()			
22	Preston North End	A	0-3	Maxwell	Price	Lee Jones	Marriott	Vickers	P Williams	Baynes	Fleming	Stewart	Darlington	Taylor	Matischok(5)	Hunt(4)	S Smith(9)		
27	**Chester City**	H	1-2	Maxwell	P Williams	Marriott	Lee Jones	Vickers	Fleming	**Stewart[1]**	Matischok	Darlington	Baynes	Taylor	Backhouse(8)	Hunt(5)	Price(9)		
29	Bury	A	0-2	Maxwell	Lee Jones	Taylor	Roche	G Evans	C Evans	Baynes	Fleming	Ma Williams	Gray	Stewart	Marriott(2)				
MAY																			
6	**Stockport County**	H	2-3	Maxwell	Baynes	Marriott	Price	Lee Jones	Matischok	P Williams	Backhouse	Stewart	**Darlington[1]**	**Taylor[1]**	Cronshaw(7)	Hunt(8)	Vickers(4)	Llwyd	

~DENOTES OWN GOAL *DENOTES WON 4-2 ON PENALTIES (AET) - PENALTY SCORERS Braisdell, Fleming, Darlington, Done #DENOTES PLAYED AT COLLIERS PARK

Coaches have been unable to focus on the Youth Alliance match properly ahead of a Saturday morning engagement. Obviously this has had a detrimental affect on results.

But there has still been some high points during the season, most notably the exhilarating penalty shoot-out win at league leaders, Oldham Athletic, in the Second Round of the prestigious F. A. Youth Cup. This brought Southampton to the Racecourse for a Third Round tie just before Christmas. The Saints boast one of the best Youth set-ups in the League and were beaten finalists in the competition the season before. Indeed their side featured a certain Gareth Bale, who went on to become the youngest Welsh international ever when he appeared as a substitute in the 2-1 defeat of Trinidad & Tobago in Graz at the end of the season. The illustrious nature of the visitors held no fears for the young Dragons and an upset looked on the cards when Aaron Braisdell and Matty Done goals opened up a 2-0 lead before the interval. The Saints were rocked even further when Michael Jones saved a penalty right on the stroke of half time.

Unfortunately the Dragons couldn't keep it going after the break and the visitors demonstrated their credentials with a five-goal blast to secure a place in the next round. But one final point on the Southampton game. In his post-match interview for the club's website Saints' Coach George Prost said that he'd reminded his players of Liverpool's epic comeback against AC Milan in the Champions League Final a few months earlier. So there you have it, they had to compare us with AC Milan in order to beat us!

And so, finally, what can we expect in the season ahead? Who better to ask than Steve Weaver himself? "We've got some good lads pushing through from the younger age groups and so we haven't wanted to clog up places for them," he said. "It's going to be an under-18 league, which should suit us. We have 10 newcomers and, hopefully, we'll have more time to work with them on a day-to-day basis and mould them into a good side. I said at the start of last season that it would be a tough season but I'm more than hopeful of a better season this time."

Football League Youth Alliance North & Midlands West Conference
Final Table 2005-2006

	P	W	D	L	F	A	GD	PTS
Oldham Athletic	30	26	1	3	102	32	70	79
Preston North End	27	18	3	6	62	28	34	57
Tranmere Rovers	28	15	5	8	59	40	19	50
Port Vale	29	14	7	8	56	45	11	49
Rochdale	29	15	3	11	58	46	12	48
Stockport County	30	14	4	12	52	45	8	46
Burnley	27	15	1	11	55	65	-10	46
Chester City	30	10	7	13	52	53	-1	37
Carlisle United	28	10	7	11	35	51	-16	37
Walsall	29	10	6	13	42	46	-4	36
Wigan Athletic	28	11	3	14	39	47	-8	36
Blackpool	28	11	2	15	25	41	-16	35
Bury	30	8	7	15	43	48	-5	31
Shrewsbury Town	29	7	5	17	34	58	-24	26
Macclesfield Town	30	6	7	17	31	69	-38	25
WREXHAM	**30**	**7**	**0**	**23**	**31**	**63**	**-32**	**21**

Everything you need to get you through the week...

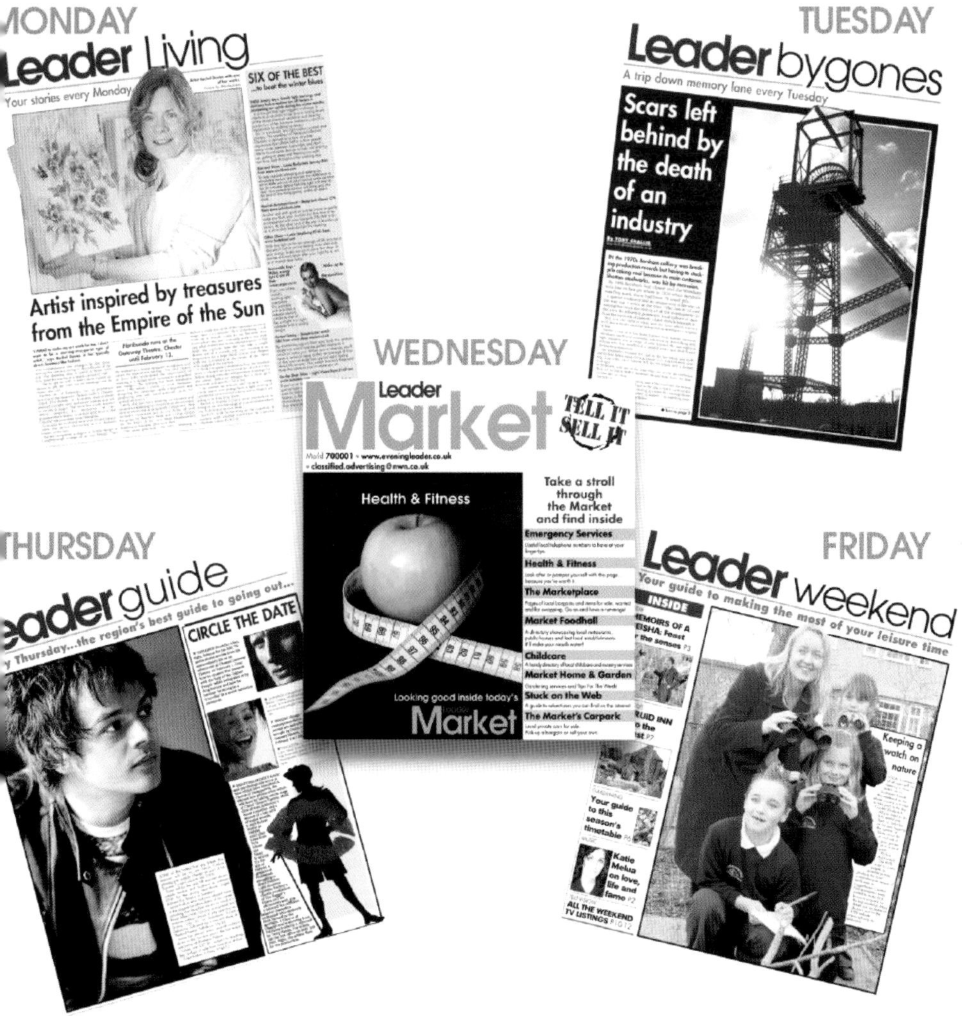

MONDAY

Leader Living

Your stories every Monday

Artist inspired by treasures from the Empire of the Sun

TUESDAY

Leader bygones

A trip down memory lane every Tuesday

Scars left behind by the death of an industry

WEDNESDAY

Leader Market

TELL IT SELL IT

Health & Fitness

Take a stroll through the Market and find inside

Emergency Services

Health & Fitness

The Marketplace

Market Foodhall

Childcare

Market Home & Garden

Stuck on the Web

The Market's Carpark

Looking good inside today's Market

THURSDAY

Leader guide

...the region's best guide to going out...

CIRCLE THE DATE

FRIDAY

Leader weekend

Your guide to making the most of your leisure time

INSIDE

Keeping a watch on nature

nd so much more, every week in your

Evening Leader

This summer saw Dennis Lawrence become the first-ever Wrexham player in the club's history to play in a World Cup finals. It was an experience that Dennis himself will never forget, and he shares some of those memories with us here.

"It was disappointing not to have reached the play-offs with Wrexham, but as our interest in the season had sadly ended early, Denis Smith allowed me to miss the last game of the season to travel home for an extended break before joining up with Trinidad's World Cup squad. It enabled me to visit my family and friends before getting down to the real business.

"The game against Peru on 10th May was a chance for the Trinidad & Tobago public to send the team off to Germany in style. It was also our chance to say thank you to the fans and, as a squad, we visited numerous places all over the twin islands of Trinidad and Tobago to thank those people for there support. We drew the Peru match 1-1 at the national stadium, which is called the Hasely Crawford Stadium, but to be honest we could not fully concentrate on the preparation for the match, because of all the activity in travelling around the islands in the build up to the games.

"We left Trinidad a couple of days later and set up camp in Cheshire at the De Vere Carden Park Hotel, just over the Welsh border. The full squad was to spend a full week there, giving the manager, Leo Beenhakker, time to assess his squad, check our fitness levels and prepare the team to focus on the task ahead. We had a great time at Carden, and unlike a lot of the players, it gave me chance to say goodbye to my wife Gloria and daughter Celine before we left to go to our training camp in Austria.

"Having arrived in Austria we began to look ahead at the job in hand. We had five matches lined up before the real thing. The whole build up was about preparation, and having the managers ideas drilled into us, and put into practice. Our first match was on 23rd May when we played Austria Vienna at Bad Radkersburg, which was near to where we were based. It was a good work-out and we won 3-2.

"The next match was of special importance to me and Carlos, as it was against Wales in Graz. It was important we did well, especially for the banter with the Welsh lads back at Wrexham. However, we lost the match 2-1, but we should have gone on and won the game. In all honesty though, it was a good work-out for us, and about us looking at the game, forgetting the negatives, and building on the positives for the next match in our build up. It was a pity Mark Jones wasn't playing, but I did have a chat with Mel Pejic after the game.

"We then travelled from our training camp by bus to Celje where we were to play Slovenia. We had really worked hard preparing for the game, but found ourselves 2-0 down after just ten minutes. We battled hard to pull one back, and was pleased with our performance in the end, despite losing 3-1. From these games we were becoming a lot stronger on set

pieces. We didn't like to lose, but it was a good test for us. Again we would take the positives from the game."

"A few days later we had our biggest test to date against the Czech Republic in Prague. It was a huge game for us, as they were a top quality team, and we knew that. However, we worked hard in our preparation, but again found ourselves disappointingly 3-0 down after 30 minutes. After the break we dug in, and didn't concede any more goals, but created one or two chances for ourselves. The manager Leo Beenhakker told us that the games had been worthwhile as they had given us an idea of what we would be up against in the World Cup. This was our last big hurdle before Germany.

"We had had two weeks in Austria, it was a beautiful country, but very quiet. We flew from Vienna to Munich, and then on to Bremen, where we were taken to our World Cup base in the German city of Rotenburg.

"We were immediately made welcome, and there was a large turn out of local people to welcome us with T & T flags at the swish Landhaus Wachtelhof Hotel. It was then that I realised; this is it. I am in a World Cup finals. The hotel was top drawer! It had first-class facilities with a games room, and we had the hotel to ourselves.

"The training ground facilities were excellent, and we would ride our bikes there every day, which only took us about five minutes. It was an excellent set up to prepare for the job in hand.

"Gloria and Celine and the other players' families were based in a hotel about 35 minutes away, and we were given time off every now and then to meet go out and meet them. We were also given tours around the local town and informed of the history of the place.

"The manager wanted us to prepare for one game at a time, and not look ahead. As soon as we played our final warm up game against Hamburg club side FC St. Pauli, which we won 2-1, we began our focus on the game against Sweden. We drove to our hotel in Dortmund by coach on the day before the game. Upon our arrival we rested, before travelling to the stadium to relax and get a feel for the pitch and the stadium in a 45 minute training session.

"We were fully prepared for the game, and we knew what we were up against and what to expect. We knew our supporters would be outnumbered, but they were fantastic. However, having warmed up on the pitch prior to the game, I came out into the tunnel, and found Shaka Hislop lining up alongside me. What had happened to Kelvin Jack? He had been named in the team, but he had apparently had his calf tighten up on him in the warm up. It was disappointing for Kelvin, but we had no concerns over his replacement, and we knew Shaka could do just a good a job for us.

"As we walked out into the stadium, the thought of me representing Trinidad & Tobago on the World's biggest stage hit me. It was a huge occasion, and the pride I felt from singing my country's national anthem was immense. I will never forget that.

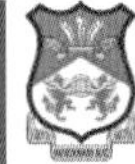

"We knew if we could stay in the game for the opening 25 minutes we could build on it and, as the game went on, the more we began to believe in ourselves. We had looked at tapes of the Swedes in our preparation in the video sessions at our hotel in Rotenburg, and we believed we could win it then.

"However, Avery John's sending off meant we had to change our tactics, and it became a different game. We had to battle for our lives, but Shaka was tremendous and Cornell Glenn came close when he hit the bar. We stuck together and held out for a scoreless draw. The final whistle saw what it meant to us all. It was a very proud moment. We were buzzing! It was a similar feeling as when we beat Bahrain to qualify. It was like we had won the World Cup!

"After the game we travelled back to our hotel in Rotenburg, and arrived in the early hours of the morning, but there were still over 300 people there to welcome us back. But the job wasn't done, and we had to remain focussed, so there was no partying for us. The following day, we were allowed to spend a relaxed day with our families, but then our minds were turned to the England game, and that brought all the media hype!

"As I've already mentioned, as well as our training sessions, we would have video sessions, and we watched England's build up games against Jamaica and Uruguay. We understood what we had to do. We had to defend the second ball, and stick with there runners, Gerrard and Lampard. We knew our jobs, and that we had to do them correctly. We were confident about defending set pieces against the likes of Peter Crouch.

"We flew over to Nuremberg, and stayed overnight, again having a 45-minute session in the afternoon before the game. The game had more significance as the press were making out the game was won before it had started. We felt we should have been given more respect. We were determined to prove we could compete, and weren't there to make up the numbers.

"Despite being outnumbered 10-1 by England fans, our fans were brilliant and the more the game went on the more we believed we could achieve something from the game. Yes, England had their chances, but so did we. If John Terry hadn't reached Stern John's header and cleared it off the line, it might have been a different story.

"For 83 minutes we frustrated England and had the English media and fans with their heads held in their hands, but when they scored it was the most demoralising feeling I had ever felt. It wasn't until after the game that I saw a video of Peter Crouch pulling down Brett Sancho's dreadlocks. If I'd seen it at the time I would have made a big complaint.

"Having conceded that goal, we felt well, let's go for it. Cornell Glenn had a couple of one on ones, but then Stevie Gerrard scored one of the best goals of the tournament. At the final whistle I was gutted, but I soon came round to thinking we had not let ourselves down. We could

walk off the pitch with our heads held high. "The trip back to Rotenburg was very quiet and subdued. Thinking of what could have been, but the point from the Sweden game had still given us a chance to qualify for the next stages if we could beat Paraguay in our final group game.

"The disappointment of the previous day soon disappeared when we decided to play a cricket match between ourselves in the afternoon. I was captain of one side, and Dwight Yorke the other, and my team whipped them! Marvin Andrews was our top scorer, and I hit a few runs myself, but the funniest moment was when Brett Sancho dropped me and Marvin back to back! He will never forget that.......well, we certainly won't let him!

"We then turned our minds to the Paraguay game in Kaiserslautern. We still had something to play for while Paraguay was playing for pride. However, we weren't anywhere near our best in the first half, but the second half we were a lot better, but it still didn't stop us losing 2-0. The biggest disappointment was that we were going home without having scored a goal in the tournament.

"The sad fact was that we had more support at that game than any other, and they were fantastic. At the end of the game it was very emotional for us when we walked round the stadium to thank the fans. It had been a tremendous adventure, and we had given it our best, and felt we'd achieved a lot. We achieved respect, not only from the smaller countries but also the bigger ones as well.

"On our journey back to Rotenburg we discussed what we had taken from the tournament, but upon getting back to the hotel we put those memories behind us, and did what Trinis do best, and that's party!

"On the Thursday we packed our belongings, and said our goodbyes. The hotel staff had been fantastic, and they really looked after us, as did the local police and community, who gave us a good send off.

"We then flew back to Trinidad, which had been at the request of the Prime Minister, as they wanted the country to honour the team. Our arrival back at Piarco Airport wasn't as big as our return from Bahrain, but the Saturday had been deemed as the big day.

"We were given a free day on Friday to chill out, and meet our family and friends, but then on the Saturday it was party time! We were given an open-top bus tour from our hotel to the Hasely Crawford stadium. It was a fantastic turn out by the Trinidadian people, and was overwhelming.

"The following day the squad dispersed. I stayed four extra days in Trinidad, and then myself and Marvin Andrews went to Miami for a short break to relax, and be a tourist for a bit.

"Looking back, my own personal highlight of the World Cup was the first game with Sweden, and singing the T&T national anthem in a World Cup finals. It gave me immense pride, but the lowest point has to be Peter Crouch's 83rd minute goal for England, which was made worse afterwards when I saw what he did to Brett to score. But overall I have too many happy memories to let that cloud my World Cup experience."

This article was written before Dennis joined Swansea. We are obviously sorry to see him go, but we are sure every Wrexham fan wishes him well for the future.

Thanks Dennis – Wrexham Legend.

In preparation for the upcoming European qualifiers Northern Ireland embarked at the end of last season on a two-match tour of the USA, where they were to play Uruguay and Romania. Included in Lawrie Sanchez's 18-man squad was our very own Michael Ingham, keen to establish his place in the Northern Ireland set up.

In his broad Belfast accent, Michael chatted about his experience of his two-match tour with the Northern Irish team to America in May; "I knew that Maik (Taylor) and Roy (Carroll) would not be making the trip, so I knew that it would be a good chance for me to impress the manager. The other keeper on the trip was Doncaster Rovers' Alan Blayney. Lawrie told us before we went, that we would both get a chance.

"Mind you, I was lucky to get there in the end, as I went to the wrong airport to get the connecting flight to Heathrow. There are two airports in Belfast; City and International, and I chose the wrong one! I really should have checked my ticket I suppose, but in the end I still managed to get to Heathrow before Lawrie and unless he's reading this book he will never know!

"There were six new caps in the party, and two or three more lads like myself with just one cap. I made my debut for Northern Ireland in the IFA's 125th Anniversary match against Germany last year."

Michael had been scheduled to make his international bow on Northern Ireland's Caribbean tour the previous year, which included a match with Trinidad & Tobago, but a broken finger ruled him out. It was well worth the wait though as Ingham was able to make his debut on his own soil in front of family and friends.

"The reaction of the crowd that night when I came on was amazing. To be honest I was holding back the tears, as I never thought I would get such a reception. I was the proudest man in the ground" Michael said of that memorable evening.

Of the tour to America, Michael said: "There is a seven-hour time difference between the UK and America. We arrived in New York late on Friday night, and did some light training on the Saturday. We were playing Uruguay at the famous Giants Stadium on the Sunday, and it was important to have a run out on the artificial pitch. It's what they call a third generation surface (polyethylene and polypropylene blend with rubber and sand infill) and it took a bit of getting used to.

"To play at the Giants Stadium itself was an amazing experience. Apparently the ground holds over 80,000 spectators, and is shared by both the Giants and Jets American football teams. I understand that they are looking to build a new ground to replace it.

"When we played Uruguay on the Sunday there were about 12-15,000 in

Left: The Giants Stadium, slightly more impressive than the Deva (right)

the ground, mainly ex-pat South Americans, although there were around 200 fans from Northern Ireland. These are guys who travel everywhere with us.

"My room mate on the tour was Steve Davis of Aston Villa, and he made history at the age of 21 as the youngest-ever player to captain Northern Ireland.

"It was the proudest moment of my career to walk out with the number ONE jersey on for that Uruguay game. I thought that we played well against the Uruguayans, and were unlucky to lose 1-0. They scored with a 35-yard wonder goal from Fabian Estoyanoss of Cadiz. Not my fault I can assure you!

"Although they were missing Juventus pairing Zalayeta and Olivera, the Uruguayans were ranked 25 in the FIFA rankings and gave us a good workout. I suppose in many ways they were a typical South American team, but they had a dark side to their game as they would nip and spit at us, which was a shame because they had ability in spades. I was particularly impressed with the young full-back Garcia who is on the books of Real Madrid.

"After that game Lawrie gave us a few days off and we did all the usual tourist stuff, Central Park and all that. We even managed to blag our way into a James Blunt concert by telling the security he was a big Northern Ireland fan, and he had come to watch us the night before, and invited us to his concert!

"We then moved on to Chicago for the second game against Romania. I sat that game out on the bench, as Lawrie let Alan Blayney play. We had James Quinn sent-off in that match, and we despite playing ok, we were unfortunate not to get more out of the game, but lost 2-0.

"Overall the games were good preparation for the up-and-coming Euro Qualifiers. Football is on a high in Northern Ireland at the moment following the win against England, and everyone is looking forward to the forthcoming campaign.

"On a personal note, I think that being involved in the international set up is a definite bonus for me. Different routines, playing with different players and the experience of playing at grounds like the Giants Stadium all help build up a player's confidence. Hopefully that will translate into promotion for Wrexham this season."

We could not mark the start of a bright new era for Wrexham without reflecting on the events of the last few years. To describe this period as traumatic would be to understate the fear and tensions felt by all Wrexham fans, as for long periods it appeared our club was about to be consigned to history.

Mark Guterman

On February 7th 2002, Mark Guterman and his associate Alex Hamilton set up a joint venture agreement in order to profit from property speculation.

Shortly after this date, Guterman informed Hamilton that the acquisition of Pryce Griffiths' shareholding in the club was the key to progressing the commercial development opportunities at the Racecourse site.

Guterman already had a tarnished record in football due to his time as Chairman of local rivals Chester. His tenure at the Deva had resulted in City in administration following a long period of cash problems including bills and wages not being paid.

Memorvale Ltd was incorporated as a vehicle for the purchase on March 11th and negotiations with Griffiths progressed. Hamilton owned all the shares in Memorvale.

Pryce had been in poor health for some time and was keen to sell his controlling shareholding.

On March 26th 2002, the board of Wrexham approved the sale of Pryce Griffiths' 78% shareholding to Memorvale Ltd, (a company described in court as the "corporate personification of Mr Hamilton"). In return he received a sum of £50,000 up front, a promise of £500,000 based on the future development of the Racecourse and an annual payment of £30,000 per annum for the next five years.

This was to be paid as a consultancy fee by the club for Griffiths services but, oddly for a consultancy, in the event of his death was to have been paid to his children.

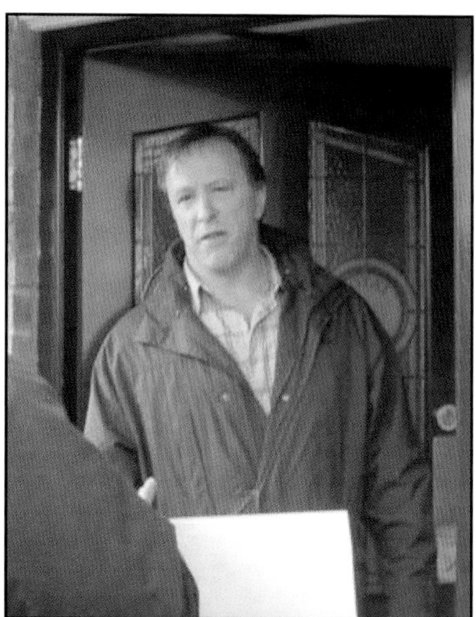
Alex Hamilton

He was also appointed to the honorary position of Club President.

With control of the football club secured, the partners turned their attention to the freehold of the Stadium, owned by Wolverhampton and Dudley brewery.

In early April 2002, negotiations began with Wolverhampton and Dudley to purchase the freehold of the Racecourse.

At this point the club already held a lease on the Racecourse Stadium that had

been negotiated by Pryce Griffiths with the brewery and, at the time, was thought to have secured the long-term future of Wrexham AFC. The club paid £750,000 to the brewery as a premium for the grant of this lease.

It had 120 years to expire and a peppercorn rent payable to Wolverhampton Dudley of £1 per annum. The lease was valued in the list of club's assets at over £3 million.

Marrying up the leasehold with the freehold would create an asset worth around £10 million and would have provided the cash-strapped club with a large measure of security in the event the club paid the brewery a sum of £300,000 for the freehold. A fantastic deal you may think.

However, it turned out to be a fantastic deal for Hamilton rather than the club. By using the club as a front in negotiations, Hamilton and Guterman were able to secure a bargain price for an asset that Hamilton had expected to pay around a million pounds for.

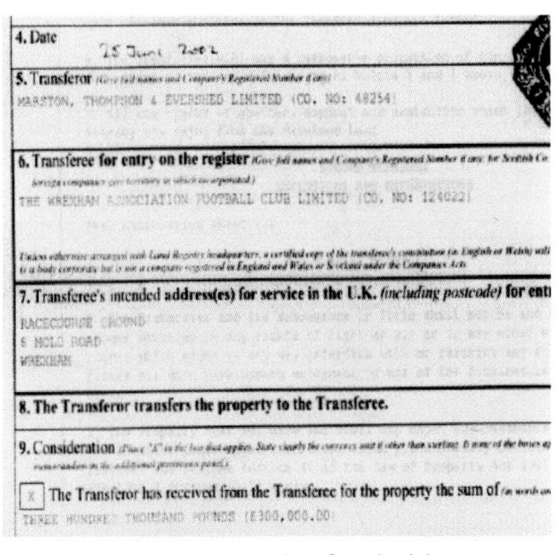

4. Date 25 June 2002

5. Transferor
MARSTON, THOMPSON & EVERSHED LIMITED (CO. NO: 48254)

6. Transferee for entry on the register
THE WREXHAM ASSOCIATION FOOTBALL CLUB LIMITED (CO. NO: 124022)

7. Transferee's intended address(es) for service in the U.K. (including postcode) for ent
RACECOURSE GROUND
MOLD ROAD
WREXHAM

8. The Transferor transfers the property to the Transferee.

9. Consideration

[X] The Transferor has received from the Transferee for the property the sum of
THREE HUNDRED THOUSAND POUNDS (£300,000.00)

On the same day as the freehold was purchased by the club it was transferred to another Hamilton company, Damens Ltd for nothing.

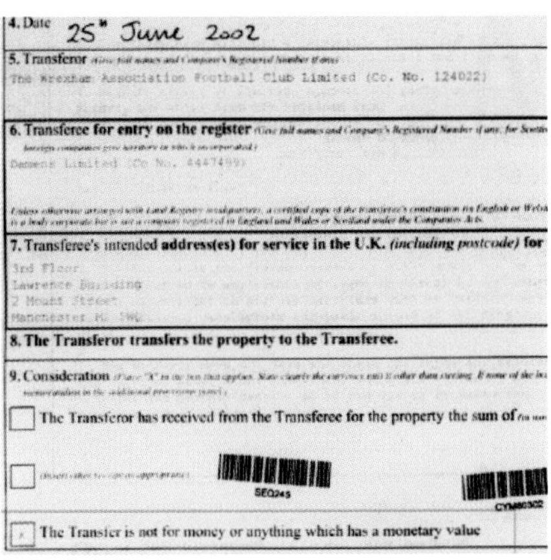

4. Date 25th June 2002

5. Transferor
The Wrexham Association Football Club Limited (Co. No. 124022)

6. Transferee for entry on the register
Damens Limited (Co No. 4447499)

7. Transferee's intended address(es) for service in the U.K. (including postcode) for
3rd Floor
Lawrence Building
2 Mount Street
Manchester M2 5WQ

8. The Transferor transfers the property to the Transferee.

9. Consideration

[ ] The Transferor has received from the Transferee for the property the sum of

[ ]

SEQ245

[x] The Transfer is not for money or anything which has a monetary value

It is true that Hamilton had used his own money to fund the purchase from the brewery but it is even more pertinent that the club's directors had not been informed about the freehold purchase or indeed even the possibility of the club purchasing the freehold.

Neither were the club's minority shareholders consulted.

Neither Guterman nor Hamilton were directors of the club at this stage, yet using the club, they had conducted the purchase and transfer of the Racecourse freehold for their own personal benefit.

This business was conducted by an acquaintance of the two men, a Salford solicitor, called Andrew Zatman. Zatman's own notes record that he was acting for both the club and Damens Ltd in this matter, although, he was not the club's regular legal advisor. Zatman was to claim later that he was not aware of the Hamilton/Guterman profit-share agreement.

On June 1st, Guterman was officially appointed as a director of the club and on June 11th held his first board meeting. At this meeting Pryce Griffiths stood down as Chairman in favour of Guterman.

Other matters discussed at the meeting were shirt sponsorship and a report on the Centre of Excellence.

There was no mention of the transactions relating to the transfer of the freehold just 10 days earlier to Damens Ltd. Neither did Guterman mention the fact that he was also a director of Damens Ltd, the club's new landlords. Surely a clear conflict of interest?

The next day Guterman resigned as a director of Damens Ltd.

It would appear that this act brought down the curtain on their first burst of activity at the club.

On the field we were relegated at the end of the 2002 season but, against all the odds, were promoted the following spring.

In the prevailing mood of celebration few, if any, Wrexham fans were calling into question any of the off-field activities at the club.

However, during the second season of Guterman's Chairmanship the financial situation at the club deteriorated.

Promoted from the second division the previous May, the new campaign was undermined by the players' wages being paid late virtually every month. The heating and hot water was cut off at the club training complex, as there were insufficient funds to pay for heating oil. The chef at the training complex was unable to provide meals for the players for the same reason. The club was also fined £12,000 for failing to renew its PRS license (which enables it to play music on match days). Guterman claimed at the time that there was no cash crisis at the club and actually banned a reporter from the *Daily Post* newspaper for suggesting that there was indeed a cash flow problem.

In March 2003, three months overdue, the club finally published its accounts for the year ending 2002. These accounts cover the period up to the Guterman/Hamilton takeover and reflect the final year of the previous Chairman's tenure.

They show that the club made a loss of £300,000 on the year and had liabilities of £2 million against assets of over £4 million.

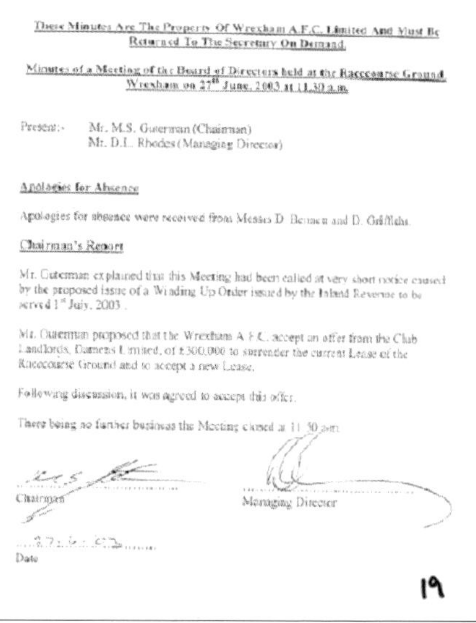

These Minutes Are The Property Of Wrexham A.F.C. Limited And Must Be Returned To The Secretary On Demand.

Minutes of a Meeting of the Board of Directors held at the Racecourse Ground Wrexham on 27th June, 2003 at 11.30 a.m.

Present:- Mr. M.S. Guterman (Chairman)
Mr. D.L. Rhodes (Managing Director)

Apologies for Absence

Apologies for absence were received from Messrs D. Bennett and D. Griffiths.

Chairman's Report

Mr. Guterman explained that this Meeting had been called at very short notice caused by the proposed issue of a Winding Up Order issued by the Inland Revenue to be served 1st July, 2003.

Mr. Guterman proposed that the Wrexham A.F.C. accept an offer from the Club Landlords, Damens Limited, of £300,000 to surrender the current Lease of the Racecourse Ground and to accept a new Lease.

Following discussion, it was agreed to accept this offer.

There being no further business the Meeting closed at 11.30 a.m.

Chairman Managing Director

27.6.03
Date

19

The bulk of the club's assets were made up of its 125-year lease on the Racecourse Stadium. At the time that this lease was purchased it was thought to have safeguarded the club's future. Pryce described it at the time as the best piece of business he had ever done.

However, in June 2003 the terms of the lease were changed.

The new lease negotiated by Messrs

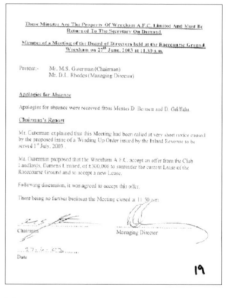

Guterman and Hamilton also had 120 years to run.

More importantly, however, a break clause was inserted into the lease that stated that the landlord (Damens) could evict the club from the ground by giving it 12 months' notice upon payment to the club of £1 million when exercising the break clause

Under the new lease, the club was obliged to pay Damens Ltd an annual rental of £30,000 which is rather more than the £1 per annum that they were paying the brewery under the terms of the old lease.

£1 million is obviously not enough to build a new stadium and would in any event go straight to the club's creditors, of whom Hamilton was one.

Damens Limited (owner Alex Hamilton) paid the club £300,000 in consideration for the change in the lease which gave Damens Limited total control over a site worth anything up to £10m subject to planning consent.

Hamilton claims that he was "approached by the club" with a proposal to surrender and re-grant the lease in return for the payment of £300,000 which the club needed to settle a VAT bill.

As he was also the majority shareholder of the club and also involved in a profit sharing agreement (based on the development of the club land) with the club Chairman Mr Guterman, we doubt that this "approach" came as any great shock to him.

Again as in the transfer of the freehold 12-months earlier, this matter was passed without a full board meeting being called. Guterman and the club secretary David Rhodes produced minutes for a "meeting" that showed the absent directors as having tendered "apologies". In reality the absent directors, Messrs Bennett and Griffiths, were unaware of the meeting, because they had not been informed that there was one.

Once again the club's minority shareholders were not consulted on this matter. Guterman as club Chairman was supposed to be acting in the interests of these shareholders, but he was in fact acting in the interests of himself and his partner Hamilton

The combined effect of the changes to the leasehold and freehold of the Racecourse Stadium, was to divorce the club from its assets. In effect the club now had a lease, determinable at any time on 12 months' notice on far worse terms than the 125-year lease, which had been surrendered.

The club's future was now heavily dependant on the plans of Messrs Hamilton and Guterman and any goodwill that they felt towards it.

On March 16th 2004, David Rhodes, the long-serving club secretary, left the club after 20 years service. It does not appear to have been an amicable split and Rhodes' severance package included a gagging clause that forbade him from discussing the terms of his departure.

At this point wages were continually paid late and in dribs and drabs. More and more fans began asking questions about the club's finances. The club's accounts for the previous season were due to be published the previous Christmas, but as the season drew to a close in May there was still no sign of any financial information.

What on earth was going on at the Racecourse?

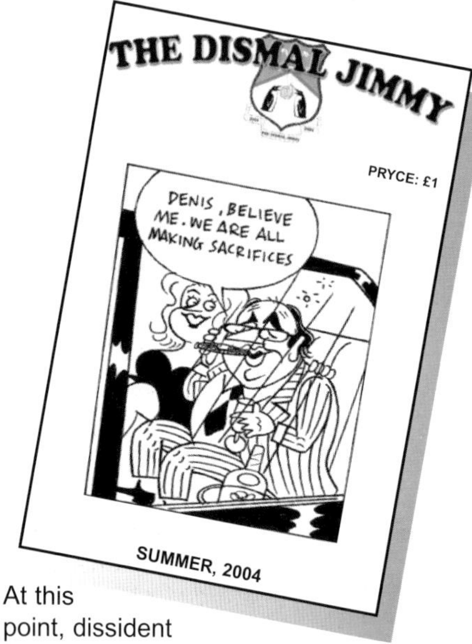

At this point, dissident Wrexham fans produced a radical new fanzine. The "*Dismal Jimmy*", was described by Chairman Guterman as a libellous magazine and it acted as a focus for discontent amongst Wrexham's fans. It detailed the relationships between Guterman and Hamilton and questioned the benefits to the club of the various land deals transacted by the two speculators.

Growing frustration at the management of the club led to a Red Card protest at the last game of the 2003-4 season against Brighton. Wrexham fans held up red cards to show their displeasure at the Guterman regime. It is fair to say that this protest was not universally supported by Wrexham fans, but was backed 100 percent by the 2,000 visiting Brighton fans. These are supporters who had suffered similar problems to us and their fight for a home still continues. Their support on that afternoon was both awesome and humbling and has lead to a special relationship between the two sets of supporters ever since.

Two weeks later Guterman left the club. His official statement claimed that he had resigned for family and personal reasons. However, in reality his one-time associate, and the real club owner, Alex Hamilton had dismissed him.

Hamilton had become increasingly concerned at the financial situation at the club and Guterman's management of it. It is believed that a consultant, John Reames, brought in to the club following Rhodes' departure, had pointed to various shortcomings in the financial management of Wrexham AFC.

Throughout his time at Wrexham, Guterman maintained to the public that he was the owner of the club, and that he was supporting it using his own money.

In fact the truth of the matter was rather different as Justice Mann heard in the Chancery Division of the High Court on Sept 6th 2004, in an action between Guterman and Hamilton and companies under Hamilton's control.

"*He (Guterman) entered into a number of agreements with the first defendant (Hamilton) whereby the first defendant provided finance for certain projects in exchange for profit share. Joint ventures entered into under the agreements included the redevelopment of Wrexham Football Club*"

Hamilton was the owner all along.

When Guterman left the club in May 2004, shareholders were still waiting for the accounts to May 2003 to be published. They should have been published at Christmas 2003 but they were eventually published in July 2004

and revealed that the club's debts had risen by over £500,000 during Mr Guterman's stewardship. This included a whopping £900,000 owed to the Inland Revenue.

Guterman had failed to pay any income tax during the proceeding 12 months and it was the Inland Revenue who would eventually petition for a winding-up order four months later.

Guterman had also achieved an economic miracle by managing to increase the attendances at the Racecourse whilst reducing the club's income.

Guterman's exit paved the way for Alex Hamilton to pick up the reins at the club and the battle to save Wrexham now began in earnest.

Hamilton stated that he had no interest in football on many occasions and that his sole interest in Wrexham was to realise as much profit as he could from his initial investment.

Fans were horrified. The scale of the betrayal was becoming apparent and the prospect of losing both the ground and the club was very real.

At a series of public meetings that summer, the Wrexham Supporters' Trust galvanised the supporters and organised the defence of the club. The first meeting was held at the Miners Institute and over 400 worried fans were electrified by the words of Racecourse legend Gary Bennett:

"*If we stick together and fight, over our dead bodies will they move the Racecourse.*"

On July 21st 2004, Damens Ltd (owner Alex Hamilton) exercised the break clause inserted in the new lease and served on Wrexham football club (owner Alex Hamilton) 12 months' notice to quit the Racecourse. There was no other alternative home for the club and neither were there any assets left with which to satisfy the creditors. Under the terms of the lease the club was entitled to a payment of £1 million from Damens, however the debts were already in excess of £2 million and the future looked hopeless.

On October 21st 2004, the Inland Revenue served the club with a winding-up order that was due be heard in the High Court on November 17th.

On November 1st 2004, Alex Hamilton resigned as Chairman after a row with the only surviving directors Dave Bennett and Dave Griffiths. This was a pivotal moment in the struggle.

Bennett and Griffiths, two local businessmen, were Wrexham supporters of many years standing and had been involved in the club for many years.

Despite their obvious distaste for Hamilton, they had retained their directorships in the hope that they could somehow influence the clubs direction in the face of Hamilton's plans. This persistence paid off at a board meeting on November 1st, when their refusal to accept Hamilton's son Jack, and his P.A., Gail Stubbs, as directors of the club was the catalyst for the events that would eventually save the club.

Hamilton was furious at the two Daves intransigence and scribbled a hasty resignation note on a Coca Cola jotter pad. This was swiftly pocketed by Dave Bennett and for the first time in two years the club was controlled by two men with its best interests at heart.

Hamilton swiftly realised that he had made a massive tactical error and tried to retract his resignation but to no avail. Messrs Bennett and Griffiths informed him that his input would no longer be necessary.

Dave Bennett later said: "*Our lawyers had stressed the importance of keeping a majority on the club board. We knew that he wanted his secretary and also his son Jack made directors. Both Dave Griffiths and myself were determined to stop this and Mr Hamilton was furious. He resigned in frustration and although he thought better of it when he had calmed down, it was too late. The resignation note was locked up in my safe and he wasn't getting it back. He had lost control of the club.*"

Hamilton no longer had a voice at the club.

He then decided to call a series of shareholder EGMs in order to remove the two Daves from the board of directors and reinstall himself as Chairman. As the majority shareholder this would have been a formality. However, the ex-solicitor botched the paperwork in calling the meetings and Wrexham's disgruntled minority shareholders made two fruitless journeys to the Racecourse for meetings that were cancelled at the last minute. At the second of these meetings they held an impromptu gathering of their own and passed a motion of no confidence in the club's owner.

The thought that Hamilton could have regained control of the club during this period is chilling and we all owe a debt of gratitude to these Wrexham men who stood up and were counted at the time their club needed them most.

It became clear to Bennett and Griffiths that the clubs financial position was precarious and that the only hope of saving it was to apply for administration.

On November 17th 2004, the winding-up petition was served, as the club indicated its intention to apply for administration in an attempt to save the oldest football club in Wales from extinction.

On December 4th 2004, the club went into administration and Begbie Traynor were appointed to run the club and to find a buyer. Wrexham became the first club to be docked 10 points by the Football League for going into administration, under recently introduced League Rules. An appeal against the points deduction was dismissed.

Under the stewardship of David Acland and Steve Williams, Joint Administrators, the club was able to trade profitably whilst they started the search for new owners and a credible legal challenge to Hamilton's ownership.

Victory in the LDV final provided much-needed revenue for the club, but the absence of a credible buyer meant that the Leagues stringent 18 months in admin ruling was starting to become a major issue.

And then a stroke of luck.

In April 2005, ex-chairman Guterman served an injunction on Wrexham supporter Ken Pemberton relating to the contents of several taped telephone conversations between the two of them. Guterman was afraid that publication of the contents of the tapes would harm his interests in his ongoing legal battle with Alex Hamilton. Not surprisingly Hamilton waded into the dispute demanding a copy of the tapes for himself.

As a result of this the two men were required to serve on Pemberton all documents relating to their own dispute. These documents proved to be a goldmine. They listed chapter and verse all the contracts and agreements entered into by Hamilton and Guterman prior to taking over the club and also during their period of control.

It was clear from these documents that they had acted in their own interests rather than the interests of the club and that they had quite frankly been sloppy in the way that they had handled the matter.

The contents of the documents were published in full in an edition of the *Dismal Jimmy* and, more significantly, forwarded to the administrators to help them in their legal battle.

They were a godsend as David Acland stated:

"There is no doubt that our case was significantly enhanced by the disclosure of certain documents in other legal proceedings. We had already commenced proceedings (trial date fixed) and had a strong case, but it almost certainly would have proceeded to full trial and summary judgement would have been an impossibility."

The value of the information was further underlined on October 20th 2005, when Judge Norris handed down summary judgement in favour of Wrexham AFC stating,

"I regard this as a straightforward case in which a fiduciary position in the club has been misused for the benefit of those interested in the exploitation of its property assets, and they must account for the Club for the benefit they have obtained."

In short we - wuz robbed!!

It is worth noting that at this point, Pemberton is still subject to the very same injunction served on him by Guterman and has spent many thousands of pounds of his own money in fighting this action.

During this period the Dickens/Moss consortium emerged as the only credible bidder for the club and the owner of choice of the majority of fans.

Naturally, Mr Hamilton appealed against the summary judgment and the case was heard in the High Court in February 2006.

The judges, hearing the appeal, considered the matter and unanimously dismissed the appeal against the summary judgement supporting the original decision by Judge Norris. They stated that:

"At the end of a meticulous and careful judgement, he (Norris) decided that summary judgement should be given against the defendant. No adequate basis for interfering with this conclusion has been demonstrated."

Victory in the appeal opened the way for the Dickens/Moss bid to go through and we were home safe at last.

The darkest period in our history is now over and we can look to the future with some optimism.

So there you have it, the perfect story ... heroes, villains but most importantly, a happy ending.

Don´t mess with the Town!!

(1) Michael Gerard Ingham

Joined Wrexham from Sunderland in the summer of 2005 after previously impressing in a loan spell at the Racecourse. Mike was the number one choice for the last campaign. He suffered a sprained wrist at Stockport in April which kept him out of the last few games of the season. A fine shot stopper, Ingham's fine form across the season saw him called up to the Northern Ireland touring part to the USA where he became the first Wrexham keeper to play at The Giants Stadium in New York.

Nationality: Northern Irish
Date of Birth: 09/07/1980
Height: 6' 4" (193cm)
Weight: 13st 10lbs (87.16kg)
Previous Clubs: Sunderland, York City (loan), Wrexham (loan), Carlisle United (loan), Doncaster Rovers (loan), Stockport County, Darlington (loan)
Position: Goalkeeper

(2) Lee Paul Roche

Lee began the season in the starting line up and scored the winner in the first game of the season against Boston. However, an ongoing hernia problem led to an operation in January that effectively put paid to his season. Lee can play in both defence and midfield and this versatility will be much needed this season in what is still a small squad. In his second spell at the Racecourse having played a full season here on loan from Manchester United in 2000/01.

Nationality: English
Date of Birth: 28/10/1980
Height: 5' 10" (178cm)
Weight: 10st 10lbs (68.0kg)
Previous Clubs: Burnley, Manchester United
Position: Defender

(3) Ryan Valentine

Ryan, from Chirk, was taken from under the noses of Wrexham. He was a product of the Everton youth set-up, and played in the same youth team as a certain Wayne Rooney. However, Ryan failed to make the grade at Goodison Park, and in the summer of 2002 he was allowed to join Darlington. Already a member of the Welsh youth team, he earned under-21 appearances whilst at Feethams, and went on to make 162 league appearances for the 'Quakers'. The tough tackling full-back jumped at the chance to join his home town club in the summer.

Nationality: Welsh
Date of Birth: 19/08/1982
Height: 5' 10" (178cm)
Weight: 11st 5lbs (72.18kg)
Previous Clubs: Everton, Darlington
Position: Defender

(4) Shaun Melvyn Pejic

After starting the season well, Shaun suffered knee ligament damage in the home game against Doncaster which kept him on the sidelines until January. After a frustrating four months for the youngster, he returned to the team for the Shrewsbury away match and remained a permenant fixture thereafter. One of our quickest defenders, he is firmly established in the first team squad and will be looking to play a big part in this season's promotion push. Injury has again kept him out of the side at the start of this campaign.

Nationality: Welsh
Date of Birth: 16/11/1982
Height: 6' 0" (183cm)
Weight: 12st 2lbs (77.18kg)
Previous Clubs: None
Position: Defender

(5) Steve Evans

Steve had spells in the Football League with Crewe Alexandra and West Bromwich Albion, but failed to make the grade. He joined TNS in the League of Wales in 1999, winning every major honour in Welsh football, including being voted the Welsh Premier League's player of the year in 2005. Impressive performances against Liverpool in the Champions League last season alerted Denis Smith. A Welsh semi-professional international, Steve was given a chance to re-launch a Football League career by joining Wrexham in the close season.

Nationality: Welsh
Date of Birth: 26/02/1979
Height: 6' 5" (195cm)
Weight: 13st 10lbs (87.16kg)
Previolus Clubs: Crewe Alexandra, West Bromich Albion, TNS, Oswestry Town (loan)
Position: Defender

(7) Mark Jones

Mark enjoyed a fantastic first full season of league football scoring 13 goals from a central midfield position. He was named in the PFA League Two Team of the Year and narrowly missed out on full international recognition when injuries ruled him out of the games against Trinidad and the Basques. Last season was his first full campaign and dispite looked tired towards the end he is sure to come back stronger this time. We will be relying on a succession of his trademark 30-yard strikes to propel us up the table.

Nationality: Welsh
Date of Birth: 15/08/1983
Height: 5' 11" (180cm)
Weight: 10st 10lbs (68.1kg)
Previous Clubs: None
Position: Midfielder

(8) Daniel Ivor Llewellyn Williams

Danny began the season in his customary midfield role. However, injuries and a shortage of centre backs saw him convert to a centre half in a 3-5-2 formation where he played until the end of the season. He did so well in this role that he was voted the Player of the Season by the fans. Scored several important goals, including a bullet header against Chester in late March. Will probably play in a midfield role this season.

Nationality: Welsh
Date of Birth: 12/07/1979
Height: 6' 1" (185cm)
Weight: 13st 0lbs (82.63kg)
Previous Clubs: Liverpool, Chester City (loan), Bristol Rovers, Doncaster Rovers (loan), Kidderminster Harriers
Position: Midfielder, Defender

(9) Lee Richard McEvilly

Lee enjoyed a stop-start first season with the Dragons. The well-built Hartson "look-a-like" began the season well. However, he sustained a broken bone in his foot at Carlisle in December, which kept him out until April. Even worse for Lee came at Chester, when just four games into his comeback he broke the same foot again and was out for the rest of the season. Seven goals in 15 games hints at a return to be welcomed by Dragon's fans. However, a pre-season injury to the same foot has scuppered Lee's chance of a return to goal scoring action for the time being.

Nationality: Northern Irish
Date of Birth: 15/04/1982
Height: 6' 0" (183cm)
Weight: 12st 8lbs (79.9kg)
Previous Clubs: Rochdale, Accrington Stanley
Position: Striker

(10) Darren Ferguson

The best passer of a ball in the division, Darren is still the hub of the midfield engine room, always calling for the ball and looking to play in a colleague. When Fergie is on top of his game Wrexham are a real force to be reckoned with. He was virtually ever present in the side until the end of January, when a hip injury ruled him out for several weeks. He returned to the side for the home game against Chester making a major contribution to our victory. Darren is currently our longest serving player with over 280 appearances to his name.

Nationality: Scottish
Date of Birth: 09/02/1972
Height: 5' 10" (178cm)
Weight: 11st 10lbs (74.45kg)
Previous Clubs: Manchester United, Wolverhampton Wanderers, Sparta Rotterdam
Position: Midfielder

(11) Chris Llewellyn

“It’s good to be back”, said Chris upon rejoining Wrexham in the close season having left the club a year earlier to join Hartlepool United for £40,000. The Swansea-born striker began his career with Norwich City, where he played alongside Craig Bellamy, and where he first won full Welsh international honours. He showed great promise at Carrow Road, but a career at the top never materialised, and he joined the Racecourse club in June 2003. ‘Izzy’ as he is nicknamed at the club, was a member of that memorable LDV winning side in 2005.

Nationality: Welsh
Date of Birth: 28/08/1979
Height: 5' 11" (180cm)
Weight: 11st 6lbs (72.64kg)
Previous Clubs: Hartlepool United, Norwich City, Bristol Rovers (loan)
Position: Striker

(12) Matthew Thomas Crowell

Matty returned to the side last November following a long term knee injury, and was employed in Wrexham's central midfield for the rest of the campaign benefiting from Danny Williams' move to the defence. Always likes to be in the heat of the battle, his enthusiastic tackling does not always meet with the referee's approval. Although not a prolific marksman he scored important goals at Carlisle, Rochdale and at home to Oxford.

Nationality: Welsh
Date of Birth: 03/07/1984
Height: 5' 9" (175cm)
Weight: 10st 10lbs (68.1kg)
Previous Clubs: Southampton
Position: Midfielder

(13) Michael Jones

Although not given too many opportunities as yet in the first team, Michael looks to have a promising future in the game. "Carrots", described by his manager Denis Smith as one of the best young prospects in the country, he is wise enough to keep his feet firmly on the ground. The 18-year-old has bags of confidence in his ability, and his attitude is first class. He appeared in two matches in September and again towards the end of the season, and will be looking to put pressure on Michael Ingham for the number one jersey this time around.

Nationality: English
Date of Birth: 03/12/1987
Height: 6' 3" (191cm)
Weight: 13st 0lbs (82.63kg)
Previous Clubs: None
Position: Goalkeeper

(14) Simon Spender

Still only 20, Simon seems to have been around for several seasons now. The departure of Carlos Edwards meant that he got more opportunities last season than previously, and he will be looking to establish himself as a regular first team choice this campaign. One of the best passers of a ball at the club, Simon likes to get forward, and got on the score-sheet against Torquay last October in a 4-2 win. He was called up to Brian Flynn's under-21 squad at the end of the season.

Nationality: Welsh
Date of Birth: 15/11/1985
Height: 5' 11" (180cm)
Weight: 11st 0lbs (69.92kg)
Previous Clubs: None
Position: Defender

(16) Levi Alan Mackin

Highly rated by Denis Smith, Levi will be looking this season for a regular place in the starting line up. The hard working midfielder came off the bench numerous times until given a start in October against Darlington. Luck was not with him, as he sustained damaged knee ligaments in the same game, which kept him on the sidelines until February. Another injury in March put him out for the rest of the season. Won his first under-21 cap at Llanelli in February against Northern Ireland.

Nationality: Welsh
Date of Birth: 04/04/1986
Height: 6' 0" (183cm)
Weight: 12st 0lbs (76.27kg)
Previous Clubs: None
Position: Midfielder

(17) Josh Johnson

Signed for Wrexham in August 2006, having impressed in pre-season training, playing wide right. He has been described as "an exciting, midfielder with electric pace". Josh represented Trinidad and Tobago at the under-20 World qualifying tournament in 2001, and has since been a member of the T&T under-23s. He made his senior debut versus China in August, 2001, and has since made three more caps for his country. Josh finished joint top scorer last season for San Juan Jabloteh.

Nationality: Trinidadian
Date of Birth: 16/04/1981
Height: 5' 10" (178cm)
Weight: 10st 7lbs (66.67kg)
Previous Clubs: San Juan Jabloteh T&T
Position: Striker

(18) Jon Newby

Out of contract, Jon Newby was signed on a short-term basis at the start of this season with a view to earning a longer contract. Newby started his career as an apprentice with Liverpool, before moving to Bury for a fee of £100,000 in 2001. He left Bury for Huddersfield in 2003 before returning to Gigg Lane a year later. Always guaranteed a 'warm' reception from the Racecourse faithful, Newby gives Dennis Smith the option of as an out and out striker or as a wide-right-attacking player. Has scored 26 goals in 206 League appearances.

Nationality: English
Date of Birth: 28/11/1978
Height: 6' 0" (183cm)
Weight: 12st 0lbs (76.27kg)
Previous Clubs: Crewe Alexandra (loan), Liverpool, York City (loan), Bury, Huddersfield Town, Kidderminster Harriers (loan), Sheffield Utd (loan)
Position: Striker

(20) Matthew Done

There has been a real buzz about Matty Done for a few years now as he is regarded as one of the most exciting prospects produced at Collier's Park. Matty made his first team debut last season at home to Northampton, and made several other appearance mainly coming off the bench. Given a full game against Darlington in the last match of the season, Matty showed in glimpses what he is capable of. An exciting and pacy winger, he is still only 18. He could be Wrexham's secret weapon this season.

Nationality: English
Date of Birth: 22/07/1988
Height: 5' 10" (178cm)
Weight: 10st 4lbs (65.32kg)
Previous Clubs: None
Position: Midfielder

(21) Marc Richard Williams

Younger brother of Mike, who is also on the club's books. Marc made his debut in the 2-0 win at Rushden in January, and almost scored when hitting a shot against the bar. Likes to hold the ball up in a Steve Watkin/Neil Roberts style, he went on to make his under-21 debut against Northern Ireland at Llanelli in February along with his brother Mike.

Nationality: Welsh
Date of Birth: 27/07/1988
Height: 5' 10" (178cm)
Weight: 11st 12lbs (75.29kg)
Previous Clubs: None
Position: Striker

(23) Neil Roberts

A welcome return to the club for the popular Wrexham-born striker signed from Doncaster Rovers in the summer. Roberts scored 17 goals in 75 games for the club in his first spell, before leaving in a big-money move to Wigan six years ago. He will prove to be a more than adequate replacement for the Jon Walters, and his leadership qualities have been recognised by Denis Smith, who has made him team captain for the coming campaign.

Nationality: Welsh
Date of Birth: 07/04/1978
Height: 5' 10" (178cm)
Weight: 11st 0lbs (69.92kg)
Previous Clubs: Wigan Athletic, Bradford City (loan), Doncaster Rovers, Hull City
Position: Striker

(24) Gareth Evans

The Wrexham-born 19-year-old has been handed his first professional contract earning a one-year deal. Gaz is a beneficiary of our exit from administration, as he was told originally that he would not be kept on following completion of his YTS. A Wrexham fan and a former season-ticket holder at the Racecourse, Gareth will be looking to put pressure on the three senior centre backs ahead of him in the pecking order. Gareth has been an unused substitute on three occasions over the past two seasons and will be desperate to get on the pitch this time around.

Nationality: Welsh
Date of Birth: 10/01/1987
Height: 6' 1" (185cm)
Weight: 12st 12lbs (81.64kg)
Previous Clubs: None
Position: Defender

(25) Michael Paul John Williams

An unflappable type of defender adept at central defence or left back. The 19-year-old made the step up from the reserves to the first team squad last season, enjoying a number of starts and not looking out of place. Made his debut as a sub in a 4-1 defeat at Wycombe last September and made his first start at Oxford in November. Made history with brother Marc by making their under-21 international debuts in the same game against Northern Ireland in February.

Nationality: Welsh
Date of Birth: 27/10/1987
Height: 5' 11" (180cm)
Weight: 12st 0lbs (76.27kg)
Previous Clubs: None
Position: Defender

(27) Jamie Lee Reed

Another fine youngster produced by Steve Weaver's School of Excellence. Young Jamie has had limited opportunities to impress thus far, making several appearances from the bench during the last campaign. The teenage striker signed for Glentoran last season and made serveral appearances until a change in management at the Northern Irish side limited his opportunities. Following our exit from administration, Jamie had shown Dennis Smith enough to be offered a one-year deal for this season.

Nationality: Welsh
Date of Birth: 13/08/1987
Height: 6' 0" (183cm)
Weight: 11st 7lbs (73.03kg)
Previous Clubs: Glentoran
Position: Striker

Football crazy

Wednesday is youth football night in the Evening Leader.
Our great Football Crazy pull-out is packed with pictures,
esults and reports from all of the youth teams around the region.
t's the best way to keep up
with the local youth
ootball scene.

very Wednesday in your

Evening Leader

Coca-Cola League 2 Fixtures

AUGUST				
Sat 5	15:00	A	Wycombe	FL2
Tue 8	**19:45**	**H**	**Grimsby Town**	**FL2**
Sat 12	**15:00**	**H**	**Peterborough**	**FL2**
Sun 20	12:00	A	Chester City	FL2
Wed 23	19:45	A	Sheffield Wed	LGCP
Sat 26	**15:00**	**H**	**Barnet**	**FL2**
SEPTEMBER				
Sun 3	12:00	A	Shrewsbury	FL2
Sat 9	**15:00**	**H**	**Swindon Town**	**FL2**
Wed 13	19:45	A	Accrington	FL2
Sat 16	15:00	A	Stockport	FL2
Sun 24	**12:00**	**H**	**Hereford**	**FL2**
Wed 27	**19:45**	**H**	**Rochdale**	**FL2**
Sat 30	15:00	A	Hartlepool	FL2
OCTOBER				
Sun 8	13:00	A	Bury	FL2
Sat 14	**15:00**	**H**	**MK Dons**	**FL2**
Sat 21	15:00	A	Mansfield Town	FL2
Sat 28	**15:00**	**H**	**Bristol Rovers**	**FL2**
NOVEMBER				
Sat 4	**15:00**	**H**	**Macclesfield**	**FL2**
Sat 18	15:00	A	Notts County	FL2
Sat 25	**15:00**	**H**	**Lincoln City**	**FL2**
DECEMBER				
Tue 5	19:45	A	Torquay United	FL2
Sat 9	15:00	A	Boston Utd	FL2
Sat 16	**15:00**	**H**	**Walsall**	**FL2**
Sat 23	**15:00**	**H**	**Darlington**	**FL2**
Tue 26	12:00	A	Rochdale	FL2
Sat 30	12:00	A	Hereford	FL2
JANUARY				
Mon 1	**15:00**	**H**	**Accrington**	**FL2**
Sat 6	**15:00**	**H**	**Stockport**	**FL2**
Sat 13	15:00	A	Swindon Town	FL2
Sat 20	**15:00**	**H**	**Hartlepool**	**FL2**
Sat 27	15:00	A	Darlington	FL2
FEBRUARY				
Sat 3	**15:00**	**H**	**Wycombe**	**FL2**
Sat 10	15:00	A	Peterborough	FL2
Sun 18	**12:00**	**H**	**Chester City**	**FL2**
Tue 20	19:45	A	Grimsby Town	FL2
Sun 25	**12:00**	**H**	**Shrewsbury**	**FL2**
MARCH				
Sat 3	15:00	A	Barnet	FL2
Fri 9	**19:45**	**H**	**Bury**	**FL2**
Sat 17	15:00	A	MK Dons	FL2
Sat 24	15:00	A	Bristol Rovers	FL2
Sat 31	**15:00**	**H**	**Mansfield Town**	**FL2**
APRIL				
Sat 7	15:00	A	Macclesfield	FL2
Mon 9	**15:00**	**H**	**Notts County**	**FL2**
Sat 14	15:00	A	Lincoln City	FL2
Sat 21	**15:00**	**H**	**Torquay United**	**FL2**
Sat 28	15:00	A	Walsall	FL2
MAY				
Sat 5	**15:00**	**H**	**Boston Utd**	**FL2**

Key

FL2 Football League Division 2
LGCP League Cup

Pontin's Holiday League Fixtures

AUGUST			
Tue 15	7.00	A	Manchester City
Mon 21	**7.00**	**H**	**Blackpool**
Mon 28	**7.00**	**H**	**Chester City**
SEPTEMBER			
Wed 6	2.00	A	Oldham Athletic
Mon 18	**7.00**	**H**	**Accrington Stanley**
OCTOBER			
Mon 9	**7.00**	**H**	**Bury**
Wed 18	7.00	A	Preston North End
NOVEMBER			
Mon 6	**7.00**	**H**	**Rochdale**
Wed 15	7.00	A	Tranmere Rovers
Mon 20	**2.00**	**H**	**Carlisle United**
DECEMBER			
Wed 6	**7.00**	**H**	**Oldham Athletic**
Wed 13	7.00	A	Chester City
JANUARY			
Mon 8	**7.00**	**H**	**Manchester City**
Wed 24	7.00	A	Blackpool
FEBRUARY			
Wed 21	7.00	A	Accrington Stanley
MARCH			
Wed 7	2.00	A	Bury
Mon 19	**7.00**	**H**	**Preston North End**
APRIL			
Wed 4	7.00	A	Rochdale
Wed 11	**7.00**	**H**	**Tranmere Rovers**
Wed 25	2.00	A	Carlisle United

Back row (L-R): Mike Williams, Levi Makin, Michael Jones, Mike Ingham, Danny Williams, Gareth Evans

Middle row (L-R): Kevin Russell, Shaun Pejic, Matty Done, Darren Ferguson, Dennis Lawrence, Steve Evans, Chris Llewellyn, Brian Carey, Mel Pejic

Front row (L-R): Ryan Valentine, Matty Crowell, Simon Spender, Dennis Smith, Neil Roberts, Mark Jones, Jamie Reed

Supporting Wrexham at all 23 league away games this season will mean you will clock up 5,638 miles in a round trip from Wrexham. (This does not include detours to pubs or dropping off your mate in Llangollen on the way home.)

Last season was not the best on the road for Wrexham with only three victories recorded away from the Racecourse and two of these came at the teams who were eventually relegated to the conference – Oxford and Rushden & Diamonds. The other win came at Rochdale when Dave Bayliss was sent off for Dale whilst on loan from Wrexham!

The away campaign starts on the opening day at the scene of last season's heaviest defeat, a 4-1 reversal at **Wycombe**. Wycombe were running away with League Two until the tragic death of promising youngster Mark Philo in January. With then manager John Gorman suffering personal tragedy of his own, added to this the sale of hot-shot Nathan Tyson to Forest and the Chairboys slipped out of the automatic promotion spots. Only their early season form secured them a play-off position. It came as no surprise that they lost out to Cheltenham in the play-off semi finals and manager John Gorman parted company with Wycombe to be replaced by former Scottish international Paul Lambert, who picked up a Champions league winner's medal whilst playing for German side Borussia Dortmund.

Next on the road for Wrexham is the most awaited away game for all Wrexham fans, as the Red Dragons make the short journey up the A483 to **Chester**, although if travelling by bus, Cheshire police insist you make a detour down the A55 and travel in via Queensferry! Although this game has been moved to a 12pm kick off on the Sunday, unlike last season it does not take place on a workday like the original game. Chester looked in dire straights until Mark Wright arrived back at the helm to steer the Deviants away to safety. The game also sees the return of familiar faces Dean Bennett and Jon Walters, who made the short journey over the border to join Chester, although Walters should expect a 'friendly reception' from the Wrexham fans due to the manner he departed the Racecourse in the summer. Wrexham fans will be expecting a greatly improved performance from the team this season.

After fitting in the first round of the Carling Cup at Sheffield Wednesday, Wrexham complete their away derby matches with the short trip to **Shrewsbury** on the first weekend in September. It is a case of watching the press for this game, as it clashes with an international weekend, which will most likely mean the game being called off due to international call-ups. Shrewsbury completed a rare double over Wrexham last season with the Shrews almost securing a play-off spot. This season they are without the services of England's under 19 goalkeeper, Joe Hart, who joined Manchester City in a deal that could be worth up to £1.5million for the Shropshire club. Manager Gary Peters has signed Scottish shot-stopper Ryan Esson as a replacement in a two-year deal in a surprise move from Aberdeen. As at Chester we will be demanding a much improved display for our last ever League trip to Gay Meadow before the Slops move to their new stadium for season 07/08

Next up for Wrexham is **Accrington Stanley**. Who are they? Well, they were the runaway Conference Champions last season and the club we signed Lee McEvilly from. This game has also been moved to a Wednesday night at Accrington's request and will be Wrexham's first visit to Stanley since October 1961 when we won 2-0 (this match is covered in more detail elsewhere in the

book). A new ground for all of us will be sure to see a bumper turn out of Wrexham fans.

Another short trip follows the Accrington game with Wrexham visiting Edgeley Park to face **Stockport County**. For the majority of last season it looked as if Stockport were heading out of the Football League but the arrival of former player Jim Gannon as manager, has turned around Stockport's fortunes. County are a Trust-owned club and we wish them well as they try to reverse the years of mismanagement by the ubiquitous local businessmen.

The last game in September sees Wrexham travel to the North East and to the scene of the most remarkable game the Red Dragons have played in recent times. When Wrexham last faced **Hartlepool**, the game in March 2005, was preceded by a hailstorm and a swirling wind off the North Sea. Despite the inclement conditions, the players, and in particular Juan Ugarte, served up a feast of football with Wrexham running out 6-4 winners with the Basque striker grabbing five of Wrexham's goals. The game sees an early return for Chris Llewellyn to the club he left in the summer after his move from Wrexham did not work out after only one year away from the Racecourse. Wrap up for this one, as even in September the temperatures are likely to hover around the sub-zero mark. It's cold oop North!

Wrexham then travel to **Bury**'s Gigg Lane where manager Chris Casper has signed experienced goalkeeper Alan Fettis to bolster his defensive options after The Shakers flirted with relegation last season. Bury's financial problems have rivalled our own over recent seasons so try and get up to Gigg Lane for this one, it's a cracking view on the away end and you are made very welcome in either the Official Social Club or the very plush Fishpool Liberal Club around the corner.

The final away game in October sees Wrexham travel to Derbyshire to face **Mansfield**. Last season after a poor start, the Stags had an uneventful season, rarely threatening a play off spot or in danger of relegation. The man to watch out for is striker Richard Barker who found the back of the net 18 times in league games in the last campaign and in the corresponding fixture last season he bagged a brace as Mansfield came back to secure a point in a 2-2 draw.

The only league away game in November sees Wrexham travel to Nottingham to face **Notts County**. The Magpies, like Wrexham, have had off the field financial problems in recent years and their flirtation with relegation on the last weekend of season resulted in their then manager, Gudjon Thordason, losing his job at Meadow Lane. Steve Thompson has returned to the club for his second spell in charge of the Magpies after previously being joint manager with Colin Murphy between June 1995 and January 1996.

A Tuesday night in December precludes the possibility of an autumn, or spring mini-break for Wrexham fans. Those who manage to make this, the longest away trip, will deserve medals and also a much-improved display from our last trip to **Torquay**. This game will see Wrexham come up against summer transfer target Jamie Ward, after the former Aston Villa youngster opted for a three-year contract on the English Devon Riviera.

The last away game before Christmas will see former goalkeeper Andy Marriott face Wrexham after his summer move from Torquay to **Boston United**. Marriott's move from Torquay came as a surprise after he was voted player of the season for Torquay last season with his performances help keeping Torquay in the League.

As we all know too well, the rivalry with **Rochdale** fans is intense and it was really inevitable that our game at Dale on Boxing Day would be moved to a noon kick off. So it's early to bed for all of us on the 25th and the chance to make it in time for tea at the in-laws, if you put your foot down after the game. Merry Christmas!!

Wrexham end 2006 on the road with a trip to **Hereford** for the first league encounter at Edgar Street since October 1992, although we have played there twice in the last five years in the FA Cup and LDV Vans. Thankfully, at the time of writing, this game has yet to be moved and it will be the traditional 3pm kick off.

The first league away game of the New Year is a visit to **Swindon**, who have been tipped for an early return to League One following their relegation last season. Now under the guidance Dennis Wise, the former Chelsea midfielder has appointed his former team mate Gus Poyet as his assistant, in an attempt to steer the Robins out of League Two. Start saving, as a ticket for this one will set you back an eye watering £20.

The visit to **Darlington** on the last game of the previous season was a strange trip and not because we had nothing to play for. The stadium itself is stunning, but with fewer than 5,000 fans in a 27,500 seater ground, there was a strange atmosphere around the TFM Arena that afternoon. The game will see Ryan Valentine come up against the team he left in the summer to join Wrexham, whilst Darlington have a former Red on their books, winger Neil Wainwright who is in his fifth season with the North-East club. Pies are only £1 and top quality, which suggests that you wait until you get into the ground before lunching.

Next up for Wrexham is the visit to **Peterborough** in February. Former Lincoln manager, Keith Alexander, took charge of the Posh during the close season after failing in the play offs with the Imps for four successive seasons. Alexander made bricks out of straw at Lincoln and the Posh faithful can expect a better showing than last season's 17th position. Lets hope their style of play is more attractive than the traditional Lincoln alehouse approach.

Wrexham then travel to last season's defeated play-off finalist **Grimsby** for a midweek game in February. Last season, Grimsby were always in the running for an automatic play off position and their failure in the final against Cheltenham resulted in manager Russell Slade departing Blundell Park with Graham Rodger, Slade's assistant, taking over in the managerial hot seat. The romantically named "Findus Stand" has recently gained a new sponsor and will be henceforth known as the "Carlsberg Stand". Let us hope that we can acquire a sponsor for the Mold Road and the new Kop in the near future.

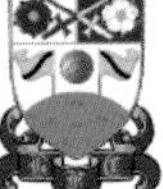

The first game in March sees Wrexham travel to North London to face **Barnet**. One thing Wrexham fans will remember from last season's visit, is to use the toilets before getting to the ground, as there were only four cubicles available inside Underhill. The visit to Underhill had been in some doubt but the club have made arrangements with their local authority for vehicle access to the stadium of match days. Barnet's famous slopping pitch has also been approved by the Football League, although they must put in place 1,000 extra seats, improve segregation and facilities to continue to play at Underhill in future seasons.

If you really must go! **MK Dons** are probably the least favourite team in the

League, and not just League Two. They are that unpopular, a number of teams have been forced to cancel friendlies against Franchise FC following complaints by their fans after they changed their name from Wimbledon and moved to Milton Keynes. This shameful decision shows up the moral vacuum at the heart of football's decision-making process, but in all honesty is just what Wrexham fans would expect from the football authorities. Former Brentford manager Martin Allen has taken over the reigns from Danny Wilson following the Dons' welcome relegation from League One last season. Martin absolutely loathes his nickname of "Mad Dog" so we won't mention it here. Craig Morgan and Matt Baker will be on hand to greet the travelling Wrexham fans.

The last game in March sees Wrexham travel down the M5 to **Bristol Rovers**. The Pirates continue with former Cardiff manager Lennie Lawrence as Director of Football, with current player Paul Trollope as first team coach. £2 off your ticket if you buy it before match day.

Easter Saturday sees Wrexham make the relatively short trip into to Cheshire to face **Macclesfield**. With the game being played in April we should not suffer the problems of last season when the game was called off due to a frozen pitch whilst Wrexham fans were half way into their journey to the Moss Rose ground. Macclesfield had scares on and off the field last season, but Brian Horton managed to steer them to safety on the field whilst the club agreed payment terms with the FA on a repayment of stadium improvement grant. We aren't sure what the stadium's improvement money was spent on but it certainly didn't fund customer service training for their catering staff. We have yet to meet a more ill-mannered and truculent set of oiks at any ground. Take a flask.

The penultimate away game of the campaign is the cross-country trip to **Lincoln**. Alehouse football has been a relative success for the Imps as Lincoln have been involved in the play offs in each of the last four seasons. However, they start this campaign without Manager Keith Alexander after he joined League two rivals Peterborough. Lincoln Supporters' Trust own a significant stake in their club and are working with the local business community to reverse the years of financial crisis and mismanagement the Imps suffered under our old friend John Reames. These days Lincoln always turns a profit, and on similar gates to Wrexham, have a turnover of £3 million. One million more than us!!

The final away trip of the season, play-offs excluded, is a trip via the M54 to **Walsall**. Walsall are another team with a new man in charge after Paul Merson and Kevan Broadhurst left following the club's relegation from League One last season. Richard Money arrived at the Bescot Stadium in May after previously holding coaching positions at Forest, Man City and Coventry. Those big advertising hoardings you see outside the ground net the Saddlers a reputed £1 million per annum, a sum that puts them into a different financial league than most other clubs in League Two. Check out their social club while you are there. It's just what we need at Wrexham.

Quiz Question:

This season we will "only" be meeting 3 of Rooster's former clubs in League action.

Who are they?

Answer:

Hereford, Notts County, Peterborough

Hereford were relegated from the Football League in 1996/97 season after a dramatic last- day encounter with our friends from Brighton. However, unlike Accrington, we have met them several times in cup competition since then.

Firstly in the televised FA Cup match in 1992, over which I will draw a discreet veil, and secondly during our triumphant march to the Millennium Stadium in the LDV.

There was a buzz around the Wrexham section of the ground at Edgar Street. Rumours spread through fans that the club was about to be saved by Surrey businessman Andy Smith. The rumour later confirmed in the next day's papers was enough to have Wrexham fans in a buoyant mood before the game had even begun as at last it seemed Hamilton's reign was over.

The game itself was the Northern Semi-Final of the LDV trophy and at the time those Wrexham fans present wouldn't have realised the significance this game, or competition, played in saving the club. This was a game that conference side Hereford United dominated for long periods - a game they really should have won.

The Wrexham side started with two changes. In goal replacing the hapless Xavi Valero was loan signing Ben Foster with Jim Whitley replacing injured Carlos Edwards. Joining the 400 strong reds fans who had made the journey was former Wrexham manager, now Wales under-21 boss, Brian Flynn, keeping an eye on Mark Jones, Matty Crowell and Craig Morgan.

From the off, it was hard to believe there were two divisions between these sides, as Hereford quickly settled into the game. A penalty claim for Hereford within four minutes was dismissed after Steve Roberts looked to have handled in the air, but the ref waved play on. Within a minute, Juan Ugarte spurned a chance at the other end, with a shot straight at the keeper.

Wrexham struggled to settle down and kept giving the ball away, so it came as no shock when Hereford took the lead on 20 minutes. Stansfield's cross was only partially cleared and Bertram drove the ball home. Within a minute Wrexham had equalised through Ugarte, but this did nothing to dent Hereford's determination. The rest of the half saw chances at both ends, but after 45 minutes it was 1-1.

In the second half Darren Ferguson came on to replace Matty Crowell in midfield, but

to no real effect. Hereford again appeared the stronger of the two sides and soon had a couple more close chances on goal with both Stansfield and Bertram having good efforts. Hereford were now pumping long balls forward and Wrexham were struggling to deal with them.

In a rare chance Chris Llewellyn managed to break forward, but with no support was forced to chance a shot from too tight of an angle. Minutes later, Dennis Lawrence and Steve Roberts worked hard to create a perfect chance for Llewellyn, who headed over when it seemed easier to score than miss. Wrexham were at least now looking stronger and yet only a brave challenge by Lawrence at the other end stopped Hereford regaining the lead.

On the 74th minute however, Wrexham fans forgave Llewellyn's earlier miss when Lawrence flicked on Holt's throw-in and the Welsh international scored from 10-yards out. The Reds were finally in front but Hereford still wouldn't lie down and played out the remainder of the game with as much passion as ever.

The last 10 minutes had Wrexham fans biting their nails as a series of corners were awarded to the home side. Hereford went closest to equalising on the 86th minute when somehow loan keeper Foster managed to grab the ball from between Bertram and Mkandwire as they both tried to force it home. The long-awaited whistle finally came and Wrexham were through to the Northern section final of the LDV trophy.

Hereford Craig Mawson, Simon Travis, Tony James, Tamika Mkandawire, Tom Smith, Mark Robinson, Robert Purdie, Jamie Pitman, Craig Stanley, Adam Stansfield, Daniel Carey-Bertram

Subs: Daniel Williams, David Brown

Wrexham: Ben Foster, Steve Roberts, Craig Morgan, Dennis Lawrence, Jim Whitley, Danny Williams, Mark Jones, Matty Crowell, Andy Holt Juan Ugarte, Chris Llewellyn.

Subs: Darren Ferguson, Scott Green

Attendance : 2,700

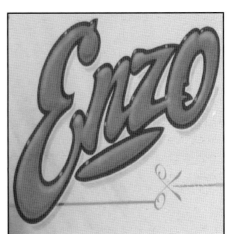

You have to go all the way back to October 31st 1961 for the last time we played Accrington Stanley. Teenage sensation Helen Shapiro was at the top of the hit parade with "Walking Back to Happiness", as the on-fire Robins made the journey up to Peel Park for the midweek fixture.

Having won their last four games, the Robins were on a roll and several hundred fans boarded the Crosville single deckers for the no-frills trip to North Lancashire. Your six shillings and sixpence ticket did not guarantee onboard TV or toilet facilities in those days, but we understand that a comfort break was made in Warrington on the return journey where fish and chip suppers were purchased and devoured with relish. Happy days!

The links between the two clubs go back to the early 20s, when Accrington Stanley along with the Town were founder members of the old Third Division North. A glance at the names of other founder members reveals a host of football names from history; Ashington, Barrow, Durham City, Nelson, Wigan Borough, Southport and Stalybridge Celtic. When you consider the fate of these clubs we haven't done badly at all at Wrexham.

In 1961, Wrexham were making great progress under Ken Barnes and all the talk around the town was of the possibility of promotion. Ken Barnes, his namesake Ron Barnes, Wyn Davies, Alan Fox and Mike Metcalfe formed the nucleus of what many older fans still consider to be our best ever team. Don't tell Denis, but Barnes even had a budget to bring in new players and Kidderminster keeper Kevin Keelan was reported to be his latest target.

Keelan was certainly keen to make the move.

"I would walk to Wrexham to get into league football. " he told the Leader. There's commitment for you!

It was a very different scenario for our opponents. Even at this early stage of the season Accrington were struggling on and off the pitch. A string of poor performances had lead to the inevitable poor attendances at Peel Park. This situation was exacerbated by a spate of bad weather leading to a series of postponed games and the fact that every home game for Stanley clashed with a home fixture for either Burnley or Blackburn, their omnipresent near neighbours. Accrington were in debt and losing money.

As the crisis grew, the Accrington club made, what looked to outside observers, a perverse decision. They invited Bob Lord the "Butcher King", Chairman of near neighbours Burnley, to advise them of their options. (Lord was later to become notorious amongst Wrexham fans for banning the playing of Welsh choir music before our 1974 FA Cup quarter-final at Turf Moor.)

And what advice do you think Lord gave the club? Well after demanding, and receiving, the resignations of the entire Stanley board he recommended the outright closure of the club.

To this end a resignation letter was drafted and swiftly despatched to Alan Hardaker the Secretary of the league and a personal friend of Lord's. The resignation was accepted and Accrington Stanley was no more. The haste in which the club were turfed out of the League was astonishing. In fact Hardaker even vetoed the club's last home game against Exeter that was due to be played the day before their resignation became effective, which he had no right to do.

The town of Accrington was appalled. Meetings were held and money pledged to pay off the debts. Even the club's creditors admitted that they had no intentions of calling in their money. The will was there from the town of Accrington to find a solution and efforts were made to rescind the resignation. However, all this effort was to no avail. The Football League were not interested and League football vanished from Accrington for over 25 years.

The club president Sir William Cocker stated: *"I did think that since Accrington were among the pioneers of the Football League, we would have been given the breathing space we asked for to put our affairs in order. It was surely not too much to ask?"*

If you were of a cynical frame of mind you may ponder what benefits the Chairman of Burnley could envisage in the closing down of a near neighbour, but we are sure that these supposed benefits played no part in Mr Lord's strategy of closing down Stanley.

Luckily we now live in a more enlightened era where the League fiercely protects the rights of all of its member clubs and has a stringent fit and proper-persons test for club owners to ensure the highest possible standards of probity and accountability. This could never happen again.

As to the game itself, the Robins duly rolled over Stanley 2-0 courtesy of goals from Mickey Metcalf and Wyn Davies in front of a crowd of 2,800 - Stanley's lowest of the season.

Four wins on the trot became five and Ken Barnes' wonder team of the early 60s were on course for the club's first ever promotion the following spring.

The points were later deducted from our total as Stanley's results for the season were expunged from the record.

So welcome back to league football Accrington Stanley. We look forward to renewing our rivalry and wish you better luck this time around.

Anyhow, what are Nelson up to these days?

"Ond pwy ti'n cefnogi go iawn?" - dyma'r cwestiwn dwi'n cael yn aml iawn gan blant Ynys Môn wedi mi ddweud fy mod i'n cefnogi Wrecsam. Ffefryn arall ydi "Ond pwy ti'n cefnogi yn yr Uwchgynghrair?"

Mae'n gallu bod yn dorcalonnus ar brydiau gweld yr holl grysau Manchester United, Lerpwl ac Everton ac, erbyn hyn, yr holl grysau Chelsea ar hyd a lled gogledd Cymru pan fo gennym glwb ein hunain i fod yn falch ohono.

Clwb Pêl-droed Wrecsam, y clwb proffesiynol hynaf yng Nghymru. Clwb gafodd ei ffurfio ymhell cyn Newton Heath; clwb oedd yn chwarae'n rheolaidd cyn i aelodau Glwb Pêl-droed St Domingo's gael ffrae am gost rhentu maes Anfield a chroesi Parc Stanley i chwarae yn Goodison.

Yn wir, erbyn i Glwb Pêl-droed Lerpwl ddod i fodolaeth, roedd pêl-droedwyr Wrecsam eisoes wedi ymddangos yn rownd derfynol Cwpan Cymru ar bum achlysur, gan godi'r tlws enwog ddwywaith.

Ac fel Cymry balch, mae'n bwysig cofio cyfraniad y clwb i ddatblygiad y tîm rhyngwladol.

Yng ngêm gyntaf rhyngwladol Cymru yn erbyn Yr Alban ym 1876, roedd dau aelod o'r tîm yn chwarae dros Wrecsam ac fe chwaraewyd y gêm ryngwladol cyntaf ar dir Cymreig ar Y Cae Ras.

Mae llond trol o enwau mawr y byd pêl-droed yng Nghymru wedi dilyn ôl troed Alfred Davies ac Edwin Cross drwy wisgo crys coch Wrecsam a chrys coch Cymru, yn eu mysg, Wyn Davies, Arfon Griffiths, Mickey Thomas, Joey Jones, Dai Davies ac yn fwy diweddar, Neil Roberts a'i frawd Stephen Roberts.

Felly fe ddylai fod yn gam amlwg i gefnogwyr pêl-droed gogledd Cymru gefnogi'r Dreigiau yn lle tyrru dros y ffin i gefnogi'r timau mawr, yn enwedig o gofio bod y clwb yn meithrin talent ifanc yr ardal hefyd.

Tymor diwethaf cafodd y ddau frawd, Marc a Mike Williams, sydd yn hanu o Fae Colwyn, eu cyfleoedd â'r tîm cyntaf a chyda chwaraewyr megis Danny Williams, Mark Jones, Matty Done, Levi Mackin a Simon Spender yn fechgyn lleol, heb sôn am Ryan Valentine a Steve Evans sydd newydd ddychwelyd i'w tref enedigol, mae'n braf gallu cefnogi clwb sydd â charfan o fechgyn lleol yn hytrach na chwaraewyr ariangar o dramor.

Mae sicrhau bodolaeth Clwb Pêl-droed Wrecsam yn golygu bod nifer fawr o chwaraewyr talentog gogledd Cymru yn cael y cyfle i ennill bywoliaeth fel pêl-droediwr proffesiynol. Ond rhywbeth sydd yr un mor bwysig yw bod y cannoedd o fechgyn a merched ifanc sydd yn tyrru i Barc Colliers ar gyfer sesiynau ymarfer yr holl dimau academi yn parhau i fod yn rhan o glwb pêl-droed proffesiynol ac i gael hyfforddiant safonol.

Wrth gwrs, mae gennym ni'n chwaraewyr egsotig hefyd - neb llai na'r cawr, Dennis Lawrence; y chwaraewr cyntaf erioed o'r clwb i chwarae yng Nghwpan y Byd - a'r gobaith yw bod y gwr o Wlad y Basg, Juan Ugarte, yn gallu profi ei ffitrwydd er mwyn cymryd ei le yn y llinell flaen unwaith eto, ond mae'n bwysig cofio mai clwb Cymreig yw Wrecsam - clwb sydd yng nghanol ei chymuned ac yn glwb i holl bobl gogledd Cymru.

Mae **Gary Pritchard** yn ohebydd chwaraeon â BBC Cymru'r Byd, gwasanaeth Cymraeg y BBC ar-lein:

www.bbc.co.uk/chwaraeon

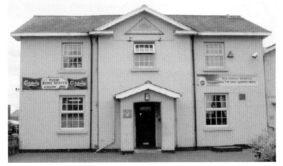

Wrexham Supporters Trust

President
Arfon Griffiths MBE

Trust Board:

Bruce Clapton (Chairman)
Mark Williams (Treasurer)
Lesley Griffiths
Terry Heath
Sally Poppit
Simon Johnson
Rob Griffiths (Vice Chairman)
Lindsay Jones (Secretary)
Wyn Griffiths
Peter Jones
Richard Purton

Co-opted:
Richard Owen
Phil Lloyd
Kevin Baugh

The Wrexham Supporters' Trust was created out of the ashes of the WINS organisation some two years ago. WINS was founded in March 2002 with the purpose of raising funds to strengthen the playing squad at the club. Members paid £10 per month under the "beer a week scheme" and over the two years in existence, the organisation contributed over £40,000 of funding to the club helping to fund the signings of Marius Rovde, Scott Green, Paul Edwards, Chris Llewellyn and Andy Dibble.

The change in the club's ownership from Pryce Griffiths to Mark Guterman led to a change in strategy for the Trust. As the full extent of the clubs troubles became apparent radical measures were called for and WINS was reborn as the Wrexham Supporters' Trust (WST) in 2004.

If we go back just two years, although it seems a lot longer, the situation facing the club was that of an owner with no interest in the club, a Chief Executive claiming that the club's debts could only be solved by a move from the ground and a generally demoralised fan base lacking organisation and focus. It was a "Summer of Discontent" that none of us had ever imagined was possible.

The WST mandate was to buy the club. Initially the Trust set about debunking the myth that we needed to move from the Racecourse. The building plan, drawn up by Charles Wardle and Nick Stockdale, proved that by developing the surplus land behind the Kop it was possible for enough money to be raised to pay off the debts and set the club up in some measure of health. This plan was unveiled to a packed public meeting at the Miners Institute and was widely reported in the press and on TV. The fight-back had begun!

Attracting a blue-chip backer for this scheme enabled the WST to put two bids to owner Hamilton to buy him out of Wrexham. Needless to say he rejected both offers in his customary graceless fashion. There was not enough money in the deal to interest him and he was not prepared to wait for his "big pay-day". Ironically, if he had accepted the offer, he would now be sitting on a tidy profit rather than the net loss he incurred on the "Wrexham Project".

This was a massive setback at the time which only hardened the fans' determination to win. Membership of the WST was growing and Wrexham fans now had a strong voice in the battle. The Wardle/Stockdale plan had shown that we did not have to move to prosper, there was support from the Council and Assembly and to all intents and purposes Hamiltons vision was dead in the water.

In the two years since becoming WST the Trust membership has grown to over 1,000 members. We have put over £60,000 into the club, whilst in administration, to help with running costs. We have raised over £200,000 to buy equity in the new club. We organise the Open Day and the Player of the Season Dinners.

We run the club merchandising, transforming a loss maker into a highly profitable business.

We underwrote the players' contracts last season. We bought the kit that the players and fans are wearing this season. We have supported the Ticket Office and commercial departments during heavy workload periods. Our members have spent a long-hot summer refurbishing the ground to roll back years of neglect. We have just taken over the running of the Junior Dragons. We have brought lager brewing back to the town and now we have just entered the world of publishing!

It's fair to say that collectively we make a difference!

At our June AGM, our membership voted to raise a total of £250,000 to buy equity in the new club and to push on for board representation. Both of these aims are crucial to ensuring that we never again have to face the battles of the last two years. We have come a long way in that time, but in truth the real work starts from here. Wrexham is a massive club waiting to be released from years of mismanagement. Not many clubs have a fan-base as committed and as passionate as ours. Can you imagine how this club will look if the energy put into saving the club is now channelled into putting it back where it belongs?

Muhammad Ali once wrote the shortest poem ever written.

Me!

We!

Our strength is in our solidarity and if we all work together, there is really no limit on what we can achieve.

C'mon the Town!!!

JOIN THE TRUST:

Wrexham Supporters' Trust
PO Box 2200
Wrexham, LL11 9WG

Phone: 07981 151958

Website: wst.org.uk

Wrexham FC Supporters' Association
Supporting Wrexham Football Club since 1926

Chairman and Treasurer:
Carroll Clark

Deputy Chairman:
Phil Davies (aka Phil Pies)

Secretary:
Richard Owen

Committee Members:
Steve Clarke, Ray Clarke
Rob Clarke, David Davies
Gareth Griffiths, Geraint Lloyd
David Price and Phil Wynn

The history of supporters' clubs in Wrexham

Wrexham AFC Supporters' Club (as it was then known) was born in August 1926 at the Black Lion pub in Wrexham. The driving force behind Wrexham's first supporters club was Jack Williams who was born in Summerhill in 1898. Jack saw his first Wrexham match in 1910, a Birmingham League encounter with Hednesford Town and was inspired to form a supporters' club. He was a man of great vision who recognised the importance of fans working together and with Tom Hodgson of Northampton Town, formulated the idea of the National Federation of Football Supporters' Clubs, which was inaugurated in 1927.

Representing fans at a national level

The 'Nat Fed' played a very important role in representing and campaigning for fans' interests before it merged with the Football Supporters' Association (FSA) to form the Football Supporters' Federation (FSF). The FSF has taken the supporters' movement forward to broaden its appeal and influence within English and Welsh football. It is appropriate that this year's FSF Conference was hosted by Wrexham Supporters' Association at Llangollen's Wild Pheasant Hotel.

The Football Supporters' Federation

One of our guest speakers was John Lloyd - former Premier League referee and now assessor - but perhaps better known to our older fans as the son of Cliff Lloyd. Cliff was 'Mr Wrexham' in the post-war era, holding the posts of Secretary and Acting Manager (on a number of occasions). He was always on duty and promoted a very positive image of Wrexham Football Club at every opportunity, something we need to recreate today. No wonder he was unanimously elected as one of the 20 inaugural members of the Hall of Fame!

The Hall of Fame

We're very proud to recognize the people who have contributed so much to Wrexham Football Club through our Hall of Fame, which you can view on our website, Wrexham Dragons. The Hall of

Fame recognises the contribution of players, officials and fans who have achieved so much for this great club. We'll be inaugurating more members to the Hall of Fame this season, so please join us to celebrate our great history – details to be announced very soon.

Our role within Wrexham Football Club

Over the years the Supporters' Association has played a major role in the success of the football club. The Association helped to fund and build the old stand on the Kop, ran the Centre Spot club shop in the old Mold Road stand and ran the Away Travel Scheme. We had over 2,500 members at the height of our success.

We've played a big role in the past success of Wrexham Football Club and want to support this club to become great once again.

Looking to the future

In the past we've given our unconditional support to Wrexham Football Club, but believe it is now time for the fans to have a much bigger say in how the club is run. That's why we're supporting the Wrexham Supporters' Trust's drive to purchase shares in the club. We believe that this yearbook is an excellent way of bringing all supporters' clubs together to raise money for this common aim.

We're still raising money for Wrexham Football Club through the 50/50 competition, helping out on match days by managing the NEWI car park and supporting the community by providing Hospital Broadcasts to Wrexham Maelor Hospital. We're also planning to build on the success of the inaugural Wrexham FC Charity Shield Competition, which helped to raise over £2,000 for local charities.

To celebrate our past and to look forward to supporting Wrexham Football Club in the future, we're planning to celebrate our 80th birthday with a very special dinner at the new Ramada Jarvis Hotel on September 10th, 2006. Look out for more details on our website Wrexham Dragons and in the local press nearer to the time.

For more information on our forthcoming plans please visit our Wrexham Dragons website at:

http://www.wrexhamdragons.co.uk

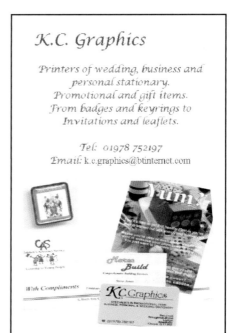

Chairman John Humphreys
Treasurer Brian Davies
Secretary Dave Jones

Can it really be twelve whole years since we took those first faltering steps? Our inaugural meeting - 20 eager souls huddled around a back-room snooker table in Shrewsbury's Telepost Club - offered up few clues of what lay in store.

Gradually, though, as our expertise grew to accompany the limitless enthusiasm, we began to make our mark; a number of genuinely innovative ventures have encouraged membership growth year on year, passing the 250 mark last January. With a total turnover now approaching a quarter of a million pounds its little wonder that we are now seen as an important cog in the Football Clubs supporters machine.

The secret of our success? Hard to say, because I don't think we've ever really set out a definite plan for ourselves. The Shreds have, quite literally, evolved naturally: we've just drifted along with the tide. We have always been careful to ensure, though, that Honesty and Respect are constantly reflected in everything we have done, and I'm proud to say that practically everyone we've met on our journey have become very good friends of ours as a result.

Now that the club is free of the shackles of administration the Shropshire Reds, just like every other supporters' group, must face up to new challenges and opportunities. Individually, very much will be asked of every single fan who claims to have Wrexham FC in their hearts to do everything possible to ensure the horrors of the past four years are never repeated.

Collectively, we're in pretty good fettle; united against a common enemy we now have an infrastructure better organised than at any time throughout the near half century that I've followed the club. The Official Supporters' Association head up the family tree, with strong healthy branches now stretching out to London, Shropshire, Manchester, Holywell, Buckley and Rhos. And of course, at the roots, there's also the awesome work undertaken by the Supporters Trust. How wonderful it would be to see further growth in the years to come as we all chase Denis dream of Championship football at the Racecourse.

The Shropshire Reds re always pleased to welcome enthusiastic, devoted fans of Wrexham Football Club. If you fit the bill, then please get in touch with us;

Visit our Website www.shropshirereds.com

e mail us shreds@wafc123.freeserve.co.uk

or write to us at: PO BOX 547,Shrewsbury,Shropshire,SY3 8YY

Remember - this is a job for ALL of us, not just the same old few, and we'll never know what we can achieve if we don't try.

The Manchester Reds was founded in November 1997 by a group of Manchester based Wrexham fans. Our famous "Manchester Reds" flag can be seen at all home games on the Turf side of the Kop.

Since our formation The Manchester Reds have contributed over £1400 to Wrexham AFC in the form of sponsorship.

1. Brian Carey's Home Shirt 2002-2003

2. Paul Barrett's Home Shirt 2001-2002

3. Lee Roche's Home Shirt 2000-2001

4. Brian Carey's Away Shirt 1999-2000

5. Craig Skinner's Away Shirt 1998-1999

6. Page Sponsorship of 2003 Wrexham AFC Calendar

7. Donation of Rucksack & Cap To Phil Hardy Testimonial Fund

8. Two bricks in the Mold Road Stand 1999–2000

9. Registration of internet name **www.wrexhamfc.co.uk**

10. Donation to the Sponsored Walk to Cardiff

As a supporters' club the Manchester Reds main function is to arrange travel to home and away games within the Greater Manchester area and further afield.

Check out the Travel Club section on our website for all travel details.

Regular meetings are held which are open to all Wrexham fans.

The Manchester Reds also produce a bi-monthly newsletter that goes out to all members. 'The Exiled Dragon' is full of our forthcoming events, the latest news and also travel arrangements for forthcoming games.

As a recognised supporters' club with Wrexham AFC, the Manchester Reds now have priority booking status on big all-ticket games - both home and away.

Membership: It is free to join the Manchester Reds and we welcome all Wrexham fans from the Greater Manchester areas. So if you already live in Greater Manchester or are about to move to Manchester then give us a shout and travel to matches with fellow Reds.

Secretary: Pete Banks

Contact Details: E-mail: Pete@feed_me_till_i_want_no_more.co.uk

Website: http://www.manchester-reds.com/

Buckley Reds at the Supporters 8-a-side tournament in May. We won it!!

The Buckley and District Reds was formed on 25th January 2006 when a total of 29 people turned up to our initial meeting. It was agreed to form the Buckley and District Reds and everybody who attended that night signed up as founder members.

Our aim is to raise funds to put into the club through sponsorship and also donations to WST and just as importantly to have a bit of fun on the way!

Buckley and District Reds Committee

Chairman: Bryn Jones
Secretary: Dave Kelsall
Treasurer: Tony Williams

Meeting Venues: To date we have held meetings at the following venues, the Hope & Anchor in Buckley (Mike Williams pub), Buckley Working Men's Club and the Royal British Legion in Penyffordd.

Membership: is just £5 for adults and £1 for children.

Contact Details: Membership is open to all. We currently have 70 members and are keen to welcome new friends. Anybody wishing to join or come to a meeting should call Bryn on 07783430301

Website:
http://www.buckleyreds.co.uk

IN MEMORY OF PAUL ANTROBUS 1964-2006

FOUNDER MEMBER & TREASURER

BUCKLEY AND DISTRICT REDS

SADLY MISSED BY ALL HIS MATES

The 'Rhos and District Reds' supporters group was formed on Thursday 27th April at the Coach and Horses Pub in Rhos. The decision to try and form a group was the result of a discussion on the unofficial Wrexham website 'Red Passion', which made us realise just how much support there is for the club in the local area.

Many of us were already members of other supporters groups such as the Shropshire Reds, Buckley & District Reds etc, and seeing the effort these groups put in and the events they enjoy, made us appreciate the fact that we live right on the doorstep of the club and yet very few of us knew each other and there was nothing in place that celebrated being a 'Jacko' and a Wrexham fan.

A number of people put in a lot of hard work to get the group up and running, whilst Ian and Lynne at the Coach and Horses being Wrexham fans, were more than happy to host the event. The night was a great success with over 40 people attending and we hope it will be the first of many.

The events of the last few years have shown that we must all take steps to ensure that history cannot repeat itself. Wrexham AFC is a fantastic club that should always be at the heart of our community. The Rhos and District Reds are committed to becoming an established supporters' group and are 110 percent behind the WST in their efforts to secure fans representation on the new board.

Here's to a new era and a fantastic season for Denis and the lads!

Aims - we are hoping to arrange social events in the People's Republic where fans can meet and talk to players and management.

We will also be arranging travel to games and fund raising for both the club and the WST.

Its going to be a great season.

Membership: Just £5

Contact: Please e-mail Steve at llanongard@aol.com for a membership form.

The London Reds was formed after the famous promotion game at Northampton way back in 1993. Following the match it was noticeable that many Wrexham fans were travelling back to London by train. We started talking and the London Reds was formed.

Our membership is drawn from across the South East of England as well as London and we are keen to welcome new members.

Wrexham AFC London Reds Committee

Chairman:	Dave Harris
Secretary:	Barry Jones
Treasurer:	Dave Jones
Webmaster:	Stuart Evans

Meeting venue

We meet at the The Bunch of Grapes St Thomas Street. (Nearest tube and rail station London Bridge) This also hosts our annual general meeting and the evening with Denis Smith.

This season we will be running trips to several games and also our 50/50 draw club, which has a top quarterly prize of over £200.

We will be running a coach to the last home game of the season, for the fourteenth year in succession. In addition there will be the ever-popular mid-winter coach trip as well as train journeys to home and away games.

(The opening game of the season sees us on the train from Marylebone station, to be met at High Wycombe station by Harris Coachways who will take us to the Bird in Hand pub, then onto the game and back to the station.)

Annual Membership

Annual membership is unchanged for the 14th season in a row at £7.50

Contact Details

Contact details You can find details of application forms, London Reds sponsorship activity, the 50/50 draw, contact details and trips to home and away games on our web site or contact Secretary Barry Jones on 07973 512258 .

Website

www.geocities.com/wrexham_london_reds

Holywell Reds: Wrexham Supporters' Clubs
8-A-Side Football Champions 2002

Holywell Reds

Chairman: Paul Evans
Secretary: John Evans

Committee: Barry Davies & Shaun Holden

The Holywell & District Reds were formed in July 2001 by brothers John and Paul Evans, from the Holywell Area.

With so many Wrexham supporters living in and around Holywell, it was decided that by forming a supporters' group we could bring fans together and support Wrexham FC as a group.

We began by organising bus trips to away matches and ironically our first match turned out to be Brian Flynn's last after Wrexham were thrashed 5-0 at Tranmere.

Although Wrexham were relegated that season, the Holywell Reds managed to attract over 50 members from the area.

Since then we have sponsored a match every season and various players. They include Waynne Phillips, Paul Whitfield and Shaun Pejic.

This season we will be backing Welsh under-21 striker Marc Williams and sponsoring the Hartlepool United match.

Although Alex Hamilton has finally gone, there is still a long road ahead and by working together we can achieve a successful outcome.

Therefore, we are urging all Wrexham supporters from the area to join the Holywell & District Reds and enjoy the new and exciting future that at one time looked a very distant prospect!

We hold regular meetings at the Abbots Arms in Holywell and all Wrexham fans are more than welcome to come along. This season we will be arranging meetings with players and officials and thus strengthening the ties between the club and the Holywell area.

Its just a £5 for adults and £3.50 for juniors to join, so if you live in the Holywell area get in touch with John Evans on jonev@supanet.com or Shaun Holden on flewog87@hotmail.com, otherwise check out the official website and programme for details of our meetings - Keep The Faith!

With the club finally out of the shackles of Administration we at the Centre for Excellence are raring to help take the club to a higher level.

It only seems like yesterday that we finished last season, and we were very pleased with the way season went for all our teams. It was very productive on all fronts, and we managed to make big strides in many areas. All teams throughout the season produced an impressive set of results with performances to match. For me, good results made by individual and team displays are what we are always aiming for.

On the tour front, trips to Holland, Repton and Glasgow proved to be very beneficial, not only for the players involved, but to the club in general. Many good contacts and friendships have been made which I'm sure will be put to good use in the future.

The general aims of the centre are to create an environment that caters for the players needs in helping them to maximise their potential, and the club ultimately will help them develop as footballers and as young men.

It is important that we all pull together and make sure that we reach our aims for the season, which is to realise the overall aim of Wrexham FC in producing home grown players for the first team.

Enjoy the season,

Steve Weaver - Head of Youth

Wrexham FC Centre for Excellence is determined to continue to produce youth players that meet the high standards necessary to continue the future development of the Club. We intend to achieve this vision by selecting young footballers from our local community by providing them with a programme designed for emphasising the full range of personal growth.

The Coaching Team – Full Time Staff

Steve Weaver - Head of Youth Development

Steve Cooper - Assistant Head of Youth (Ages 9-16)

Mark Morris - Head of Goalkeepers

Ben McKenzie - Head of Sports Science

Centre of Excellence Staff

Richie Buchanan & Ritson Lloyd – Physiotherapists

Tricia Deary-Furber – Administrator

John Reardon – Chief Scout

Evan Evans – North Wales Scout

Phil Boyle & Danny Copnall – Under-8/9s coaches

James Parry – Under-10s coach

Kevin Quigley & Mark Cox – Under-11s coaches

Ben Heath & Danny Williams – Under-12s coaches

Brian Potts & Darren Ferguson – Under-13s coaches

Lee Jones & Neil Roberts – Under-14s coaches

Steve O'Shaughnessy & Gary Speed – Under-15s coaches

Andy Davies – Under-16s coach

Steve Weaver & George McGowan – Under-18s coaches

Mark Morris & Tim Roberts - Goalkeeping coaches

Youth Fixtures 2006/07

2006		Home	Away
3rd Sept	Stockport County	9, 11, 13, 15	10, 12, 14, 16
10th Sept	Macclesfield Town	14, 16	13, 15
17th Sept	Tranmere Rovers	10, 12, 14, 16	9, 11, 13, 15
24th Sept	Port Vale	9, 11, 13, 15	10, 12, 14, 16
1st Oct			
8th Oct	Walsall	10, 12, 14, 16	9, 11, 13, 15
15th Oct	Shrewsbury Town	11, 13, 15	10, 12, 14
22nd Oct	Chester City	10, 12, 14, 16	9, 11, 13, 15
29th Oct			
5th Nov	Chester City	9, 11, 13, 15	10, 12, 14, 16
12th Nov	Stockport County	9, 11, 13, 15	10, 12, 14, 16
19th Nov	Macclesfield Town	13, 15	14, 16
26th Nov	Tour		
3rd Dec	Tranmere Rovers	9, 11, 13, 15	10, 12, 14, 16
10th Dec	Port Vale	10, 12, 14, 16	9, 11, 13, 15
17th Dec			
2007			
7th Jan	Walsall	9, 11, 13, 15	10, 12, 14, 16
14th Jan	Shrewsbury Town	10, 12, 14, 16	9, 11, 13, 15
21st Jan			
28th Jan	In Service Training		
4th Feb	Stockport County	9, 11, 13, 15	10, 12, 14, 16
11th Feb	Walsall	14, 16	13, 15
18th Feb	Tranmere Rovers	10, 12, 14, 16	9, 11, 13, 15
25th Feb			
4th Mar	Port Vale	9, 11, 13, 15	10, 12, 14, 16
11th Mar	Walsall	10, 12, 14, 16	9, 11, 13, 15
18th Mar			
25th Mar	Shrewsbury Town	9, 11, 13, 15	10, 12, 14, 16
1st Apr			
8th Apr	Chester City	10, 12, 14, 16	9, 11, 13, 15

The Centre for Excellence are always looking to improve all departments, and over the past four years we have worked extremely hard in providing the best facilities and provisions for the players. The Centre has organised Golf Days, social evenings and had two very successful pre-season friendly games against Liverpool FC.

The money raised by these events have been earmarked for projects that would benefit players and running of the Centre. Over the past two years we have seen significant progress in the quality of the pitches, facilities, equipment and overall look of the Centre. Money has also gone into providing our own resource centre for game analyses and smartboard. Both of which will be used to full effect this season.

The Centre is in the process of our most ambitious and biggest project to date of replacing our three quarter size astro turf with a brand new state-of-the-art full-size playing surface. Planning permission has been granted and work is about to commence.

This season we will be looking to raise more money and we will be running activities throughout the year. Anyone who can help with sponsorship or with fundraising support for us will be much appreciated.

The Playing Squads 2006/07

Under-9s

Nathan Paul Broadhead
Jack Chambers
Matthew Clewley
John Davies
Kieran Joseph Evans
Ryan Hughes
Thomas Hughes
Rakim Yasir Newton
Stephen David Rimmer
Shaun William Trousdale

Under-10s

Todd Barron
Danny Burgess
Jonathan Crump
Matthew Dunbabin
Jake Fernandez-Hart
Matthew Graham-Hammons
Jack Ireland
Daniel Jones
Scott Munro
Jake Phillips
Daniel Reynolds
Ben Richards
Joshua Robertson
Jordan Sheerin

Under-11s

Thomas Batten
Iwan Cartwright
Oliver Cooke
Ryan Crump
Jack Driver
Jordan Evans
Declan Fulton
Robert Gilroy
James Littlemore
Jordan Maddock
Daniel Miller
Jack Smith
Curtis Strong
Richard Tomassen
Jordan Williams

Under-12s
Adam Bailey
Wesley Bennett
Oliver Bentley
Luke Douglas
Robert David Evans
Conor Patrick Fay
Tom Freeman
Conner Luke Kendrick
Adam Lee
Joshua Lyth
Gregory Patrick Mills
Kyle Parle
Aled Parry
Jonathan Parry
Jonathan Royle
Max Tatler

Under-13s
Naim Arsan
George Baxter
Jared Bennett
Chris Boswell
Ryan Edwards
Max Fargin
Naser Farhat
Elliott Hewitt
Mattew Regan
Kieran Murphy
Nathan Nicholls
Matthew Owen
Christopher Pulford
Connor Shutt
Stephen Tomassen

Under-14s
Thomas Boam
Paul Cain
Niall Challoner
Jack Chaloner
James Colbeck
George Cowell
Owen Davies
Stephen Ferrigan
Michael Jones
Connor Hunter
Jon-Paul Molyneux
Louis Moss
Joshua O'Connell
Max Penk
Liam Rice
Thomas Woodward

Under-15s
Thomas Bainbridge
Daniel Birks
Ryan Catahan
Leon Clowes
Matthew Cross
Phillip Davies
Joshua Griffiths
Joseph Imlach
Edward Moss
Joshua Kyle Rush
Nicholas Rushton
Ben Smith
Kieran Smith

Under-16s
Andreas Alvarado
Benito Apollonio
Robert Bennett
Thomas Bonnett
River Cass
Michael Cronshaw
Kai Edwards
Daniel Hughes
Matthew Hurdman
Jack Jones
Rhys Llwyd
Rob Pearson
Arran Pritchard
Simon Williams

Youth Players
Steven Backhouse
John Hunt
Lee Jones
Christopher Marriott
Thomas Matischok
Christopher Maxwell
Jamie Price
Simon Smith
Mark Stewart
Thomas Vickers
Vincent Whelan
Paul David Williams

I'm not surprised that the question of Wrexham's formation comes up now and again. The club badge states 1873, but many books, and even in our own programme at times I have seen 1872. The Supporters' Trust even branded 1872 on some of their clothing that they were once selling. So why, is there a question mark over the year we were born?

I went out to find Peter Jones, who has wrote five books on the club and ask him why this was the case. He informed me:

"In the early 1970's a 15-year-old lad by the name of Anthony Jones, brought out a book called the 'Robins Story'. It was the first book that was really written on Wrexham Football Club, apart from club handbooks.

"I knew Anthony from selling programmes, as he was in fact the programme editor at that time, which was a remarkable achievement for someone so young. In his book, Anthony backed up the theory that the club was founded in 1873, and following on from this, the club decided that they would have a new club badge to celebrate our centenary, to replace the town's 'Wrexham Regis' crest that they wore on the club's shirt. The Wrexham Leader newspaper, even ran a competition to find the new crest, from which the winner came up with the badge that we still wear on our shirts......with 1873 on it.

"Going back to Anthony's book, when he wrote it, and we must remember his age, as he would not have been able to look further a field than our very own Wrexham Library. So when I first began researching the club's history, the Library was one of my first port of calls. However, I found that the main newspaper of that time was the 'Wrexham Guardian', but the Wrexham Library only kept that newspaper back to.........1873.

"I found out that the 'Wrexham Guardian' actually went back to 1865, and copies of these were kept at Colindale in London, the National Library of Wales in Aberystwyth, and also at the Clwyd Records Office in Ruthin. I travelled to Ruthin, to look back through old copies of the paper. I looked all the way back to 1865, scouring the paper for anything connected with football. It was here that I found the first ever mention of Wrexham Football Club.

"It was in the 'Wrexham Guardian' dated 5th October 1872. The actual script stated; "Wrexham Foot-ball Club – A meeting, chiefly composed of members of the cricket club, was held at the Turf Hotel on Saturday last (28th September), for the purpose of starting the foot-ball club for the ensuing season. The attendance was large and the following gentlemen were appointed to the management, viz:- President: F. Page, Esq.; Hon.Sec, Mr W.H. Pritchard. Committee: Messrs T. Walker, N. Humphreys, B. Dale, E. Cross, G. Pritchard, and E. Evans. The opening game will be played this day (Saturday) at 3pm, when a good muster is expected.

"This obviously seems to be the very first meeting of the Football Club, and that the club badge should read '1872'. I know it would be low on the agenda, but maybe the club's new directors can put this right one day soon, as it would certainly stop the confusion and the question of 'what year where we formed?' coming up."

Opposite is the actual clipping from the Wrexham Guardian - see highlighted area. [Warning, don't read the news item above the football clip whilst eating your breakfast!]

SATURDAY, OCTOBER 5, 1872.

His remarks were met with a general storm of disapprobation, resulting in the total discomfiture of the speaker, who had to resume his seat. Truly the Radical cause must be extremely weak if it requires to be bolstered up by such unseemly displays as these, and we are afraid it will require more than the assistance of Sir Robert Cunliffe to "strengthen the Liberal cause in Denbighshire." Are we to presume that the reception accorded to the Hon. G. T' Kenyon at the agricultural dinner has so aroused the indignant feelings of Mr Williams that his political passion cannot even be checked at a social dinner. We join in wishing the Lord Lieutenant and his amiable bride a happy and prosperous life, and trust the day is far distant when Conservatives and Liberals will be precluded from meeting together and sinking their political differences to celebrate the marriage of their landlord and neighbour.

LOCAL TAXATION.

AMONGST the various topics discussed at the recent agricultural meetings, the question of local taxation naturally suggested itself. Mr Cavendish Bentinck, at Whitehaven, made a sensible reference to it, showing that through the resolu-

...vices, which, we are glad to say, are remarkably well attended, and it was agreed that they accounts should be postponed until the Easter vestry.

FATAL ACCIDENT ON THE RAILWAY AT RUABON.—On Thursday, as Robert Boast, of Rhos, was walking along the branch line which communicates with the Great Western Railway, the up coal train knocked him down and he was fearfully mutilated, his legs being severed from his body, death resulting instantaneously. Deceased was about 56 years of age, and was by trade a painter. It seems he had been painting at Gardden, and was returning from his work along the line when the accident occurred.

WREXHAM FOOT-BALL CLUB.—A meeting, chiefly composed of members of the cricket club, was held at the Turf Hotel on Saturday last, for the purpose of starting the foot-ball club for the ensuing season. The attendance was large, and the following gentlemen were appointed to the management, viz:—President: F. Page, Esq.; hon. sec., Mr W. H. Pritchard. Committee: Messrs T. Walker, N. Humphreys, B. Dale, E. Cross, G. Pritchard, and E. Evans. The opening game will be played this day (Saturday) at 3 p.m., when a good muster is expected.

CHURCH SERVICES AT ROSSETT.—On Tuesday night a meeting was held in connection with the Local Association for Foreign Missions, the Society for the Propogation of the Gospel with its usual liberality supplying all the

Matt Crowell (b. Bridgend 3rd July 1984)

Season	League apps	League gls	FA Cup apps	FA Cup gls	WPC apps	WPC gls	Carling Cup apps	Carling Cup gls	LDV apps	LDV gls	Total apps	Total gls
2003/04	9/6	1	-	-	1/1	0	0/1	0	1/1	0	11/9	1
2004/05	22/6	0	1	0	2	0	-	-	5/1	0	30/7	0
2005/06	26/3	3	-	-	2	0	-	-	-	-	28/3	3
2006/07												
Total	57/15	4	1	0	5/1	0	0/1	0	6/2	0	69/19	4

Matty Done (b. Shrewsbury 22nd June 1988)

Season	League apps	League gls	FA Cup apps	FA Cup gls	WPC apps	WPC gls	Carling Cup apps	Carling Cup gls	LDV apps	LDV gls	Total apps	Total gls
2005/06	1/5	0	-	-	-	-	0/1	0	-	-	1/6	0
2006/07												
Total	1/5	0	-	-	-	-	0/1	0	-	-	1/6	0

Gareth Evans (b. Wrexham 10th January 1987)

Season	League apps	League gls	FA Cup apps	FA Cup gls	WPC apps	WPC gls	Carling Cup apps	Carling Cup gls	LDV apps	LDV gls	Total apps	Total gls
2006/07												
Total												

Steve Evans (b. Wrexham 26th February 1979)

Season	League apps	League gls	FA Cup apps	FA Cup gls	WPC apps	WPC gls	Carling Cup apps	Carling Cup gls	LDV apps	LDV gls	Total apps	Total gls
2006/07												
Total												

Darren Ferguson (b. Glasgow 9th July 1972)

Season	League apps	League gls	FA Cup apps	FA Cup gls	WPC apps	WPC gls	Carling Cup apps	Carling Cup gls	LDV apps	LDV gls	Total apps	Total gls
1999/00	37	4	5	1	5	1	-	-	-	-	47	6
2000/01	43	9	1	0	6	4	2	1	1	0	53	14
2001/02	37/1	3	-	-	2	0	1	0	2	0	42/1	3
2002/03	41	2	1	0	2	0	2	0	3	0	49	2
2003/04	39	1	1	0	2/1	0	1	0	1	0	44/1	1
2004/05	40	3	2	0	-	-	2	1	5/1	2	49/1	6
2005/06	36/3	2	1	0	1	0	1	0	1	1	40/3	3
2006/07												
Total	273/4	24	11	1	18/1	5	9	2	13/1	3	324/6	35

Michael Ingham (b. Preston 9th July 1980)

Season	League apps	League gls	FA Cup apps	FA Cup gls	WPC apps	WPC gls	Carling Cup apps	Carling Cup gls	LDV apps	LDV gls	Total apps	Total gls
2003/04	11	0	-	-	-	-	-	-	-	-	11	0
2005/06	40	0	1	0	3	0	1	0	1	0	46	0
2006/07												
Total	51	0	1	0	3	0	1	0	1	0	57	0

Josh Johnson (b. Carenage, Trinidad 16th April 1981)

Season	League apps	League gls	FA Cup apps	FA Cup gls	WPC apps	WPC gls	Carling Cup apps	Carling Cup gls	LDV apps	LDV gls	Total apps	Total gls
2006/07												
Total												

Mark Jones (b. Wrexham 15th August 1983)

Season	League		FA Cup		WPC		Carling Cup		LDV		Total	
	apps	gls	apps	gls	apps	gls	apps	gls	apps	gls	apps	gls
2002/03	0/1	0	-	-	-	-	-	-	-	-	0/1	0
2003/04	0/13	1	-	-	0/1	0	-	-	-	-	0/14	1
2004/05	18/9	3	1/1	0	3	1	0/1	0	6/1	1	28/12	4
2005/06	42	13	1	0	3	2	1	0	1	2	48	17
2006/07												
Total	60/23	17	2/1	0	6/1	3	1/1	0	7/1	3	76/27	22

Michael Jones (b. Liverpool 3rd December 1987)

Season	League		FA Cup		WPC		Carling Cup		LDV		Total	
	apps	gls	apps	gls	apps	gls	apps	gls	apps	gls	apps	gls
2004/05	0/1	0	-	-	-	-	-	-	-	-	0/1	0
2005/06	6/1	0	-	-	-	-	-	-	-	-	6/1	0
2006/07												
Total	6/2	0	-	-	-	-	-	-	-	-	6/2	0

Chris Llewellyn (b. Merthyr 29th August 1979)

Season	League		FA Cup		WPC		Carling Cup		LDV		Total	
	apps	gls	apps	gls	apps	gls	apps	gls	apps	gls	apps	gls
2003/04	46	8	1	0	3	1	1	0	1/1	0	52/1	9
2004/05	44	7	2	1	1	0	1/1	1	7	3	55/1	12
2006/07												
Total	90	15	3	1	4	1	2/1	1	8/1	3	107/2	21

Levi Mackin (b. Chester 4th April 1986)

Season	League		FA Cup		WPC		Carling Cup		LDV		Total	
	apps	gls	apps	gls	apps	gls	apps	gls	apps	gls	apps	gls
2003/04	1	0	-	-	-	-	-	-	-	-	1	0
2004/05	5/5	0	-	-	1	0	0/1	0	-	-	6/6	0
2005/06	3/13	0	-	-	0/1	0	0/1	0	0/1	0	3/16	0
2006/07												
Total	10/18	0	-	-	1/1	0	0/2	0	0/1	0	10/22	0

Lee McEvilly (b. Liverpool 15th April 1982)

Season	League		FA Cup		WPC		Carling Cup		LDV		Total	
	apps	gls	apps	gls	apps	gls	apps	gls	apps	gls	apps	gls
2005/06	14/9	7	1	1	-	-	-	-	0/1	0	15/10	8
2006/07												
Total	14/9	7	1	1	-	-	-	-	0/1	0	15/10	8

Shaun Pejic (b. Hereford 16th November 1982)

Season	League		FA Cup		WPC		Carling Cup		LDV		Total	
	apps	gls	apps	gls	apps	gls	apps	gls	apps	gls	apps	gls
2000/01	1	0	-	-	-	-	-	-	-	-	1	0
2001/02	11/1	0	-	-	1	0	-	-	-	-	12/1	0
2002/03	23/4	0	1	0	1	1	2	0	2	0	29/4	1
2003/04	20/1	1	-	-	-	-	1	0	1	0	22/1	0
2004/05	30/5	0	2	0	2	0	2	0	4/1	1	40/6	1
2005/06	26	0	-	-	2/1	0	-	-	1	0	29/1	0
2006/07												
Total	111/11	1	3	0	6/1	1	5	0	8/1	1	133/13	2

Jamie Reed (b. Chester 13th August 1987)

Season	League apps	League gls	FA Cup apps	FA Cup gls	WPC apps	WPC gls	Carling Cup apps	Carling Cup gls	LDV apps	LDV gls	Total apps	Total gls
2004/05	-	-	-	-	0/1	0	-	-	-	-	0/1	0
2005/06	0/3	0	-	-	-	-	-	-	-	-	0/3	0
2006/07												
Total	0/3	0	-	-	0/1	0	-	-	-	-	0/4	0

Neil Roberts (b. Wrexham 7th April 1978)

Season	League apps	League gls	FA Cup apps	FA Cup gls	WPC apps	WPC gls	Carling Cup apps	Carling Cup gls	LDV apps	LDV gls	Total apps	Total gls
1997/98	29/5	8	3/1	1	6/3	1	-	-	0/1	0	38/7	10
1998/99	11/11	3	3	1	3	1	1	1	2/1	2	20/12	8
1999/00	18/1	6	5	2	2	1	-	-	-	-	25/1	9
2006/07												
Total	58/17	17	11/1	4	11/3	3	1	1	2/2	2	83/20	27

Lee Roche (b. Bolton 28th October 1980)

Season	League apps	League gls	FA Cup apps	FA Cup gls	WPC apps	WPC gls	Carling Cup apps	Carling Cup gls	LDV apps	LDV gls	Total apps	Total gls
2000/01	41	0	1	0	7	0	2	0	1	0	52	0
2005/06	17/1	1	1	0	-	-	-	-	-	-	18/1	1
2006/07												
Total	58/1	1	2	0	7	0	2	0	1	0	70/1	1

Simon Spender (b. Mold 15th November 1985)

Season	League apps	League gls	FA Cup apps	FA Cup gls	WPC apps	WPC gls	Carling Cup apps	Carling Cup gls	LDV apps	LDV gls	Total apps	Total gls
2003/04	3/3	0	-	-	-	-	-	-	-	-	3/3	0
2004/05	9/4	0	2	0	0/1	0	0/2	0	2	0	13/7	0
2005/06	15/3	2	1	0	1/2	1	-	-	1	0	17/5	3
2006/07												
Total	27/10	2	3	0	1/3	0	0/2	0	3	0	33/15	2

Ryan Valentine (b. Wrexham 19th August 1982)

Season	League apps	League gls	FA Cup apps	FA Cup gls	WPC apps	WPC gls	Carling Cup apps	Carling Cup gls	LDV apps	LDV gls	Total apps	Total gls
2006/07												
Total												

Danny Williams (b. Wrexham 12th July 1979)

Season	League apps	League gls	FA Cup apps	FA Cup gls	WPC apps	WPC gls	Carling Cup apps	Carling Cup gls	LDV apps	LDV gls	Total apps	Total gls
1999/00	24	1	4	1	4/1	0	2	0	1	0	35/1	2
2000/01	14/1	2	-	-	4	0	2	0	-	-	20/1	2
2004/05	20	0	-	-	2	0	2	0	3/1	1	27/1	1
2005/06	45	4	1	0	3/1	0	1	0	1	0	51	4
2006/07												
Total	103/1	7	5	1	13/2	0	7	0	5/1	1	133/3	9

Marc Williams (b. Bangor 27th July 1988)

Season	League apps	League gls	FA Cup apps	FA Cup gls	WPC apps	WPC gls	Carling Cup apps	Carling Cup gls	LDV apps	LDV gls	Total apps	Total gls
2005/06	2/2	0	-	-	-	-	-	-	-	-	2/2	0
2006/07												
Total	2/2	0	-	-	-	-	-	-	-	-	2/2	0

Mike Williams (b. Bangor 27th October 1986)

Season	League apps	League gls	FA Cup apps	FA Cup gls	WPC apps	WPC gls	Carling Cup apps	Carling Cup gls	LDV apps	LDV gls	Total apps	Total gls
2005/06	7/5	0	-	-	1	0	-	-	-	-	8/5	0
2006/07												
Total	7/5	0	-	-	1	0	-	-	-	-	8/5	0

Individual appearance milestones for the season:

Matt Crowell	28 league games to his 100th league appearances & 12 games to his 100th appearance for the club
Darren Ferguson	23 league games to his 300th league appearance & 20 games to his 350th appearance for the club
Mark Jones	17 league games to his 100th league appearance
Chris Llewellyn	10 league games to his 100th league appearance & 41 games to his 150th appearance for the club
Levi Mackin	22 league games to his 50th league appearance & 28 games to his 50th appearance for the club
Shaun Pejic	28 league games to his 150th league appearance & 4 games to his 150th appearance for the club
Neil Roberts	25 league games to his 100th league appearance for the club
Lee Roche	29 games to his 100th appearance for the club
Simon Spender	13 league games to his 50th league appearance & 2 games to his 50th appearance for the club
Danny Williams	14 games to his 150th appearance for the club

Team	P	W	D	L	F	A	W	D	L	F	A
Accrington Stanley	66	23	5	5	75	34	9	6	18	40	[illegible]
Aldershot	34	13	4	0	42	11	3	3	11	17	[illegible]
Ashington	16	5	2	1	21	6	1	5	2	11	[illegible]
Aston Villa	4	0	0	2	2	5	1	0	1	4	[illegible]
Barnet	8	3	0	1	10	4	1	1	2	5	[illegible]
Barnsley	32	12	4	0	38	13	0	4	12	17	[illegible]
Barrow	70	20	11	4	68	25	7	14	14	50	[illegible]
Birmingham City	4	1	1	0	2	1	0	0	2	2	[illegible]
Blackburn Rovers	14	2	4	1	7	6	1	5	1	6	[illegible]
Blackpool	28	2	5	7	18	22	2	3	9	12	[illegible]
Bolton Wanderers	10	1	0	4	4	8	1	1	3	3	[illegible]
Boston United	4	1	1	0	3	1	0	1	1	4	[illegible]
Bournemouth	42	11	3	7	32	23	7	4	10	18	[illegible]
Bradford City	64	16	7	9	50	42	5	7	20	44	[illegible]
Bradford Park Avenue	44	16	3	3	51	20	8	3	11	24	[illegible]
Brentford	38	7	4	8	27	29	3	5	11	12	[illegible]
Brighton HA	28	4	5	5	14	15	2	4	8	18	[illegible]
Bristol City	24	5	3	4	12	13	2	1	9	9	[illegible]
Bristol Rovers	40	13	4	3	32	19	3	3	14	17	[illegible]
Burnley	30	4	4	7	15	23	4	3	8	16	[illegible]
Bury	34	10	6	1	29	12	8	4	5	29	[illegible]
Cambridge United	34	10	5	2	39	14	6	3	8	24	[illegible]
Cardiff City	30	6	2	7	20	20	2	4	9	11	[illegible]
Carlisle United	74	28	7	2	99	42	11	10	16	42	[illegible]
Charlton Athletic	12	3	2	1	11	8	1	3	2	5	[illegible]
Chelsea	6	2	0	1	3	4	0	1	2	3	[illegible]
Cheltenham Town	2	1	0	0	2	0	0	1	0	2	[illegible]
Chester City	72	20	10	6	65	41	8	8	20	44	[illegible]
Chesterfield	104	23	15	14	87	67	10	9	33	59	[illegible]
Colchester United	50	11	7	7	43	39	7	8	10	39	[illegible]
Coventry City	8	2	1	1	10	6	0	0	4	3	[illegible]
Crewe Alexandra	98	26	11	12	92	52	10	15	24	48	[illegible]
Crystal Palace	16	0	3	5	9	16	0	1	7	6	[illegible]
Darlington	86	26	11	6	109	48	6	13	24	52	[illegible]
Derby County	8	1	2	1	6	6	1	0	3	2	[illegible]
Doncaster Rovers	66	14	9	10	52	37	3	15	15	35	[illegible]
Durham City	14	6	1	0	17	3	0	1	6	5	[illegible]
Exeter City	32	7	7	2	27	11	3	5	8	18	[illegible]
Fulham	12	1	3	2	6	9	2	2	2	4	[illegible]
Gateshead	46	13	3	7	48	28	3	9	11	29	[illegible]
Gillingham	32	10	4	2	27	13	5	4	7	20	[illegible]
Grimsby Town	50	14	4	7	46	25	5	7	13	16	[illegible]
Halifax Town	108	31	13	10	112	62	12	14	28	46	[illegible]
Hartlepool United	98	32	7	10	116	62	13	9	27	62	[illegible]
Hereford United	28	5	6	3	18	11	1	5	8	7	[illegible]
Huddersfield Town	14	2	3	2	9	6	1	1	5	6	[illegible]
Hull City	38	13	3	3	47	17	4	4	11	21	[illegible]
Kidderminster Harriers	2	0	0	1	0	2	1	0	0	2	[illegible]
Leicester City	6	0	2	1	0	1	0	1	2	1	[illegible]
Leyton Orient	26	6	3	4	22	16	5	5	3	16	[illegible]
Lincoln City	78	18	11	10	61	43	6	12	21	39	[illegible]
Luton Town	30	10	3	2	24	11	3	3	9	20	[illegible]
Macclesfield Town	6	1	1	1	4	5	2	0	1	5	[illegible]
Maidstone United	6	1	2	0	6	4	2	0	1	6	[illegible]
Manchester City	2	0	0	1	0	1	0	1	0	0	[illegible]
Mansfield Town	60	17	7	6	64	31	5	8	17	30	[illegible]
Millwall	26	5	6	2	24	14	4	5	4	17	[illegible]
Milton Keynes Dons	2	0	1	0	0	0	0	0	1	0	[illegible]
Nelson	18	7	2	0	30	13	2	0	7	8	[illegible]
New Brighton	42	10	6	5	38	24	4	8	9	20	[illegible]
Newcastle United	8	2	2	0	5	2	1	0	3	3	[illegible]

am	P	W	D	L	F	A	W	D	L	F	A
wport County	20	5	3	2	18	7	2	2	6	11	21
rthampton Town	32	7	2	7	20	23	7	5	4	23	25
rwich City	6	0	0	3	4	7	0	1	2	3	9
tts County	44	13	6	3	46	24	2	8	12	19	36
dham Athletic	66	14	11	8	55	48	10	9	14	56	65
ford United	20	5	5	0	18	12	4	3	3	16	14
terborough United	50	9	10	6	39	32	6	5	14	29	47
mouth Argyle	26	5	4	4	30	22	5	4	4	15	16
rt Vale	56	13	9	6	40	27	6	6	16	25	44
rtsmouth	6	2	0	1	4	2	2	0	1	2	3
eston North End	30	5	7	3	15	14	3	2	10	13	23
een's Park Rangers	18	3	2	4	9	12	2	2	5	8	16
ading	26	6	1	6	19	17	2	2	9	8	26
chdale	108	37	11	6	124	50	14	9	31	80	116
therham United	70	22	6	7	73	39	10	10	15	42	62
shden & Diamonds	6	2	1	0	6	1	2	1	0	7	4
arborough	12	3	0	3	8	6	2	1	3	10	11
unthorpe United	44	12	3	7	32	21	3	7	12	24	40
effield United	4	2	0	0	8	1	0	1	1	1	3
effield Wednesday	14	2	2	3	11	9	2	0	5	9	14
rewsbury Town	40	9	5	6	27	21	7	4	9	26	30
uthampton	4	1	0	1	3	4	1	0	1	2	4
uthend United	38	11	6	2	50	24	5	6	8	20	26
uthport	72	23	9	4	86	43	8	11	17	38	60
alybridge Celtic	4	2	0	0	4	1	0	0	2	0	5
ockport County	92	23	8	15	70	53	9	11	26	53	95
oke City	12	0	0	6	4	10	1	0	5	4	12
nderland	4	0	0	2	1	3	0	1	1	1	2
ansea City	30	10	4	1	25	9	5	3	7	15	19
indon Town	30	7	4	4	25	20	3	3	9	17	29
rquay United	32	9	3	4	30	23	5	2	9	21	29
anmere Rovers	102	26	15	10	99	53	13	10	28	60	106
alsall	60	19	6	5	58	25	9	7	14	31	52
atford	20	6	2	2	17	6	1	2	7	7	18
est Ham United	6	2	1	0	7	5	0	1	2	1	3
gan Athletic	12	1	3	2	7	9	2	2	2	8	9
gan Borough	20	8	1	1	24	10	0	4	6	7	25
olves	6	1	2	0	6	4	2	0	1	5	3
orkington	24	7	3	2	30	8	1	2	9	8	26
combe Wanderers	20	5	3	2	11	6	1	5	4	7	18
rk City	94	24	16	7	89	58	7	14	26	49	87
tal	**3464**	**914**	**435**	**383**	**3202**	**1915**	**381**	**438**	**913**	**1915**	**3141**

Overall:

Games	P	W	D	L	F	A
me	1732	914	435	383	3202	1915
ay	1732	381	438	913	1915	3141
tal	**3464**	**1295**	**873**	**1296**	**5117**	**5056**

Overall %

Games	Win%	Draw%	Loss%
me	52.8%	25.1%	22.1%
ay	22.0%	25.3%	52.7%

ams currently in the Football League that Wrexham have never played in a football league match are: senal, Everton, Ipswich Town, Leeds United, Liverpool, Manchester United, Middlesbrough, ttingham Forest, Tottenham Hotspur, West Bromwich Albion & Yeovil Town (11).

Players with 200 or more League appearances

1 Arfon Griffiths 585/6
2 Alf Jones 503
3 Gareth Davies 482/7
4 Aly McGowan 408
5 Mickey Evans 368/15
6 Joey Jones 378/1
7 Mel Sutton 355/5
8 Karl Connolly 337/21
9 Alan Fox 350
10 Graham Whittle 331/19
11 Gareth Owen 298/52
12 Phil Hardy 346/3
13 Eddie May 330/4
14 Brian Carey 298/6
15 Kevin Russell 256/26
16 Brian Tinnion 265/14
17 Darren Ferguson 273/4
18 Brian Lloyd 266
19 Mickey Thomas 251/13
20 Albert Kinsey 245/8
21 Wayne Phillips 219/26
22 Neil Salathiel 243/1
23 Mark McGregor 237/7
24 Gren Jones 241
25 Billy Tunnicliffe 236
26 Ron Hewitt 231
27 Fred Davis 230
28 Steve Buxton 179/50
29 Peter Jones 226/1
30 Tommy Bannan 226
31 Archie Longmuir 223
32 Eddie Tunney 220
33 Billy Ashcroft 196/23
34 Albert Parker 216
35 Andy Marriott 213
36 Les Speed 211
37 George Snow 207
38 Tommy Bamford 204
39 Steve Watkin 167/33

The figures after the slashes denote substitute appearances.

Leading League Goalscorers with 40 goals or more

1 Tommy Bamford 174
2 Arfon Griffiths 120
3 Ron Hewitt 95
4 Graham Whittle 91
5 Karl Connolly 88
6 Albert Kinsey 84
7 Tommy Bannan 83
8 Gary Bennett 82
9 Billy Tunnicliffe 74
10 Billy Ashcroft 72
11 Ray Smith 60
11 Kevin Russell 60
13 Mike Metcalf 58
14 Jim Steel 57
15 Jack Boothway 55
16 Steve Watkin 55
17 Dixie McNeil 54
18 Brian Tinnion 54
19 Sammy McMillan 52
20 Bernard Evans 47
21 Steve Buxton 46
22 George Snow 45
23 Ernie Phythian 44
24 Albert Mays 41
25 Harold Lapham 40
26 Tommy Lewis 40
27 Don Weston 40
28 Andy Morrell 40

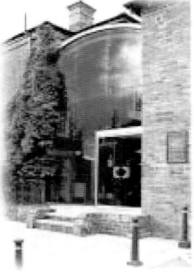

Promotions
1961-62 3rd in Division Four
1969-70 2nd in Division Four
1977-78 Third Division Champions
1992-93 2nd in Division Three
2002-03 3rd in Division Three

Qualified for Play-offs
1988-89 Lost Final to Leyton Orient (0-0, 1-2)

Relegations
1959-60 23rd in Division Three
1963-64 23rd in Division Three
1981-82 21st in Division Two
1982-83 21st in Division Three
2001-02 22nd in Division Three
2004-05 19th in League One (Final position 22nd after deduction of 10 points)

Highest League Position
1978-79 15th in Division Two

Lowest League Position
1965-66, 1990-91 24th in Division Four

LDV Vans Trophy
2004-05 Winners Southend United 2-0 aet (Ugarte, Ferguson)
1998-99 Northern Finalists Wigan 0-2, 2-3 (Brammer, J Edwards)

European Cup Winners Cup
1975-76 Quarter-finalists

F.A. Cup
1973-74, 1977-78, 1996-97 Quarter-finalists

League Cup
1977-78 Quarter-finalists

Welsh Cup Winners (23 times - record number of victories)
1877-78 Druids 1-0 (Davies)
1882-83 Druids 1-0 (Roberts)
1892-93 Chirk 2-1 (Pritchard, R. Davies)
1896-97 Newtown 2-0 (Williams, Robinson pen)
1902-03 Aberamon 8-0 (Griffiths 3, Davies 2, Gordon 2, Owens pen)
1904-05 Aberdare 3-0 (Griffiths, Davies, Owens)
1908-09 Chester City 1-0 (Huffadine)
1909-10 Chester City 2-1 (Mason, Allman)
1910-11 Connah's Quay 6-0 (Goode 3, Davies 2, Cooke)
1913-14 Llanelli 3-0 (Replay) (Uren, Cooke, Hughes)
1914-15 Swansea 1-0 (Replay) (Goode)
1920-21 Pontypridd 3-1 (Replay) (Edwards 2, Goode)
1923-24 Merthyr Tydfil 1-0 (Replay) (Cotton)
1924-25 Flint Town 3-1 (Jones 2, Goode)

1930-31 Shrewsbury Town 7-0 (Lewis 2, Taylor, Bamford 2, Mustard, Hughes)
1956-57 Swansea Town 2-1 (Thompson, McNab)
1957-58 Chester City 2-1 (Replay) (Murray, Bannan)
1959-60 Cardiff City 1-0 (Replay) (Griffiths)
1971-72 Cardiff City 2-1(Whittle (pen), Own goal), 1-1 (Kinsey)
1974-75 Cardiff City 2-1(Tinnion, Lyons), 3-1 (Ashcroft 2, Whittle)
1977-78 Bangor City 2-1(Shinton, Cartwright), 1-0 (Lyons)
1985-86 Kidderminster Harriers 1-1(Horne), 2-1 (Steel 2)
1994-95 Cardiff City 2-1 (Bennett 2)

Welsh Cup Runners-up 22 times - record number of appearances in final (45)

1878-79 White Stars 0-1
1889-90 Chirk 0-1
1890-91 Shrewsbury Town 2-5 (Davies, Turner)
1894-95 Newtown 2-3 (Harrison, Own goal)
1895-96 Bangor City 1-3 (Williams)
1897-98 Druids 1-2 (Replay) (Harrison)
1898-99 Druids 0-1 (Replay)
1901-02 Wellington 0-1
1919-20 Cardiff City 1-2 (Uren, Cooke, Hughes)
1931-32 Swansea Town 0-2
1932-33 Chester City 0-2
1949-50 Swansea Town 1-4 (Tunnicliffe)
1961-62 Bangor City 1-3 (Replay) (Barnes pen)
1964-65 Cardiff City 0-3 (Replay)
1966-67 Cardiff City 2-2 (Kinsey, Own goal), 1-2 (Kinsey)
1970-71 Cardiff City 0-1, 1-3 (Smith)
1978-79 Shrewsbury Town 1-1(Fox), 0-1
1982-83 Swansea City 1-2(Dowman), 0-2
1983-84 Shrewsbury Town 1-2(Edwards), 0-0
1987-88 Cardiff City 0-2
1989-90 Hereford United 1-2 (Gary Worthington)
1990-91 Swansea City 0-2

Welsh Premier Cup Winners - 5 times (record number of victories)

1997-98 Cardiff City 2-1 (Wilson, Owen)
1999-00 Cardiff City 2-0 (Faulconbridge 2)
2000-01 Swansea City 2-0 (Trundle, McGregor)
2002-03 Newport County 6-1 (Lawrence, Morrell, Whitley, Trundle 2, Pejic)
2003-04 Rhyl 4-1 (Carey, Barrett, Sam 2)

Welsh Premier Cup Runners-up - 2 times (record number of appearances in final - 8)

1998-99 Barry Town 1-2 (Connolly)
2004-05 Swansea City 1-2 (Ugarte)
2005-06 Swansea City 1-2 (Spender)

Debenhams Cup Runners-up

(The Debenhams Cup was a short-lived trophy from the late 70s contested by the two underdogs who had progressed furthest in the previous years FA Cup.)

1977-78 Blyth Spartans 1-2(Whittle), 1-1 (Lyons)

Wales return to the Racecourse this season for only the second time this century. Our visitors will be Liechtenstein for the first ever meeting between the two countries. Here is a rundown of all the International matches played at the home of Welsh football.

1877 Wales 0 - 2 Scotland
1879 Wales 0 - 3 Scotland
1880 Wales 2 – 3 England
1881 Wales 1 – 5 Scotland
1882 Wales 7 – 1 Ireland
1882 Wales 5 – 3 England
1883 Wales 0 – 3 Scotland
1884 Wales 6 – 0 Ireland
1884 Wales 0 - 4 England
1885 Wales 1 – 8 Scotland
1886 Wales 5 – 0 Ireland
1886 Wales 1 – 3 England
1887 Wales 0 – 2 Scotland
1888 Wales 11 – 0 Ireland
1889 Wales 0 – 0 Scotland
1890 Wales 1 – 3 England
1891 Wales 3 – 4 Scotland
1892 Wales 0 – 2 England
1893 Wales 0 - 8 Scotland
1894 Wales 1 – 5 England
1895 Wales 2 – 2 Scotland
1896 Wales 6 – 1 Ireland
1897 Wales 2 – 2 Scotland
1898 Wales 0 – 3 England
1899 Wales 0 – 6 Scotland
1901 Wales 1 – 1 Scotland
1902 Wales 0 – 0 England
1904 Wales 2 – 2 England
1905 Wales 3 – 1 Scotland
1906 Wales 4 – 4 Ireland
1907 Wales 1 – 0 Scotland
1908 Wales 1 – 7 England
1909 Wales 3 – 2 Scotland
1910 Wales 4 – 1 Ireland
1912 Wales 0 – 2 England
1913 Wales 0 – 0 Scotland
1914 Wales 1 – 2 Ireland
1922 Wales 2 – 1 Scotland
1923 Wales 0 – 3 Ireland
1925 Wales 0 – 0 Ireland
1927 Wales 3 – 3 England
1927 Wales 2 – 2 Scotland
1929 Wales 2 – 2 Ireland
1930 Wales 0 – 4 England
1931 Wales 3 – 2 Ireland
1931 Wales 2 – 3 Scotland
1932 Wales 0 – 0 England
1932 Wales 4 – 1 Ireland
1935 Wales 3 – 1 Ireland
1937 Wales 4 – 1 Ireland
1939 Wales 3 – 1 Ireland
1946 Wales 3 – 1 Scotland
1948 Wales 2 – 0 Ireland
1950 Wales 0 – 0 Ireland (WC)
1951 Wales 3 – 2 Switzerland
1954 Wales 1 – 2 Ireland (WC)
1955 Wales 1 – 2 Austria (EC)
1960 Wales 3 – 2 Ireland
1965 Wales 4 – 2 Denmark (WC)
1968 Wales 2 – 0 Ireland (EC)
1969 Wales 3 – 5 Scotland
1972 Wales 0 – 0 Ireland
1973 Wales 0 – 2 Scotland
1974 Wales 1 – 0 Ireland
1975 Wales 1 – 0 Austria (EC)
1976 Wales 1 – 2 England
1977 Wales 3 – 0 Czechoslovakia (WC)
1977 Wales 0 – 0 Scotland
1977 Wales 0 – 0 Kuwait
1978 Wales 1 – 0 Ireland
1978 Wales 7 – 0 Malta (EC)
1978 Wales 1 – 0 Turkey (EC)
1979 Wales 0 – 2 West Germany (EC)
1981 Wales 4 – 1 England
1981 Wales 0 – 0 USSR (WC)
1982 Wales 3 – 0 Ireland
1983 Wales 1 – 0 Bulgaria (EC)
1983 Wales 5 – 0 Romania
1984 Wales 1 – 0 England
1985 Wales 1 – 1 Norway
1985 Wales 3 – 0 Spain (WC)
1986 Wales 0 – 0 Uruguay
1987 Wales 4 – 0 Finland (EC)
1987 Wales 1 - 1 Czechoslovakia (EC)
1989 Wales 0 – 2 Sweden
1989 Wales 1 – 2 Holland (WC)
1991 Wales 0 – 3 Republic of Ireland
1994 Wales 0 – 2 Sweden
1999 Wales 0 – 2 Switzerland (EC)
2004 Wales 1 – 0 Canada

This is a full list of Wrexham players who have earned international caps for their countries whilst on the books of Wrexham Football Club along with the national team they represented. The overall number of caps regardless of club is shown in brackets. Within each table is the cap; date, opponents, score and venue.

Tommy Bamford (Wales)
5 appearances (5)
25/10/1930 Scotland 1-1 Glasgow
22/11/1930 England 0-4 Wrexham
22/04/1931 Ireland 3-2 Wrexham
05/12/1931 Ireland 0-4 Belfast
25/05/1933 France 1-1 Paris

Dan Bennett (Singapore)
Unknown Appearance record

Horace Blew (Wales)
22 appearances (22)
04/03/1899 Ireland 0-1 Belfast
18/03/1899 Scotland 0-6 Wrexham
20/03/1899 England 0-4 Bristol
22/02/1902 Ireland 0-3 Cardiff
15/03/1902 Scotland 1-5 Greenock
02/03/1903 England 1-2 Portsmouth
09/03/1903 Scotland 0-1 Cardiff
29/02/1904 England 2-2 Wrexham
12/03/1904 Scotland 1-1 Dundee
21/03/1904 Ireland 0-1 Bangor
06/03/1905 Scotland 3-1 Wrexham
08/04/1905 Ireland 2-2 Belfast
03/03/1906 Scotland 2-0 Edinburgh
19/03/1906 England 0-1 Cardiff
02/04/1906 Ireland 4-4 Wrexham
04/03/1907 Scotland 1-0 Wrexham
07/03/1908 Scotland 1-2 Dundee
16/03/1908 England 1-7 Wrexham
11/04/1908 Ireland 0-1 Aberdare
01/03/1909 Scotland 3-2 Wrexham
15/03/1909 England 0-2 Nottingham
14/03/1910 England 0-1 Cardiff

Tom Boden (Wales)
1 appearance (1)
15/03/1880 England 2-3 Wrexham

Tom Burke (Wales)
5 appearances (8)
03/02/1883 England 0-5 Kennington Oval
29/03/1884 Scotland 1-4 Glasgow
14/03/1885 England 1-1 Blackburn
23/03/1885 Scotland 1-8 Wrexham
11/04/1885 Ireland 8-2 Belfast

Les Cartwright (Wales)
2 appearances (7)
18/04/1978 Iran 1-0 Tehran
25/10/1978 Malta 7-0 Wrexham

Wynne Crompton (Wales)
3 appearances (3)
25/10/1930 Scotland 1-1 Glasgow
22/11/1930 England 0-4 Wrexham
22/04/1931 Ireland 3-2 Wrexham

Edwin Cross (Wales)
2 appearances (2)
25/03/1876 Scotland 0-4 Glasgow
05/03/1877 Scotland 0-2 Wrexham

Alf Davies (Wales)
2 appearances (2)
25/03/1876 Scotland 0-4 Glasgow
05/03/1877 Scotland 0-2 Wrexham

Alfred Owen Davies (Wales)
1 appearance (9)
15/04/1889 Scotland 0-0 Wrexham

Dai Davies (Wales)
28 appearances (52)
12/10/1977 Scotland 0-4 Liverpool
16/11/1977 Czechoslovakia 0-1 Prague
14/12/1977 West Germany 1-1 Dortmund
18/04/1978 Iran 1-0 Tehran
13/05/1978 England 1-3 Cardiff
17/05/1978 Scotland 1-1 Glasgow
19/05/1978 Northern Ireland 1-0 Wrexham
25/10/1978 Malta 7-0 Wrexham
29/11/1978 Turkey 1-0 Wrexham
02/05/1979 West Germany Wrexham
19/05/1979 Scotland 3-0 Cardiff
23/05/1979 England 0-0 Wembley
25/05/1979 Northern Ireland 1-1 Belfast
02/06/1979 Malta 2-0 Valletta
11/09/1979 Republic of Ireland 2-1 Swansea
17/10/1979 West Germany 1-5 Cologne
21/11/1979 Turkey 0-1 Izmir
17/05/1980 England 4-1 Wrexham
21/05/1980 Scotland 0-1 Glasgow
23/05/1980 Northern Ireland 0-1 Cardiff
02/06/1980 Iceland 4-0 Reykjavik
15/10/1980 Turkey 4-0 Cardiff
19/11/1980 Czechoslovakia 1-0 Cardiff
24/02/1981 Republic of Ireland 3-1 Dublin
25/03/1981 Turkey 1-0 Ankara
16/05/1981 Scotland 2-0 Swansea
20/05/1981 England 0-0 Wembley
30/05/1981 Russia 0-0 Wrexham

Gareth Davies (Wales)
3 appearances (3)
18/04/1978 Iran 1-0 Tehran
13/05/1978 England 1-3 Cardiff
19/05/1978 Northern Ireland 1-0 Wrexham

Revd/ Hywel Davies (Wales)
1 appearance (1)
04/02/1928 Ireland 2-1 Belfast

James Davies (Wales)
1 appearance (1)
23/03/1878 Scotland 0-9 Glasgow

John Davies (Wales)
1 appearance (1)
07/04/1878 Scotland 0-3 Wrexham

Llew Davies (Wales)
11 appearances (13)
23/02/1907 Ireland 3-2 Belfast
05/03/1910 Scotland 0-1 Kilmarnock
14/03/1910 England 0-1 Cardiff
11/04/1910 Ireland 4-1 Wrexham
02/03/1912 Scotland 0-1 Edinburgh
11/03/1912 England 0-2 Wrexham
23/04/1912 Ireland 2-3 Cardiff
18/01/1913 Ireland 1-0 Belfast
03/03/1913 Scotland 0-0 Wrexham
17/03/1913 England 3-4 Bristol
19/01/1914 Ireland 1-2 Wrexham

Oswald Davies (Wales)
1 appearance (1)
22/03/1890 Scotland 0-5 Paisley

Robert Davies (Wales)
3 appearances (3)
17/03/1883 Ireland 1-1 Belfast
09/02/1884 Ireland 6-0 Wrexham
11/04/1885 Ireland 8-2 Belfast

Robert O Davies (Wales)
2 appearances (2)
27/02/1892 Ireland 1-1 Bangor
05/05/1892 England 0-2 Wrexham

Walter Davies (Wales)
1 appearance (1)
09/02/1884 Ireland 6-0 Wrexham

William Davies (Wales)
2 appearances (11)
28/03/1903 Ireland 0-2 Belfast
08/04/1905 Ireland 2-2 Belfast

Carlos Edwards (Trinidad & Tobago)
29 appearances (53)
29/06/2000 Barbados -0-0 Bridgetown
02/07/2000 St/Vincents 1-2 Kingstown
04/07/2000 Cuba 4-1 Tunapuna
08/07/2000 Jamaica 2-4 Port of Spain
16/07/2000 Canada 2-0 Edmonton
16/08/2000 Panama 6-0 Port of Spain
15/11/2000 Panama 1-0 Port of Spain
25/02/2001 Cayman Islands 3-0 Georgetown
28/02/2001 Jamaica (a) 0-1 Kingston
19/05/2001 Martinique 1-2 Port of Spain
10/06/2001 Panama 0-0 San Francisco
16/06/2001 Honduras 2-4 Port of Spain
24/06/2001 Bermuda 5-0 Prospect
26/03/2003 Antigua/Barbuda 2-0 Port of Spain
28/03/2003 Guadeloupe 1-0 Port of Spain
30/03/2003 Cuba 1-3 Marabella
31/05/2003 Kenya 1-1 Nairobi
10/06/2003 Botswana 0-0 Gaborone
14/06/2003 South Africa 1-2 Port Elizabeth
04/07/2003 Venezuela 2-2 Port of Spain
10/09/2003 Morocco 0-2 Marrakesh
31/03/2004 Egypt 1-2 Cairo
23/05/2004 Iraq 0-2 West Bromwich
30/05/2004 Scotland 1-4 Edinburgh
06/06/2004 Northern Ireland 0-3 Bacolet
13/06/2004 Dominican Republic 2-0 Santa Domingo
09/02/2005 United States 1-2 Port of Spain
26/03/2005 Guatemala 1-5 Guatemala City
30/03/2005 Costa Rica 0-0 Mucurapo

Charles Edwards (Wales)
1 appearance (1)
23/03/1878 Scotland 0-9 Glasgow

Henry Valentine Edwards (Wales)
7 appearances (8)
15/03/1880 England 2-3 Wrexham
27/03/1880 Scotland 1-5 Glasgow
13/03/1882 England 5-3 Wrexham
25/03/1882 Scotland 0-5 Glasgow
12/03/1883 Scotland 0-3 Wrexham
09/02/1884 Ireland 6-0 Wrexham
12/03/1887 Ireland 1-4 Belfast

Ian Edwards (Wales)
1 appearance (4)
21/11/1979 Turkey 0-1 Izmir

Robert Ernest Evans (Wales)
2 appearances (10)
03/03/1906 Scotland 2-0 Edinburgh
19/03/1906 England 0-1 Cardiff

Robert Owen Evans (Wales)
4 appearances (10)
22/02/1902 Ireland 0-3 Cardiff
02/03/1903 England 1-2 Portsmouth
09/03/1903 Scotland 0-1 Cardiff
28/03/1903 Ireland 0-2 Belfast

John Arthur Eyton-Jones (Wales)
4 appearances (4)
17/03/1883 Ireland 1-1 Belfast
09/02/1884 Ireland 6-0 Wrexham
17/03/1884 England 0-4 Wrexham
29/03/1884 Scotland 1-4 Glasgow

Dick Finnigan (Wales)
1 appearance (1)
01/02/1930 Ireland 0-7 Belfast

Sam Gillam (Wales)
2 appearances (5)
27/04/1889 Ireland 3-1 Belfast
08/02/1890 Ireland 5-2 Shrewsbury

George Glascodine (Wales)
1 appearance (1)
18/01/1879 England 1-2 Kennington Oval

George Godding (Wales)
2 appearances (2)
17/03/1923 Scotland 0-2 Glasgow
14/04/1923 Ireland 0-3 Wrexham

Arfon Griffiths (Wales)
17 appearances (17)
21/04/1971 Czechoslovakia 1-3 Swansea
04/09/1974 Austria 1-2 Vienna
30/10/1974 Hungary 2-0 Cardiff
20/11/1974 Luxembourg 5-0 Swansea
16/04/1975 Hungary 2-1 Budapest
01/05/1975 Luxembourg 3-1 Luxembourg
21/05/1975 England 2-2 Wembley
23/05/1975 Northern Ireland 0-1 Belfast
19/11/1975 Austria 1-0 Wrexham
24/03/1976 England 1-2 Wrexham
24/04/1976 Yugoslavia 0-2 Zagreb
06/05/1976 Scotland 1-3 Glasgow
08/05/1976 England 0-1 Cardiff
14/05/1976 Northern Ireland 1-0 Swansea
22/05/1976 Yugoslavia 1-1 Cardiff
06/10/1976 West Germany 0-2 Cardiff
17/11/1976 Scotland 0-1 Glasgow

Llewelyn Griffiths (Wales)
1 appearance (1)
15/03/1902 Scotland 0-1 Greenock

Billy Harrison (Wales)
5 appearances (5)
20/03/1899 England 0-4 Bristol
03/02/1900 Scotland 2-5 Aberdeen
24/02/1900 Ireland 2-0 Llandudno
26/03/1900 England 1-1 Cardiff
23/03/1901 Ireland 1-0 Belfast

Abel Hayes (Wales)
2 appearances (2)
08/02/1890 Ireland 5-2 Shrewsbury
24/02/1894 Ireland 4-1 Swansea

Tom Hewitt (Wales)
3 appearances (8)
28/01/1911 Ireland 2-1 Belfast
06/03/1911 Scotland 2-2 Cardiff
13/03/1911 England 0-3 Millwall

Shaun Holmes (Northern Ireland)
1 appearance (1)
27/03/2002 Liechtenstein 0-0 Vaduz

Ted Hughes (Wales)
4 appearances (16)
03/03/1906 Scotland 2-0 Edinburgh
02/03/1912 Scotland 0-1 Edinburgh
11/03/1912 England 0-2 Wrexham

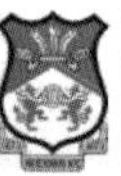

Ted Hughes (Wales) (cont.)
23/04/1912 Ireland 2-3 Cardiff

Barry Hunter (Northern Ireland)
6 appearances (15)
26/04/1995 Latvia 1-0 Riga
03/09/1995 Portugal 1-1 Opporto
11/10/1995 Liechtenstein 4-0 Eschen
15/11/1995 Austria 5-3 Belfast
24/04/1996 Sweden 1-2 Belfast
29/05/1996 Germany 1-1 Belfast

Michael Ingham (Northern Ireland)
1 appearances (3)
21/05/2006 Uruguay 0-1 New Jersey

Gordon Jones (Wales)
2 appearances (2)
23/02/1907 Ireland 3-2 Belfast
04/03/1907 Scotland 1-0 Wrexham

James Jones (Wales)
1 appearance (1)
18/04/1925 Ireland 0-0 Wrexham

Joey Jones (Wales)
29 appearances (72)
25/10/1978 Malta 7-0 Wrexham
29/11/1978 Turkey 1-0 Wrexham
02/05/1979 West Germany Wrexham
19/05/1979 Scotland 3-0 Cardiff
23/05/1979 England 0-0 Wembley
25/05/1979 Northern Ireland 1-1 Belfast
02/06/1979 Malta 2-0 Valletta
11/09/1979 Republic of Ireland 2-1 Swansea
17/10/1979 West Germany 1-5 Cologne
21/11/1979 Turkey 0-1 Izmir
17/05/1980 England 4-1 Wrexham
21/05/1980 Scotland 0-1 Glasgow
23/05/1980 Northern Ireland 0-1 Cardiff
02/06/1980 Iceland 4-0 Reykjavik
15/10/1980 Turkey 4-0 Cardiff
24/02/1981 Republic of Ireland 3-1 Dublin
25/03/1981 Turkey 1-0 Ankara
16/05/1981 Scotland 2-0 Swansea
20/05/1981 England 0-0 Wembley
30/05/1981 Russia 0-0 Wrexham
09/09/1981 Czechoslovakia 0-2 Prague
14/10/1981 Iceland 2-2 Swansea
18/11/1981 Russia 0-3 Tblisi
24/03/1982 Spain 1-1 Valencia
27/04/1982 England 0-1 Cardiff
24/05/1982 Scotland 0-1 Glasgow
27/05/1982 Northern Ireland 3-0 Wrexham
02/06/1982 France 1-0 Toulouse
22/09/1982 Norway 1-0 Swansea

Sam Jones (Wales)
1 appearance (1)
12/03/1887 Ireland 1-4 Belfast

Samuel Jones (Wales)
2 appearances (6)
18/03/1893 Scotland 0-8 Wrexham
05/04/1893 Ireland 3-4 Belfast

Fred Kelly (Wales)
2 appearances (3)
04/03/1899 Ireland 0-1 Belfast
18/03/1899 Scotland 0-6 Wrexham

Dennis Lawrence (Trinidad & Tobago)
49 appearances (63)
25/02/2001 Cayman Islands 3-0 Georgetown
28/02/2001 Jamaica 0-1 Kingston
25/04/2001 Mexico 1-1 Port of Spain
15/05/2001 Barbados 5-0 Port of Spain
17/05/2001 Jamaica 2-1 Port of Spain
19/05/2001 Martinique 1-2 Port of Spain
22/05/2001 Cuba 2-0 Port of Spain
25/05/2001 Haiti 3-0 Port of Spain
10/06/2001 Panama 0-0 San Francisco
16/06/2001 Honduras 4-2 Port of Spain
19/06/2001 USA 0-2 Foxborough
24/06/2001 Bermuda 5-0 Prospect
26/03/2003 Antigua/Barbuda 2-0 Port of Spain
28/03/2003 Guadeloupe 1-0 Tunapuna
30/03/2003 Cuba 1-3 Port of Spain
04/07/2003 Venezuela 2-2 Port of Spain
10/09/2003 Morocco 0-2 Marrakesh
31/03/2004 Egypt 1-2 Cairo
23/05/2004 Iraq 0-2 West Bromwich
13/06/2004 Dominican Republic 2-0 Santa Domingo
20/06/2004 Dominican Republic 4-0 Port of Spain
18/08/2004 St Vincent & the Grenadines 2-0 Arnos Vale
04/09/2004 St Kitts/Nevis 2-1 Basseterre
08/09/2004 Mexico 1-3 Port of Spain
13/10/2004 Mexico 0-3 Puebla
17/11/2004 St Vincent & the Grenadines 2-1 Port of Spain
26/03/2005 Guatemala 1-5 Guatemala City
30/03/2005 Costa Rica 0-0 Port of Spain
25/05/2005 Bermuda 4-0 Port of Spain
27/05/2005 Bermuda 1-0 Port of Spain
04/06/2005 Panama 2-0 Port of Spain
08/06/2005 Mexico 0-2 Monterrey
06/07/2005 Honduras 1-1 Miami
10/07/2005 Panama 2-2 Miami
12/07/2005 Colombia 0-2 Miami
17/08/2005 USA 0-1 Connecticut
07/09/2005 Costa Rica 0-2 San Jose
08/10/2005 Panama 1-0 Panama City
12/10/2005 Mexico 2-1 Port of Spain
12/11/2005 Bahrain 1-1 Port of Spain
16/11/2005 Bahrain 1-0 Manama
28/02/2006 Iceland 2-0 London
10/05/2006 Peru 1-1 Port of Spain
27/05/2006 Wales 1-2 Graz
31/05/2006 Slovenia 1-3 Celje
03/06/2006 Czech Republic 0-3 Prague
10/06/2006 Sweden 0-0 Dortmund
15/06/2006 England 0-2 Nuremberg
20/06/2006 Paraguay 0-2 Kaiserslautern

Arthur Lea (Wales)
4 appearances (4)
23/02/1889 England 1-4 Stoke
07/02/1891 Ireland 2-7 Belfast
21/03/1891 Scotland 3-4 Wrexham
05/04/1893 Ireland 3-4 Belfast

Ben Lewis (Wales)
7 appearances (10)
27/02/1892 Ireland 1-1 Bangor
05/05/1892 England 0-2 Wrexham
26/03/1892 Scotland 1-6 Edinburgh
13/03/1893 England 0-6 Stoke
24/02/1894 Ireland 4-1 Swansea
12/03/1894 England 1-5 Wrexham
24/03/1894 Scotland 2-5 Kilmarnock

Thomas Lewis (Wales)
2 appearances (2)
26/02/1881 England 1-0 Blackburn
14/03/1881 Scotland 1-5 Wrexham

Chris Llewellyn (Wales)
2 appearances (4)
27/05/2004 Norway 0-0 Oslo
30/05/2004 Canada 1-0 Wrexham

Brian Lloyd (Wales)
3 appearances (3)
19/11/1975 Austria 1-0 Wrexham
24/03/1976 England 1-2 Wrexham
06/05/1976 Scotland 1-3 Glasgow

Jimmy Lloyd (Wales)
1 appearance (2)
07/04/1879 Scotland 0-3 Wrexham

Albert Lumberg (Wales)
3 appearances (4)
02/02/1929 Ireland 2-2 Wrexham
26/10/1929 Scotland 2-4 Cardiff
20/10/1929 England 0-6 Stamford Bridge

Andy Marriott (Wales)
5 appearances (5)
24/04/1996 Switzerland 0-2 Lugano
27/05/1997 Scotland 1-0 Kilmarnock
11/10/1997 Belgium 2-3 Brussels
11/11/1997 Brazil 0-3 Brasilia
06/03/1998 Tunisia 0-4 Tunis

Tommy Matthias (Wales)
12 appearances (12)
28/02/1914 Scotland 0-0 Glasgow
16/03/1914 England 0-2 Cardiff
14/02/1920 Ireland 2-2 Belfast
26/02/1920 Scotland 1-1 Cardiff
15/03/1920 England 2-1 Highbury
12/02/1921 Scotland 1-2 Aberdeen
14/03/1921 England 0-0 Cardiff
09/04/1921 Ireland 2-1 Swansea
04/02/1922 Scotland 2-1 Wrexham
13/03/1922 England 0-1 Liverpool
01/04/1922 Ireland 1-1 Belfast
17/03/1923 Scotland 0-2 Glasgow

Albert Mays (Wales)
1 appearance (1)
02/02/1929 Ireland 2-2 Wrexham

Tom McCarthy (Wales)
1 appearance (1)
27/04/1889 Ireland 3-1 Belfast

Tracey Morgan (Wales)
1 appearance (1)
08/04/1905 Ireland 2-2 Belfast

Joe Owens (Wales)
1 appearance (1)
15/03/1902 Scotland 1-5 Greenock

Harry Phoenix (Wales)
1 appearance (1)
25/03/1882 Scotland 0-5 Glasgow

George Poland (Wales)
2 appearances (2)
15/03/1939 Ireland 3-1 Wrexham
20/05/1939 France 1-2 Paris

David Powell (Wales)
1 appearance (11)
08/05/1968 West Germany 1-1 Cardiff

Haydn Price (Wales)
3 appearances (5)
01/03/1909 Scotland 3-2 Wrexham
15/03/1909 England 0-2 Nottingham
20/03/1909 Ireland 3-2 Belfast

John Price (Wales)
12 appearances (12)
05/03/1877 Scotland 0-2 Wrexham
23/03/1878 Scotland 0-9 Glasgow
18/01/1879 England 1-2 Kennington Oval
15/03/1880 England 2-3 Wrexham
27/03/1880 Scotland 1-5 Glasgow
26/02/1881 England 1-0 Blackburn
14/03/1881 Scotland 1-5 Wrexham
25/02/1882 Ireland 7-1 Wrexham
13/03/1882 England 5-3 Wrexham
25/03/1882 Scotland 0-5 Glasgow
12/03/1883 Scotland 0-3 Wrexham
17/03/1883 Ireland 1-1 Belfast

Harry Pugh (Wales)
4 appearances (7)
29/02/1896 Ireland 6-1 Wrexham
21/03/1896 Scotland 0-4 Dundee
06/03/1897 Ireland 3-4 Belfast
20/03/1897 Scotland 2-2 Wrexham

James Roberts (Wales)
2 appearances (2)
18/01/1913 Ireland 1-0 Belfast
03/03/1913 Scotland 0-0 Wrexham

Neil Roberts (Wales)
1 appearances (4)
09/10/2000 Switzerland 0-2 Wrexham

Bob Roberts (Wales)
2 appearances (2)
27/02/1886 Ireland 5-0 Wrexham
12/03/1887 Ireland 1-4 Belfast

Steve Roberts (Wales)
1 appearance (1)
09/02/2005 Hungary 2-0 Cardiff

Bill Roberts (Wales)
4 appearances (4)
27/02/1886 Ireland 5-0 Wrexham
29/03/1886 England 1-3 Wrexham
10/04/1886 Scotland 1-4 Glasgow
12/03/1887 Ireland 1-4 Belfast

Joe Rogers (Wales)
3 appearances (3)
29/02/1896 Ireland 6-1 Wrexham
16/03/1896 England 1-9 Cardiff
21/03/1896 Scotland 0-4 Dundee

Billie Rogers (Wales)
2 appearances (2)
25/10/1930 Scotland 1-1 Glasgow
22/11/1930 England 0-4 Wrexham

Hector Sam (Trinidad & Tobago)
12 appearances (19)
08/10/2000 Mexico 0-7 Mexico City
15/11/2000 Panama 1-0 Port of Spain
31/05/2003 Kenya 1-1 Nairobi
10/06/2003 Botswana 0-0 Gaborone
14/06/2003 South Africa 1-2 Port Elizabeth
04/07/2003 Venezuela 2-2 Port of Spain
31/05/2004 Egypt 1-2 Cairo
17/11/2004 St/Vincent & Grenadines 2-1 Port of Spain
26/03/2005 Guatemala 1-5 Guatemala City
30/03/2005 Costa Rica 0-0 Port of Spain
27/05/2005 Bermuda 1-0 Port of Spain
08/06/2005 Mexico 0-2 Monterrey

Herbert Sissons (Wales)
3 appearances (3)
11/04/1885 Ireland 8-2 Belfast
27/02/1886 Ireland 5-0 Wrexham
10/04/1886 Scotland 1-4 Glasgow

David Smallman (Wales)
3 appearances (7)
11/05/1974 England 0-2 Cardiff
14/05/1974 Scotland 0-2 Glasgow
18/05/1974 Northern Ireland 1-0 Wrexham

John Taylor (Wales)
1 appearance (1)
28/03/1898 England 0-3 Wrexham

George Thomas (Wales)
2 appearances (2)
14/03/1885 England 1-1 Blackburn
23/03/1885 Scotland 1-8 Wrexham

Mickey Thomas (Wales)
12 appearances (51)
06/10/1976 West Germany 0-2 Cardiff
17/11/1976 Scotland 0-1 Glasgow
30/03/1977 Czechoslovakia 3-0 Wrexham
28/05/1977 Scotland 0-0 Wrexham
03/06/1977 Northern Ireland 1-1 Belfast
20/09/1977 Kuwait 0-0 Kuwait City
12/10/1977 Scotland 0-2 Liverpool
16/11/1977 Czechoslovakia 0-1 Prague
18/04/1978 Iran 1-0 Tehran
13/05/1978 England 1-3 Cardiff
19/05/1978 Northern Ireland 1-0 Wrexham
25/10/1978 Malta 7-0 Wrexham

Harry Trainer (Wales)
3 appearances (3)
16/03/1895 Ireland 1-4 Belfast
18/03/1895 England 1-4 Kensington
23/03/1895 Scotland 2-2 Wrexham

Joe Turner (Wales)
1 appearance (1)
05/05/1892 England 0-2 Wrexham

Dick Turner (Wales)
2 appearances (2)
07/02/1891 Ireland 2-7 Belfast
07/03/1891 England 1-4 Sunderland

Bill Turner (Wales)
5 appearances (5)
26/02/1887 England 0-4 Kennington Oval
12/03/1887 Ireland 1-4 Belfast
22/03/1890 Scotland 0-5 Paisley
07/03/1891 England 1-4 Sunderland
21/03/1891 Scotland 3-4 Wrexham

Joby Wilding (Wales)
6 appearances (9)
14/03/1885 England 1-1 Blackburn
23/03/1885 Scotland 1-8 Wrexham
11/04/1885 Ireland 8-2 Belfast
20/03/1886 Ireland 5-0 Wrexham
29/03/1886 England 1-3 Wrexham
26/03/1892 Scotland 1-6 Edinburgh

George Williams (Wales)
1 appearance (1)
23/02/1907 Ireland 3-2 Belfast

Jack Williams (Wales)
1 appearance (1)
21/05/1939 France 1-2 Paris

Leslie Williams (Wales)
1 appearance (1)
22/11/1930 England 0-4 Wrexham

George Wynn (Wales)
3 appearances (11)
01/03/1909 Scotland 3-2 Wrexham
15/03/1909 England 0-2 Nottingham
20/03/1909 Ireland 3-2 Belfast

With the new season now under way, we look at former players who have made first team appearances for Wrexham, and where they are now involved in football, either playing, coaching or managing etc:

Danny Allsopp	Melbourne Victoria	Hyundai A League (Australia)
Matt Baker	MK Dons	League Two
Steve Basham	Oxford United	Conference
David Bayliss	Lancaster City	Conference North
Dean Bennett	Chester City	League Two
Michael Blackwood	Kidderminster Harriers	Conference
Phil Boersma	Newcastle United	Premier League (Coaching Staff)
Emad Bouanane	Barnt Green Spartak	Midland Combination League
Jon Bowden	Luton Town	Championship (Physio)
Dave Brammer	Stoke City	Championship
Mark Cartwright	Leek Town	Unibond Premier League (Manager)
Steve Charles	Spalding United	Unibond First Division (Player/Asst-Manager)
Karl Connolly	Prescot Cables	Unibond Premier League
Terry Cooke	Colorado Rapids (USA)	Major Soccer League
Malcolm Crosby	Middlesbrough	Premier League (Reserve Team Coach)
Terry Darracott	Blackburn Rovers	Premier League (Chief Scout)
Kevin Dearden	Brentford	League One (Goalkeeping Coach)
Andy Dibble	Accrington Stanley	League Two
Carlos Edwards	Luton Town	Championship
Jake Edwards	Crawley Town	Conference League
Paul Edwards	Oldham Athletic	League One
Stuart Elliott	Northwich Victoria	Conference League
Mark Evans	Caernarvon Town	League of Wales
Mickey Evans	Caersws	League of Wales (Manager)
Brian Flynn	Wales under-21 manager	
Ben Foster	Manchester United	Premier League
Robin Gibson	Stafford Rangers	Conference League
Scott Green	Ashton United	Unibond Premier League (Player/Manager)
Carl Griffiths	Braintree Town	Conference South
Seamus Heath	Northern Ireland (Youth Development Officer)	
Shaun Holmes	Derry City	Irish League
Andy Holt	Northampton Town	League One
George Horan	Rhyl	League of Wales
Bryan Hughes	Charlton Athletic	Premier League
Simon Hunt	Southampton	Championship (Assistant-Manager)
Barry Hunter	Portadown	Irish League
Clayton Ince	Walsall	League Two
Jason Jarrett	Preston North End	Championship
Graham 'Ossie' Jones	NEWI Cefn Druids	League of Wales (Coach)

Lee Jones	Caernarfon Town	League of Wales
James Kelly	Lancaster City	Conference North
Chris Killen	Hibernian	Scottish Premier League
Dennis Lawrence	Swansea City	League One
Stuart Lee	FC Seattle Storm (USA)	Director of Coaching
Paul Linwood	Chester City	League Two
Andy Marriott	Boston United	League Two
Mark McGregor	Port Vale	League One
Dixie McNeil	NEWI Cefn Druids	League of Wales (Manager)
Jim McNulty	Macclesfield Town	League Two
Craig Madden	Stockport County	League Two (Youth Team Manager)
Adrian Moody	Rhyl	League of Wales
Craig Morgan	MK Dons	League Two
Andy Morrell	Blackpool	League One
Eddie Niedzwiecki	Blackburn Rovers	Premier League (First Team Coach)
Armand One	Raith Rovers	Scottish League Division Two
Gareth Owen	Airbus UK	Welsh Premier League (Player/Manager)
Waynne Phillips	Caernarfon Town	Welsh Premier League (Player/Manager)
Andy Preece	Worcester City	Conference South (Player/Manager)
Roger Preece	Newtown	League of Wales (Manager)
Paul Raynor	Boston United	League Two (Assistant Manager)
Kevin Reeves	Swansea City	League One (Chief Scout)
Paul Roberts	Bangor City	League of Wales
Steve Roberts	Doncaster Rovers	League One
Kristian Rogers	Port Talbot	League of Wales
Marius Rovde	Hamarkameratene	Norwegian First Division
Hector Sam	Walsall	League Two
Mark Sertori	Bolton Wanderers	Premier League (Club Masseur)
Ron Sinclair	Stoke City	Championship (Assistant Academy Director)
Alex Smith	Southport	Conference League
Ian Stevens	Fleetwood Town	Unibond Premier Division
Mark Taylor	Bolton Wanderers	Premier League (Physio)
Andy Thackeray	Mossley	Unibond Premier Division
Andy Thomas	Airbus UK	League of Wales
Lee Trundle	Swansea City	League One
Jon Walters	Chester City	League Two
Peter Ward	Stockport County	League Two (Assistant-Manager)
Paul Warhurst	Barnet	League Two
David Warren	Cobh Ramblers	Irish League
Paul Whitfield	Rhyl	League of Wales
Jeff Whitley	Cardiff City	Championship
Neil Wainwright	Darlington	League Two
Mark Wilson	FC Dallas (USA)	Major Soccer League

Wrexham football club was formed in October 1872 by members of the town's cricket team who needed something to occupy their leisure time in the winter months. Since that day, the Racecourse club have always produced more than their fair share of Welsh international footballers. Here we look back at the pioneers of Welsh international football.

The FA of Wales was actually formed in Wrexham at the Wynnstay Hotel during February 1876, and only a few weeks later the first Welsh side to take to the International stage contained two Wrexham men. ***Edwin Alfred Cross*** and ***Alfred Davies*** were part of the Welsh team that faced Scotland in Glasgow on March 25th 1976.

Cross, although primarily a cricketer, was to prove a very instrumental figure in helping to form Wrexham Football Club and also the FAW. Edwin also appeared in the first Welsh Cup Final, with a number of reports describing him as being the first footballer to play in the position of centre half. He gave up soccer in 1879 but continued as a batsman for Wrexham Cricket Club for a number of years. A clerk with the Alliance Insurance Company at the time, he later became an accountant. His nephew, who also had the same name E. A. Cross, was later a director of Wrexham AFC and a Wrexham Alderman. Edwyn played in the first home game on Welsh soil in 1877. He was born in Wrexham in 1848 and died at Old Colwyn in 1924.

Alf Davies along with his brother James (more of later) was another member of the Wrexham Cricket Club who saw football as a way of keeping fit during the winter months. He was involved in the 16-a-side matches in the days when the goalposts were connected by a tape! A robust half-back who backed up his forwards well, Alf was a Sunday school teacher and a Lieutenant in the Wrexham Volunteer Fire Brigade; not forgetting his trade as a stone mason. He also represented North Wales against Sheffield, Birmingham and Staffordshire, all in 1877, and like Cross also played in the opening two fixtures for Wales.

The initial Wales home game was held at the Racecourse. On 5th March 1877, Wales entertained the Scots and the legendary ***Johnny Price*** joined the aforementioned duo as a Welsh international. For the next five seasons Price was an automatic choice for Wales and only missed three of the first 15 internationals. In 1882 at Wrexham, he created a goal scoring record by notching four goals against Ireland which has only been matched to date by Johnny Doughty (Newton Heath) in 1888, Mel Charles (Cardiff) in 1962 and by Ian Edwards (Chester) in 1978. Price started his career as a full back for Wrexham Grosvenor and Wrexham Civil Service, but Charles Murless the Wrexham Captain persuaded him that he stood a better chance of Welsh Cup success if he changed allegiance. (Note: there being no organised league programme in those days the Welsh Cup was the absolute pinnacle for the Welsh and surrounding English area's club footballer) Murless decided to move Price to centre forward where contemporary reports stated that his remarkable speed made him "a difficult opponent to stop in front of goal". The strength of the Wrexham forward line allowed Murless to pull one of his front men to the half-back line to field a revolutionary 2-3-5 formation, a pattern not adopted by other clubs until around 1880! Johnny Price is believed to have been employed in a Wrexham leather works. The match report of the first International at Wrexham makes fascinating reading referring to the fact that a number of "Coach & Horses lined up along the touchlines swelling the crowd", while just as much 'copy' was spent discussing the after match banquet as the match itself! (Mark Currie eat your heart out!). A year later back up in Scotland (together with a 9-0 defeat) ***James Davies, Edward Phennah*** and ***Charles Edwards*** were the next Wrexham representatives who entered the International fray.

James, like his brother Alf Davies and Edwin Cross was also one of the members of the Wrexham Cricket Club who were involved in

his is a photograph of the Wrexham team that had just become the first Welsh Cup winners 1878. It contains a number of the internationals highlighted in this article.

Back row: (L-R) Charles Edwards, Alf Davies, E. Evans Snr
iddle row: (L-R) Edwin Cross, Ted Phennah, James Davies, Charles Murless (C), T.W.Davies.
Front row: (L-R) Johnny Price, H. Loxham and E. Evans Jnr

the original formation of the football club. He served on the committee from 1873 and did much to nurture the game in the town. Davies was a fearless player and a 'deadly shot at goal'. The Athletic News (the famous contemporary sports paper) described him as an "excellent centre forward, very fast and thoroughly unselfish." Rather like a Victorian Andy Morrell! On his retirement in 1880, he was said to have scored more goals for Wrexham than any other player with the exception of Johnny Price. No doubt the most important of his goals was in the final moments of the first Welsh Cup Final of 1878 at Acton Park which gave Wrexham the trophy. The trophy itself was not actually awarded until a year later as the fledgling FAW did not have the funds to purchase one, or the medals either, at the time of the final. In 1876, Davies helped Llewellyn Kenrick establish the FAW and served as president in 1891. He was also chairman of the Welsh League, the first soccer league in North Wales. James Davies was in business in the town as a stone mason and employed several men.

It is good to see that the spirit of James Davies still lives on today, his great granddaughter Mrs Nan Williams has kept up the tradition of football in the family being a regular at Wrexham matches for many years. She resides at Ruabon living a few doors away from Blackburn manager Mark Hughes mother! Nan's house is called Cae Ras and she has a cat called Dixie McNeill.

The third game in the embryo stage of Welsh International matches also introduced Charles Edwards as the latest Wrexham participant.

Edwards only enjoyed a short spell in football and was a bank clerk by profession. He played in the Wrexham side which won the first ever Welsh Cup competition. Edwards gained his only cap in somewhat unusual circumstances! The FAW had informed the Scottish F. A. that they were unable to field a side, but the determined Scottish secretary Mr Dick was of the opinion that the game should be played. At his prompting FAW officials toured the Wrexham area to finally round up a team! Edwards, who later took the name Gore-Edwards, retired from the game in 1881 and moved to London to work. He was a brother to Sir Francis Edwards one time Liberal MP for Radnorshire, and brother in law to Alfred George Edwards, Archbishop of Wales from 1920-34.

Ted Phennah's one and only Welsh cap came in a 9-0 defeat against Scotland in Glasgow on 23rd March 1878. A week later he played in the first ever Welsh Cup final for Wrexham against the Druids, in which he gained more success than the previous week by keeping a clean sheet in Wrexham's 1-0 win at Acton Park.

Born in Birkenhead in 1859, Ted was a leading member of the Wrexham Civil Service, a junior football and cricket club that played its matches at Rhosddu Recreation Ground, before being asked by Edwards Evans to throw his lot in with the Wrexham club for the 1877/78 season.

Following the Welsh Cup success he rejoined the Wrexham Civil Service club, but he dislocated his arm in a practice match. The injury was so bad that he was forced to give up playing, and instead became a referee and a cricket umpire, and subsequently channelled his enthusiasm for the game into the administration side.

He became Treasurer of Wrexham FC, and also a member of the FA of Wales, positions he held for a number of years, and on 15th March 1890 he chaired the meeting at the Lion Hotel, Wrexham, to launch the first association football league in North Wales. Many years after giving up the game, Ted made the following observation on goalkeeping in the early days of Welsh football: "Modern goalkeepers would be surprised if they were suddenly called upon to play under the conditions that obtained when I played. It was the practice for one forward to charge the goalkeeper and another to deliver the shot."

Ted was later steward at the Wrexham Conservative Club followed by keeping the Masons Arms in Ruabon until he died on 18th May 1923.

For the first-ever encounter with England on 18th January 1879, ***George William Glascodine*** was selected between the posts, although the record that he was with Wrexham at the time is somewhat tenuous! A native of Yarmouth he moved to Wales at a very young age and began playing football as a centre forward for St. Oswalds in 16 a side matches. George was one of nine Oswestry players who faced England at the Kennington Oval in a match played in a snowstorm in front of 150 spectators. Glascodine was also attached to Wrexham at the same time and his selection, and that of so many Oswestry men, owed a lot to the refusal of most of Wrexham's players to be considered. The fact that the selection committee was chaired by the Oswestry chairman in an Oswestry hotel may also have had some bearing! Only capped the once he trained as a teacher at Chester College and had a teaching post in Lincoln for 43 years.

John Davies, another one cap wonder, was custodian for the final international of the 1870s against the Scots at Wrexham. Davies had only a brief career as a goalkeeper and played out his most important role as FAW Secretary from 1897-1903. He succeeded John Taylor, the previous incumbent, who had entered a period of imprisonment! A senior official at Wrexham County Court, Davies brought a much-needed integrity to the position of FAW Secretary and put the governing body back on an even keel. In 1905 he became President of the Welsh FA holding the post for five years. He played in the Welsh Cup Final of 1881 and was a North

John Davies

Wales representative player.

In the same game, ***James William Lloyd*** was gaining the first of his two caps. An early starter in soccer, Jimmy Lloyd played for Ruabon at 16 against Newtown White Star in the inaugural Welsh Cup competition. During 1877 he joined the North and South Wales bank at Wrexham changing football clubs as he moved from bank branch to bank branch. Noted as a "splendid dribbler", Lloyd was said to have improved his game by a "systematic course of training and running", which no doubt played a part when he helped the Druids to a quarter final place in the English FA Cup in 1883. Jimmy went on to serve as FAW Treasurer from 1889-1891. ***Tom Boden*** was the next Wrexham player to turn out for his country, winning his only cap

James William Lloyd

in the first visit by England to play at the Racecourse in mid-March 1880. A brewery worker in the town he played for local clubs Pen y Bryn Wanderers, Grosvenor Boys and Wrexham Hare and Hounds before moving to Wrexham and developing a good understanding up front with Johnny Price. This understanding lead to his selection alongside Price for the England Test. However, Tom was the victim of a bad foul early on and in the days before substitutes was forced to limp through the rest of the game as a virtual passenger. He also represented North Wales against Staffordshire, Lancashire (as Captain) and Cheshire also in 1880.

Thomas Lewis held the distinction of being the first Wrexham representative to appear in a winning Welsh team when England were defeated at Blackburn in late February 1881 by one goal to nil. His career was short lived, but eventful, he was noted as a fast and skilful player, and a hard worker who supplied a stream of accurate crosses for the inside men. He was rewarded with a second cap against Scotland only two weeks after his first. However this time Wales went down to a heavy defeat. Tom did not appear in the following campaign and it is probable that he moved away to pursue employment outside Wales. A native of Wrexham he too was a North Wales county player.

To complete this first part on Wrexham footballers participating on the Welsh international stage, we come across ***Henry Valentine Edwards*** who had already tasted international football whilst playing for Wrexham Civil Service. Henry won eight caps in all, six with Wrexham and his final one with Wrexham Olympic, which was the cloak name for the club from 1884-89 because of the original club's expulsion. Described as a "splendid athlete" Harry Edwards was a solid half back who had a "fine engine" and an ability to back up his forwards. Captain of the Civil Service Wrexham team, he moved to the senior Wrexham club in 1879, and four years later skippered them to their second Welsh Cup success.

With the welcome news that the national team are returning to their spiritual home for a game against Liechtenstein we reflect on one of the greatest performances ever witnessed at the Racecourse.

Wales versus Spain
World Cup Qualifier - 30th April 1985.

There have been many tales of woe but nothing sums up the roller coaster ride of the Welsh international football fan than 1985. A tight qualifying group saw Wales fail to qualify for the 1986 Mexico World Cup by the narrowest of margins against Scotland at Ninian Park in a game forever overshadowed by the tragic death of Jock Stein.

The events that led to Wales being in a position to qualify were possibly even more remarkable than that Cardiff night. The pivotal game was the one that took place at the Racecourse on a pleasant spring night in front of 23,493.

Wales, under Mike England, opened the campaign with away defeats to Iceland (1-0) and Spain (3-0) and, hard though it might be hard to believe now, a squad with players like Southall, Ratcliffe, Joey, Robbie James, Flynn, Thomas, Blackmore, Hughes and Rush, seemed once again doomed to miss out.

A narrow win (2-1) against Iceland steadied the ship and hopes rose slightly after a battling victory away against Scotland. Qualification hardly seemed likely though when Wales lined up in April against a Spanish team who had already beaten them by three goals and who, although known to travel badly (witness their defeat in Scotland in the same group), topped the group.

As a life-long Mold Road paddock man tickets were hard to come by for that game and I found myself in the Yale paddock for the first and only time in my football-watching career. I should perhaps have done it more often if this was the outcome!

There was a buzz around the Racecourse of the like we didn't often get during the dark days of the 1980s. I long ago concluded that one of the reasons that Welsh players have cited for enjoying playing here - the tight ground - was only part of the story. Club rivalries that returned when boredom struck at the Vetch or Ninian seemed to disappear up North as fans united as one.

In such an atmosphere the fact that the football was cagey for the first 30 minutes didn't matter. Friends from Cardiff and I were distracted and spotted the legendary Joey Jones about 20 yards away with friends. Their hysterical laughter drew looks from all and it took a while to register that the squeaky refrain of "Hello Bally" in the style of a parrot was aimed at English football legend, Alan Ball, sat above in the Directors' box. Ball looked utterly unamused at the impersonation of his high-pitched rasp and tried desperately to ignore Joey to no avail.

However, in the last quarter of an hour Spain began to press Wales and, after a few near misses, Wales broke and Rush gave them an unlikely lead in the 44th minute (1-0). The goal created a sudden buzz around the ground that we could have a chance of beating this Spanish lot. Although we were still sufficiently distracted to note with amusement immediately after half-time that 'Bally' seemed to have disappeared, our minds were suddenly on football.

Wales pressed early on but Spain looked

sharper on the counter and it was a relief that play stopped in the 51st minute for a free kick outside the Spanish box. As the ball floated in no-one knew that what would happen next would be the pivotal moment in the game, undoubtedly set up the group for a grand finale, and, kicked up a gear the career of the man who would become the legend - 'Sparky'

Heads craned Kopwards. I vaguely recall the ball being headed away and then... there it was... Sparky rose with his back to goal and produced one of the great Welsh goals and certainly of one the greatest ever seen at the Racecourse. An almost impossible to repeat, aggressive, full-powered overhead bicycle kick that flew into the net. There was a collective gasp of breath before the Racecourse burst into out and out euphoria. (2-0) The noise level was now deafening. For Wrexham fans only the thrashing of Rotherham to win promotion and the winning of the LDV could ever compare. The rest of the game was a blur. Spanish heads dropped as they chased and Wales rode their luck. Rushy added a breakaway third but it didn't matter (3-0). We knew we'd seen something we'd never forget and most of the crowd floated out of the ground and home.

Sparky went on to win trophies with his club, win PFA young player of the year and move to Barcelona. It was the key year of his career. The goal that night was the crowning moment. Wales, of course, failed to qualify both that time and subsequently in even more promising circumstances! The Racecourse though will never forget that night.

Wales:
Neville Southall [Everton]
Neil Slatter [Bristol Rovers]
Joey Jones [Chelsea]
Kenny Jackett [Watford]
Kevin Ratcliffe [c] [Everton]
David Phillips [Manchester City]
Robbie James [Queen's Park Rangers]
Peter Nicholas [Luton Town]
Ian Rush [Liverpool]
Mark Hughes [Manchester United]
Mickey Thomas [Chelsea]

Coach: Mike England.

Spain:
Arconada [c] [Real Sociedad]
Gerardo [Barcelona]
Liceranzu [Athletic Bilbao]
Maceda [Sporting Gijón]
Andoni Goicoechea [Athletic Bilbao]
Julio Alberto [Barcelona]
Víctor Muñoz [Barcelona]
Ricardo Gallego [Real Madrid]
Gordillo [Betis]
Juan Carlos Rojo [Barcelona]
Rincón [Betis]

Coach: Miguel Muñoz.

Referee: Jan Keizer (Netherlands).

Alexandra Ewan Fenton 1929 – 2006

Ewan Fenton was born in Dundee on 17 November 1929 and he began his senior football career with Scottish junior side Lochee Harp FC from where Blackpool signed him on 23rd November 1946 for a donation of £85. This was despite having also been wanted by Manchester United, and they offered him the same weekly terms at Blackpool, which £6 plus £1 extra if and when he played in the first team. However, Blackpool also offered him the chance to complete an apprenticeship in carpentry for which he had already served two years.

After making some appearances in the junior sides he made his senior debut in the Central League side against Liverpool reserves on 30th November 1947 when Blackpool lost 3-0. Ewan continued to make progress through the ranks at Blackpool, eventually coming to prominence with a team, which included the legendary Stanley Matthews in the 1950s. It took him nearly two years to make his Football League debut, when he played in a home draw with Derby County in September 1948. A cultured right-half, Ewan was mainly an understudy to Hugh Kelly and Harry Johnston for the next few years, but his patience was rewarded when he appeared in the famous 1953 'Matthews' F.A.Cup final, as Blackpool beat Bolton Wanderers 4-3 at Wembley.

Ewan eventually earned a regular place with the 'Tangerines', and in 1956 he was appointed club captain. He was described as a 'shrewd passer of the ball and enjoyed joining the attack, scoring some crucial goals'. However, rather disappointingly to Ewan, he did not achieve international honours with Scotland, the nearest he came was representative honours playing for the British Army XI.

When Jim Kelly replaced him in the side during the 1957/58 season Ewan had a transfer request turned down, but a year later he was allowed to join Wrexham for £3,000 in May 1959, having made over 200 appearances for Blackpool. He was immediately appointed as club captain upon his arrival, but he was to spend just one season at the Racecourse before losing his place in the side to George Evans, and it came as no surprise when he was released at the end of 1959/60, although he did apply for the vacant manager's post following the departure of John Love. The job was eventually handed to Billy Morris. Of his time at Wrexham, Ewan once said; "In all honesty it was a disastrous 12 months. I was injured for most of the time. We were happy there, but I didn't enjoy the style of football."

That summer Ewan qualified as an FA coach, and joined Irish League side Limerick during that summer. He later became player/manager, and experienced playing in the European Cup, picking up an F.A.I. Cup Winners' medal in 1965. In May 1967 he was appointed manager of Linfield, inspiring them to the Irish League championship in 1969, the Irish F.A.Cup in 1970, the City Cup in 1968, the Gold Cup in 1968 & 1969 and the Ulster Cup in 1968. He also led them into Europe in each of the three seasons he held sway at Windsor Park - against Leipzig in 1967, Setubal in 1968, and Red Star Belgrade in 1969. Ewan left Linfield at the end of 1969/70, when Billy Bingham succeeded him. Ewan was also chosen to manage the League of Ireland representative XI on a number of occasions.

He returned to Limerick as manager, leading them to an F.A.I. Cup win in 1971, beating Drogheda United 3-0 in the final replay, after a scoreless draw. Having settled in Limerick, Ewan had started up in his own School of Motoring in 1965, the first in Limerick, and it was this business that he concentrated on when he retired from football in 1977. He retired from the business last year after 40 years service. Sadly, Ewan passed away on 3rd April 2006, aged 75, and is survived by wife Vera, son Ewan and grandchildren Sarah, Ewan and David.

League		F.A.Cup		Welsh Cup		Total	
apps	gls	apps	gls	apps	gls	apps	gls
24	0	1	0	2	0	27	0
24	0	1	0	2	0	27	0

Phillip Arthur Gwatkin 1929 - 2006

Phil Gwatkin originated from Harrow, London, where he was born on 5th August 1929. Phil and his family moved north to Merseyside in the 1930s after his father was offered a better job. However, the outbreak of the Second World War saw Phil and his six brothers and sisters evacuated to Ynys Môn (Anglesey) to live on their grandparents' farm, where they remained throughout the hostilities.

While in North Wales he attended the Holyhead County School, which he represented at football, before leaving to take up employment as an apprentice fitter at Liverpool docks. He spent five years there before being called up for his National Service with the Army. Until that time his football career had consisted of playing park football in his home town of Wallasey, although he had been invited for trials with Everton, which came to nothing. He joined the Army's R.E.M.E. Battalion, and underwent his basic training at Honiton in Devon.

Phil then served at Malvern, and in Germany before returning to his home base at the Dale Barracks in Chester.

It was whilst playing for his Battalion team that he was spotted and invited to sign for Chester F.C. However, after four weeks and no further contact from the Sealand Road club, he joined Wrexham! Phil had been recommended to the club by its reserve team full-back Bob Hawkins, and he was signed in October 1952 at the age of 23, remaining in the Army until he was demobbed.

Phil made his first appearance for the 'Robins' second XI in a Cheshire County League game against Macclesfield Town in August 1953, scoring four goals! The local press reported at the time, 'Gwatkin led the attack skilfully, distributed the ball cleverly and showed coolness and excellent judgment in the vicinity of goal.'

After such a good start it was only a matter of time before Phil appeared in the first team, and his opportunity soon came against Chesterfield on the Racecourse the following week, when he replaced Glyn Hughes in a 2-1 defeat. Hughes returned for the following game, but Gwatkin was back in first team action in December and he celebrated with two goals in a 5-0 win over Halifax Town.

He was regarded at the time as one of the fastest wingers in the Third Division North, and as the team began to hit peak form he played his part in Wrexham's run of seven wins from ten games, enabling the club to climb the table and finish in eighth place. The 1954/55 season was to see him contesting the outside-right position with Hughes but, by the end of the term, a change of manager had resulted in a new right winger being installed, Gren Jones. Phil was limited to just ten League games in 1955/56, and this led to the player and club parting company in the summer.

He was described at Wrexham as 'often having to make way for new signings, but he never failed to give a wholehearted display when called upon. A brilliant ball player who can easily be a match winner. However, he was by far a more prolific goalscorer with the Cheshire League team'.

Phil moved on to Tranmere Rovers in June 1956, joining them as a part-timer and taking up work with BNFL at Capenhurst. He made his Rovers' debut in a 4-1 defeat at Hull in the opening game of the 1956/57 season, scoring the consolation goal. A further 20 League appearances followed, in which he notched five more goals before leaving Prenton Park at the end of the season after a disagreement over travel arrangements.

Phil then joined Cheshire County League side Northwich Victoria for a short spell, before linking up with Lancashire Combination League side New Brighton, where he spent almost two seasons before joining West Kirby, coaching the second XI during his three year spell. He left Capenhurst in 1969 to work at Vauxhall, from where he retired in 1993 after completing 24 years with the company. He loved playing golf and was a member of Bidston Golf Club for a number of years. Sadly, Phil Gwatkin passed away on 9th July 2006 at the Aynsley Nursing Home in Wallasey. He was 76.

League		F.A.Cup		Welsh Cup		Total	
apps	gls	apps	gls	apps	gls	apps	gls
22	4	1	0	2	2	25	6
24	4	1	0	3	2	28	6
10	0	-	-	1	0	11	0
56	8	2	0	6	4	64	12

Stuart James Mason 1948-2006

It was a great shock when the news of Stuart Mason's sudden passing away on 5th February 2005 was received. Stuart was only 56, having been born in Whitchurch, Shropshire on 2nd June 1948. In the months leading up to his premature demise, Stuart had been working with the Centre of Excellence at Chester at the under-16s coach.

It was rather surprising really that Stuart actually made it as a professional footballer, as he attended Whitchurch grammar school, where football was a forbidden word in the rugby orientated school.

However, Stuart overcame this obstruction to sign for his local side Whitchurch Alport in the Shropshire County League, and it was whilst with them that he quickly came to the attention of Wrexham who snapped up the promising youngster in November 1964, as he was about to go to teaching training college in Birmingham.

At the Racecourse Stuart quickly graduated through the junior ranks and made his first team debut, deputising for Reg Holland at right back, on New Years Day 1966, at the age of 17. His rapid progression was recognised when he represented England Youth against Scotland, Wales and Northern Ireland, and the youngster signed professional terms for Wrexham in July. He continued his run of form into the following season, and a remarkable year was completed in October 1966 when along with Peter Wall, he was signed by Liverpool manager Bill Shankly for a combined fee of £30,000.

For just under two seasons at Anfield Stuart was a regular in the Central League side, being kept out of the first team due to the consistency of Chris Lawler. In 1967 he had a brief loan spell with Doncaster Rovers, making one league appearance in a 2-0 defeat at Rochdale in February 1968. At the end of that season Stuart was to rejoin Wrexham on a free transfer, and over the next five years at the Racecourse Ground he figured in a promotion winning team, returned to Anfield to play against his former club in a FA Cup third round match, and also gained a Welsh Cup winners medal as well as featuring in the club's first venture into Europe, playing in the 'Robins' very first European match in Zurich.

Stuart was allowed to leave the Racecourse for £2,000 in June 1973 to sign for local rivals Chester, where he became a prominent part of one of there 1975 promotion winning team, the first ever promotion winning team in Chester's history! He also played a major part in helping the 'Seals' reaching the semi-finals of the Football League Cup.
In the cup run he was given the role of man marking Bobby Charlton in the Preston tie and Leeds United's Billy Bremner in the famous 3-0 victory. He

performed both tasks with typical quiet efficiency as both players were marked out of the game. In the semi-final at Aston Villa Stuart scored his first goal of the season with a stunning 30-yard strike that temporarily gave Chester hope of a first Wembley appearance before their narrow 5-4 aggregate defeat.

Following promotion to Division Three Stuart was in and out of the Chester side, and after loan spells at Rochdale and Crewe, he joined Bangor City in December 1977. After two years at Farrar Road he moved along the coast to Rhyl where he played for 12 months under ex-Chester full back Ray Jones. Finally, in the early 1980's, Stuart again linked up with Ken Roberts at Oswestry Town where he himself took the position of player-manager in the 1984/85 season. He later managed Coedpoeth in the Welsh National League, and also played for Wrexham veterans and Chester Nomads.

Stuart was also a talented cricketer and played for Whitchurch as well as captaining Shropshire, but he lived in the Borras Park area of Wrexham, where he was a well respected figure in the business community and ran the Stuart Mason Sports shop in Wrexham town centre for 20 years, and at one time he was assistant commercial manager at Wrexham football club.

Following his father's shock death, son Simon spoke warmly of his father, on behalf of Stuart's widow Anne, and sister Joanne, remembering the proud moments he spent watching his dad play. "He was a fantastic father to myself and my sister Joanne. We used to go everywhere with him when he was playing football. I can remember going to watch him play for Chester in the 70s at the time when they were beating the likes of Newcastle and Leeds in the League Cup. I used to like going to watch him play cricket, too. He was everything you could wish a father to be. He was a happy-go-lucky guy and was very much looking forward to playing cricket this summer. He made a lot of good friends through football and cricket, and he will be greatly missed. I feel very proud of everything he has achieved and passed on to me over the years."

League		F.A.Cup		Welsh Cup		League Cup		ECWC		Total	
apps	gls	apps	gls	apps	gls	apps	gls	apps	gls	apps	gls
19	0	-	-	1	0	-	-	-	-	20	0
9	0	-	-	-	-	1	0	-	-	10	0
19/2	0	-	-	-	-	-	-	-	-	19/2	0
32/7	1	2/2	0	2	0	2/1	0	-	-	38/10	1
26/4	0	1	0	2/1	0	2	0	-	-	31/5	0
39	2	3	0	4	0	-	-	-	-	46	2
28	0	2	0	-	-	2	0	4	0	36	0
172/13	3	8/2	0	9/1	0	7/1	0	4	0	200/17	3

Aloysius 'Aly' McGowan 1930 - 2005

Born in the Lanarkshire town of Whiterigg on 22nd January 1930, Aly McGowan was one of a large mining family, whose brother Jimmy played in the Scottish League for Partick Thistle. Aly actually went to the same school as another former future Wrexham player, Tommy Bannan, but upon leaving school he

took up work in the coal mines, while continuing to play football in the local leagues around Airdrie for Fauldhouse United.

It was playing for Fauldhouse that Aly was spotted by St.Johnstone manager Jimmy Crapnell, and he signed professional forms for the Perth club at the age of 19, making his debut at Stenhousmuir in March 1951 in a 2-0 win.

Aly would train in Airdrie, and travel the two and a half hours to Perth just on match days. He went on to make a total of 52 Scottish League appearances for St.Johnstone, as well as earning international recognition with a Scottish 'B' cap against the Irish League XI at Windsor Park, which they won 6-0.

The arrival of Jimmy Portillo as the new manager at the Perth club saw 25 out of 27 of the clubs players given free transfers, but by this time Tommy Bannan was at Wrexham, and mentioned Aly to manager Peter Jackson, who in turn invited Aly for a trial to join Wrexham.

Despite interest from Raith Rovers for him to remain in Scotland, he signed for the 'Robins' in May 1953, and switched mines to Bersham Colliery, where he was to work for five more years before becoming a full time professional in 1958.

He made his League debut for Wrexham against Crewe on the Racecourse in the first match of the 1953/54 season, establishing himself immediately as a regular in the Wrexham side, where he remained for the next eleven seasons, making a total of 408 League games, which has only been bettered by three other players. During his time at the Racecourse, Aly played in the famous F.A.Cup match against Manchester United's Busby Babes, which saw the biggest ever crowd assembled on the Racecourse Ground, and the League Cup match against Liverpool in 1961. He also helped the club to promotion in 1962 as well as winning the Welsh Cup three times.

He was regarded as a 'hard tackling defender, who never knew when he was beaten', and was also described as being 'on the small side for a defender, but his lack of inches was discounted by the fact he never knew when he was beaten'. His career came to an unexpected end, when he broke his leg at Watford in September 1963. He made a comeback, but soon realised that he would never be quite the same, and retired. Aly was given two benefit matches, the first was a joint one against Falkirk, with Billy Waters, Gren Jones and Fred Davis and the second was against Chester before taking charge of the club's 'A' team in 1966 after a spell playing for Bethesda Athletic.

Aly later became groundsman at the Racecourse, combining those duties with running the club's Northern Floodlit League side. It was once said of Aly, "His whole hearted endeavour made him a great favourite with the supporters. He was a tenacious tackler, with a very keen sense of anticipation." Aly later became steward at the Centenary Club for a short while, and was also once the steward at the St.Mary's Catholic Club in the Town. A great and well loved character in the town he passed away on 4th July 2005 aged 75. He was taken back to his native

Scotland to be buried in Whiterigg.

There were many tributes made to Aly, who made 408 league appearances for the club, only two other players have done that; one of them is Arfon Griffiths who said; "I can remember when I first came to the club in 1956, Aly was one of the established players in the team.

"When I became a part-time professional, Aly was the one who looked after the younger players. He helped me a lot in the early days, and made sure I kept my feet on the ground. If you listened to what he said, you would not go far wrong." Len Willett also played with Aly, he told us "All football clubs have a history their ground, players, sometimes administrators and of course their fans.

"Some have had outstanding players, we have been fortunate at Wrexham to have had many, one such I feel needs an special mention, he was Aly Mcgowan. The Scot who made Wrexham his home and gave the club such wonderful service. No Wrexham team of any generation could be picked without Aly being in it. Aly is no longer with us in life but will never be forgotten by we who knew him and played with him for Wrexham.A great Wrexham player sadly missed".

Season	League		F.A.Cup		Welsh Cup		League Cup		Total	
	apps	gls	apps	gls	apps	gls	apps	gls	apps	gls
1953/54	38	0	4	0	1	0	-	-	43	0
1954/55	44	0	1	0	4	0	-	-	49	0
1955/56	35	1	1	0	2	0	-	-	38	1
1956/57	43	0	7	0	5	0	-	-	55	0
1957/58	43	0	1	0	5	0	-	-	49	0
1958/59	38	0	1	0	4	0	-	-	43	0
1959/60	46	1	3	0	5	0	-	-	54	1
1960/61	43	0	1	0	3	0	6	0	53	0
1961/62	42	0	3	0	6	0	1	0	52	0
1962/63	35	0	4	0	1	0	1	0	41	0
1964/65	1	0	-	-	-	-	-	-	1	0
	408	2	26	0	36	0	8	0	478	2

Thomas Copeland McNab 1933 - 2006

Born in Glasgow on 15th July 1933 Tom McNab attended Hamilton Crescent Secondary school, where he was to play regularly on the same pitch that the first Scotland v. England match was played on in the 1800's. He represented Glasgow Schoolboys, but upon leaving school at 15, he took up working as a painter and decorator, while continuing to play football for a local side called, Gordon Park Church of Scotland, for whom he played between 1948 and 1950. Tom then joined a Scottish Junior team called Balliston Juniors, with whom he spent twelve months before joining Partick Thistle.

He went on to make over twenty Scottish League appearances for the 'Jags' before being called up for his National Service in 1953, enlisting in the R.A.F. He was later posted near to Nottingham, where he was invited to sign amateur forms in March 1954, with Nottingham Forest, playing a few reserve team games.

Upon being demobbed, Tom rejoined Partick Thistle, which coincided with the 'Jag's' triumphant run to the League Cup

final in 1956, but there was no place for him in the team, as he had to contest his position with Scottish international centre-half, J.A.Davidson.

In March 1957, Tom left Firhill, after being recommended to Wrexham by Aly McGowan's brother, Jimmy, who was playing for Partick at the time. Wrexham paid £2,500 for Tom, who went straight into the team for his Football League debut at home to Tranmere Rovers, in place of the injured Alan Fox, in a 1-0 win. Following Fox's return, Tom was switched to play at half-back, where he played in the 1957 Welsh Cup final against Swansea, who Wrexham beat 2-1, scoring the winning goal. The following season saw Tom playing regularly in the side up until February, when he lost his place in the side to Ken Murray. He never really regained a regular place in the side, and in March 1959 was transferred to Barrow for a £1,500 fee.

He spent eighteen months with the Cumbrian team, scoring four goals in 44 League appearances before returning to Scotland in the close season of 1960 to join Second Division side, East Stirlingshire. He then went on to become a regular in the 'Shire' team for the next four seasons in which time he helped them to promotion to the First Division in 1963, when they finished runners-up to St.Johnstone. Tom played right-back in a team that included a very young Eddie McCreadie, who later went on to play for and manage, Chelsea.

With his career coming to an end, he decided to emigrate to New Zealand in 1964, where he became player/coach of Eastern Suburbs, who he led to the National Cup final three times in five years, as well as winning the League title.

In 1967, Tom captained New Zealand against a Manchester United team that included George Best, Bobby Charlton and Denis Law etc; a year later they won the European Cup! Tom also toured South East Asia with the Kiwi's National side, and won eight caps for his adopted country in total.

He was coach to the National side, when they played a Wales XI touring party in 1971. In 1978, disaster was to strike for Tom, as he suffered a building site accident that left him a paraplegic. However, Tom's spirit showed through as he would not let that deter him, and he still coached a First Division side from his wheelchair. He was later given a testimonial in which a number of the All Black's rugby Union side turned out to play with the round ball, and in 1983 he had a inter-club trophy named after him, which is played for between clubs from the Counties Manukau and Auckland.

For many years Tom never forgot his roots, and he was secretary of the New Zealand branch of the Glasgow Rangers Supporters Club. However, he did have one regret; he vividly remembered the time and the place and the name of the referee who had booked him almost 40 years earlier. That referee has the dubious honour of being the only referee to have written the name of 'T McNab' in his notebook for misconduct!

Sadly, Tom passed away in Pakuranga on Wednesday 5th April 2006. He was 72.

Season	League		F.A.Cup		Welsh Cup		Total	
	apps	gls	apps	gls	apps	gls	apps	gls
1956/57	11	0	-	-	1	1	12	1
1957/58	27	5	-	-	1	0	28	5
1958/59	5	0	-	-	2	0	7	0
	43	5	-	-	4	1	47	6

Albert Edward Parker 1927 - 2005

Born in Liverpool on 13th September 1927, Albert impressed enough at football in school to be signed up by Everton as a schoolboy. However, his progression was halted when he was not taken on by the club upon leaving school. Instead, Albert was to later join South Liverpool where he became a hit as a centre-half in the Cheshire League.

His performances for them soon attracted the attention of Football League clubs, and in December 1948 he was signed by Crewe Alexandra. With Crewe, Albert made his Football League debut on the 15th January 1949 in a home match with Carlisle United, and he went on to make a total of 111 Football League appearances with the 'Railwaymen'.

One of few players to wear contact lenses when playing in the Football League, he spent three seasons at Gresty Road before joining Wrexham in November 1951, after a fall out with his Chairman at Crewe.

He went straight into the Wrexham team at right-back in place of Les Speed, for the away match at Darlington in November 1951 which the 'Robins' lost 2–1. Albert then made just seven more league appearances that season before taking over the right berth on a permanent basis the following season, forming a formidable full-back partnership with another great Wrexham servant, Aly McGowan. Albert, a tough tackling full-back, was quite at home in either full-back position, and remained at the Racecourse until 1959, sometimes deputising at centre-half when required to do so. During that time he helped Wrexham to win the Welsh Cup in 1957 and 1958, and also played in the great match of the 1950's against Manchester United's 'Busby Babes' in front of the biggest ever crowd assembled on the Wrexham Racecourse, 34,445. Albert scored just one goal for Wrexham, and what a goal it was! A 70-yard 'shot' that bounced over the head of the Workington 'keeper, who could only watch in amazement as the ball entered the net. In 1957, Albert had a joint benefit match with Ron Hewitt against Coventry City. In 1959 he left Wrexham, and joined Holywell Town. However, in December 1960 he returned to the Racecourse as the club's new groundsman. A position he held for two years.

Albert later took up refereeing and after progressing through the Welsh League's he was appointed linesman for the Fairs Cup match between Athletico Bilbao and Sparta Prague in 1970. Albert later stood as a Conservative candidate for the Wats Dyke Ward in the 1968 local elections.

He later worked for the local council up until his retirement. In 1977, Albert returned to the Racecourse to work as a turnstile operator, a job he did until the early 1990's. Sadly, Albert passed away on 29th October 2005, he was 78. Arfon Griffiths, who was at the club as a ground staff lad in Albert's last season at the Racecourse said; "He always had a smile for people because he was a typical Scouser. He always had a joke to tell, and loved the area of Wrexham. Albert stayed in the area and continued to work in different roles after he had retired from playing." Alan Fox, who played in the same defence as Albert said "He was a nice gentleman off the field, but a tough tackler on it. He was a clean kicker of the ball and a very neat player. I remember looking up to him, and thought a great deal of him."

Season	League		F.A.Cup		Welsh Cup		Total	
	apps	gls	apps	gls	apps	gls	apps	gls
1951/52	8	0	3	0	1	0	12	0
1952/53	34	1	2	0	1	0	37	1
1953/54	18	0	-	-	1	0	19	0
1954/55	23	0	2	0	4	0	29	0
1955/56	31	0	1	0	-	-	32	0
1956/57	40	0	7	0	5	0	52	0
1957/58	38	0	1	0	4	0	43	0
1958/59	24	0	-	-	-	-	24	0

Walter Roberts 1917 – 2006

Born in Wrexham during the First World War on 23rd November 1917, Walter Roberts took up playing football whilst at the Victoria and Alexandra schools in his home town. Upon leaving school he took up employment as a shop assistant, but continued playing football in the local park just for fun with his friends. He was invited to play in a few representative matches for Wrexham Police, and it was following one of those matches that Walter was recommended to Wrexham by the Chief Constable for the Wrexham Police. He was invited for trials, and played a few reserve team matches, before being signed in August 1938.

He was a regular member of the reserve team in his first season at the club, but was given first team chance on New Years Eve, when he replaced the injured Archie Burgon at outside-left against Doncaster in a scoreless draw. He made one more first team appearance that season against New Brighton in a Northern Section Cup match before the Second World War interrupted Walter's career.

Whilst playing for Wrexham, Walter had also joined the Territorial Army, serving in the Royal Artillery; so when the War began he was one of the first to be called up. He was initially posted to France, and was a Dunkirk veteran, and later served in the Middle-East. Football continued over the war period as it was regarded as 'good for morale', and when home on leave Walter was to make nineteen appearances for Wrexham over that period.

After the War was over Walter was re-signed by Wrexham, and he was to miss only five matches of that season. The following campaign saw him play in every game until he was injured against Mansfield on Boxing Day 1947. However, when fit again, he struggled to regain his first team place. He was offered new terms at the end of the season, but manager Tom Williams couldn't guarantee Walter a first team place, and he asked to be transfer listed.

Third Division South side, Bournemouth

showed an interest, and whilst visiting his wife's family near Hartlepool, the Bournemouth manager, Harry Lowe, arranged a meeting with Walter, and he agreed terms with the South Coast club. Fred Rowell moved in the opposite direction in the part- exchange deal, but throughout his time with the Dorset club he remained living in Wrexham, and would travel by train to each match!

Walter was to make twelve League appearances for Bournemouth, but at the end of the season he was allowed to leave Dean Court, as the club couldn't find him more secure accommodation. Walter then joined Cheshire League side Ellesmere Port in the close season of 1949, but spent just one season with the Wirral club before signing for Welsh League side, Blaenau Ffestiniog.

Peter Jackson then invited him back to the Racecourse as reserve team coach, but he relinquished that position when Jackson left the club. Walter then returned to his old job as a shop assistant in Wrexham, to which he continued to do until his retirement, though Jack Rowley did invite him to return to football in a coaching capacity at the Racecourse around 1966, but he turned it down. Walter remained in the town until passing away in March 2006, aged 89. His Grandson was on Wrexham's books, Nicky Ward, who went on to play for Shrewsbury Town and TNS.

Season	League		F.A.Cup		Welsh Cup		N.S.C.	
	apps	gls	apps	gls	apps	gls	apps	gls
1938/39	1	0	-	-	-	-	1	0
1946/47	37	1	4	0	2	0	-	-
1947/48	22	0	2	0	-	-	-	-
	60	1	6	0	2	0	1	0

Robin Kenneth Thomas 1938 - 2006

Born the son of a farmer in Nebo, nr Caernarfon on 23rd September 1938, 'Robin Ken' played his early football for Penygroes Secondary school, and did enough to make his debut Nantlle Vale in the tough learning school of the Welsh League North, and it proved to be a baptism of fire as they lost 14-1! Rob did score the Vale goal though!

Upon leaving school at the age of 16, he joined fellow Welsh League North side, Porthmadog, being signed by three of the club's committee members whilst shearing sheep on his father's farm! Rob spent five seasons with Porthmadog, during which time he was a reserve for the Welsh amateur side. His football career took a lift when Porthmadog played Chester in a Welsh Cup match in February 1961. Despite losing 2-1, he did enough to be approached by both Chester and Wrexham, whom he had been recommended by another Caernarfon born player on Wrexham's books, Wyn Davies, and he signed for the Racecourse club in May 1961.

His first team debut eventually came in January 1962 when he replaced regular half-back George Evans for a Welsh Cup

tie, ironically against his former club Porthmadog, which Wrexham won 2-0.

However, that proved to be Rob's one and only senior appearance, although he did play in a first team friendly against the Danish touring team, Bronshoj before his release at the end of the season.

Former Welsh international Tommy G Jones, who was then manager of Bangor City, then snapped up Rob on a full-time contract for their European Cup-Winners' Cup campaign, but he disappointingly missed the matches with Naples because of an ankle injury.

Rob later went on to play for Caernarfon Town, Blaenau Ffestiniog, Pwllheli, and finally where it all began for him.......Nantlle Vale. He was to play for the Vale until the ripe old age of 44 years-old! At Vale he played alongside some tough characters like Orig Williams, and Idris 'Tarw Nefyn' Evans, who were feared opponents in Welsh League football. Rob himself was nicknamed 'Tarw', meaning 'The Bull'.

After quitting professional football with Bangor City, Rob took up employment with a local sand and gravel company, as well as sheep farming the mountain slopes above Caernarfon, which was one of the great loves of his life. Sadly, Rob died in his native Nebo on 22nd April 2006. The popularity of the man was shown by the fact that the church in Nebo was packed to the rafters.

Season	League		F.A.Cup		Welsh Cup		League Cup		Total	
	apps	gls	apps	gls	apps	gls	apps	gls	apps	gls
1961/62	-	-	-	-	1	0	-	-	1	0
	-	-	-	-	1	0	-	-	1	0

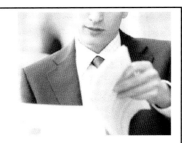

Everybody knows that the biggest ever gate at the Racecourse was 34,445 for a fourth round cup tie against Manchester United in 1958. However, less is known about the battle with Reading in the previous round. Len Willett made the long journey to Berkshire for the third round replay and recounts his memories of that important game.

"We boarded the football special train at Wrexham General for the trip south to Reading for a cup replay that was to start Wrexham's long history of FA Cup success. Young and old we were keen to cheer our team on to victory, because the winners would be playing at home against the Busby Babes in the next round. The first game at the Racecourse had ended in a 1-1 draw with Bernard Evans scoring for us in front of 24,160 fans. The replay at Elm Park was to become a very important date in the history of our club.

"As the train left Wrexham, we passed the coal mines of Bersham and Hafod. The colliers were out in force to wave and cheer us on. They had put banners up on buildings and at Hafod with a large banner that read "Come on the Town. The Pride of North Wales" which had been fixed to the colliery winding gear. Cup fever had gripped the town and it felt as if the whole of North Wales was willing us on to victory.

"Several of us youngsters (taking a day off from our studies) had found an empty guards van on the train, and after speaking to the guard a small ball was produced and six of us began a football game. One of our number would go on to become one of Wrexham's greatest heroes - Arfon Griffiths. He'd never placed in such a strange stadium, and never has.

"On the journey down south we went rolling through New Street Station Birmingham where we woke the station up with our chanting and singing.

"In those days Reading was famous for its biscuit making and although they are now k$nown as the 'Royals' but in the 1950s Reading were known as the 'biscuit men'.

"One of the lads on the train came up with an idea: We arrived in Reading and many of us were carrying packets of biscuits which we proceeded to eat as we walked through central Reading chanting 'we're going to munch you tonight'. I suppose it was an early version of football hooliganism, but it was given and received in good humour.

"We then took up our places inside Elm Park, which was a far more humble venue than Reading's current Madjeski Stadium. As we got closer to kick-off, more and more Wrexham fans started to arrive in the ground and stories started to circulate amongst us that Reading were already selling tickets for the game against the mighty Manchester United – incidentally this was before they had even beaten us!

"We did not believe it at first, but then an announcement was made in the ground telling the home fans that they could purchase their United tickets after the game. We were outraged. We had never heard anything like it. Although Reading were the clear favourites to win the tie, it was a very disrespectful thing to do.

"Reports of this had obviously filtered back to the Wrexham dressing room. When our team came out for the kick in before the start several of them, including Ronnie Hewitt and Johnny Anderson ran over to the Wrexham supporters and in

Action from the Elm Park replay.

quite basic terms told us what they thought that Reading could do with their tickets and where they could put them!

"I will not repeat what they said here, but suffice to say that the 2,000 Wrexham fans at the game were in total agreement.

"The arrogance of the Southerners backfired on them. The Wrexham side was galvanised by this slight and dominated the game from start to finish before running out the eventual 2-1 winners. Hewitt and Anderson scoring the goals. Anderson's goal in particular is deserving of special mention as he beat three Reading defenders on a mazy 40-yard dribble, before thumping a shot past the keeper. One-nil to the Town!

"Reading never did get to sell their tickets and it was to be Wrexham who would play United in the next round.

"The journey home was very enjoyable with much speculation about the forthcoming clash with United. However, before we had even left the station something unusual happened. The Wrexham captain Albert Parker turned up on the platform carrying his kit bag. He was coming back on the train with the fans. Not something we would see today I think! Anyway we were thrilled to see one of our cup heroes and Albert was hoisted high up on shoulders and passed from one end of the packed Reading station to the other with Wrexham fans chanting his name all the while. Perhaps that was not the best post-match warm down that a player could have but Albert took it in good part and no harm came to him. The rumour was that Albert was moving house the next day and wanted to get home early but I could not confirm that.

"This game was surely the start of the great cup tradition that has endured to this day. The victory sparked off mayhem in the town. Over 18,000 fans turned up for a Cheshire League game against Winsford as Manchester United tickets were only issued to spectators at this game. 'One per person' - fans broke down the fences to get out of the ground and queue again for another ticket. We drew 1-1 with Winsford by the way - Happy days!"

Wrexham lined up at Reading that day as follows:

Billy Waters	Aly McGowan
Albert Parker	Bill Green
Alan Fox	Fred Davies
Gren Jones	Ron Hewitt
Peter Thompson	Johnny Anderson
David Jones